Newcastle Out of Toon

Newcastle Out of Toon

The Inside Story of Newcastle at War

Harry Harris

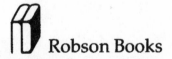

Robson Books

First published in 1999 by Robson Books, 10 Blenheim Court, Brewery Road, London N7 9NT

A member of the Chrysalis Group plc

British Library Cataloguing in Publication Data
A catalogue record for this title is available from the British Library

ISBN 1 86105 287 1

Typeset by SX Composing DTP, Rayleigh, Essex
Printed and bround in Great Britain by Butler & Tanner Ltd, London and Frome

Contents

To a loving mother, Sarah

Credits

To Ruud for being a friend and a warm human being. Special thanks to the Smith brothers, Jon and Phil. As well as being very close friends, they represented Ruud Gullit with a combination of affection and professionalism. Jon was on holiday with his family in Cyprus and after the Sunderland match had his bags packed ready to come home, uncertain whether Ruud might quit there and then and whether he would be needed back in Newcastle, a long-awaited break with his family about to be wrecked. I was glad I convinced him to stay. Jon and Phil were in constant touch with Freddy Shepherd and Freddie Fletcher and knew how much they wanted Ruud to succeed.

Thanks, of course, to Jeremy Robson at Robson Books. He commissioned me to spend the year following Ruud's fortunes on Tyneside. The original concept for the book was a diary of his first year in charge. But as the dramatic events of the first few games of the new season unfolded, all credit to the publishers in having the foresight to make an immediate decision to completely change the format and overhaul the concept of the book. Tim Glynne-Jones, who edits the BBC magazine *Match of the Day*, edited the material. With the help of Lorna Russell and Stella Caldwell at Robson Books, the book was able to emerge so soon after Ruud's resignation. I should also like to thank all on the *Mirror* picture desk, particularly John and Greg, for the picture selection.

Introduction

The Shearer factor

Alan Shearer heard the news of Ruud Gullit's resignation at 8.45am. If nothing else Shearer is precise and he is also meticulous. He recalls the exact moment he received the call concerning his manager's resignation. However, he was not the first at the club to be notified of a decision that those close to Gullit knew at 7.30am. One can imagine Shearer's reaction . . . perhaps a wry smile, a sense of satisfaction – someone with a touch more emotion might have raised their right hand and run around the living room as if he'd just scored! Maybe that's being a little unkind, but it's hard to imagine any other reaction. Gullit's decision to hand in a team sheet minus the name of Shearer for the derby with Sunderland was branded a suicide note. Even before this gamble though, there had been talk that the Toon wasn't big enough for the two of them.

In reality there was little more than a professional relationship between Gullit and Shearer for some months. The body language at pre-season team photo shoots and whenever the two were in public together told of a frosty relationship. In private, it was clear both men increasingly mistrusted each other. Shearer, however, denied a personal rift with Gullit, but conceded that they did not 'see eye-to-eye'. They certainly rarely looked at each other. Obviously Shearer was not happy with Gullit's decision to leave him out of the Sunderland match, but it goes deeper than that. Shearer got wise to the fact that Gullit wanted to sell him very soon after the Dutchman arrived at St James's Park. On the training ground Gullit talked about a lack of commitment, and Shearer believed the reference was made to him.

Gullit's extensive farewell speech, which he personally dictated to his secretary, never mentioned Shearer. However, the truth about their relationship becomes apparent as this book charts Gullit's time in charge of Newcastle United. Gullit lasted precisely one year and one day as Newcastle United manager. Could there possibly have been a more dramatic and controversial year in charge of any club anywhere in the world? Kenny Dalglish lasted two games of last season and Gullit survived just five games of this season. Enter 66-year-old Bobby Robson, the third boss in a year. It was a romantic homecoming for the Geordie who couldn't wait to return to his roots for a final post in management. But he inherited a club in deep crisis, after one of the most acrimonious and high profile feuds between England and Newcastle captain Alan Shearer and Gullit.

It was a traumatic fortnight for Shearer, of that there can be no dispute. Shearer was dropped for the first time in his illustrious career, prompting England coach Kevin Keegan to mutter darkly of 'character assassination'. The question was whether Shearer was the inspirational figure everyone believed or a disruptive influence, wielding far too much influence over club and country, and eventually bringing about Gullit's downfall.

For someone with such immense stature and respect, some believe that Shearer has, in reality, declined to a player of limited footballing resources. However when he scored a hat-trick in the England-Luxembourg game Keegan boldly pronounced that Shearer is in fact as good as the day he spent £15m of Newcastle United's money on the striker. There are few managers with that amount of money to spend on one player that would risk it on Shearer at the moment, but there has been no greater advocate to the Shearer fan club than Keegan. 'Alan is a most amazing character, so strong . . . I take my hat off to him. I see a bit of myself in him, and a bit of Bill Shankly, who would say "go on son, you write the stories." He's certainly written the stories with a hat-trick. And fair do's; he's had his chance and he's taken it. I'm delighted.'

Shearer has faced nothing equivalent to the personal as well as professional scrutiny of recent months. After being dropped by Gullit for the vital Tyne-Wear derby game, came his stony-faced response on the bench when Kieron Dyer opened the scoring against Sunderland in contrast to the jubilation expressed by his boss and fellow sub Duncan Ferguson beside him on the bench. After being fingered for his role in Gullit's downfall came blistering personal attacks from first Malcolm Macdonald, who publicly chastised Shearer as not being fit to be England captain because of his over physical approach and excessive use of the elbows, and then from Graham Kelly who revealed Shearer's threat to walk out of the World Cup team if he was punished by the FA for the kick on Neil Lennon. Kelly branded his attitude 'childish'. By the end of a week of Shearer baiting, Robson had arrived as the new boss. Speaking of Shearer's harsh treatment from the media in the wake of the England-Luxembourg game, Keegan said: 'They are entitled to their opinions. Alan has had it for two or three days, sometimes I think it's been two or three years. He is resilient but I wish sometimes they would look at the good points rather than decimate him. We need to back our heroes. But he knew how to respond, he had a bottle of champagne in one hand as man of the match and the match ball in the other.' Little wonder that Shearer was in the mood for a sarcastic and enigmatic response when he said: 'I'm part of a Newcastle side that has not started very well, we know that . . . I don't have to answer to anyone, least of all discredited people.' Who he was referring to he did not make clear, but he also said: 'The only people I have to prove myself to are Bobby Robson and Kevin Keegan.'

Shearer got an early chance to meet his new boss as Robson was guest of honour at Wembley. As Robson warmly greeted old friends like Pearce and Adams who played for him four England managers removed, and encouraged debutant Dyer, and welcomed Shearer, the mind wandered back to those heady days of Italia '90. Robson inadvertently mixed up so many names ten years ago. There is an old story about how he greeted his World Cup captain Bryan Robson with 'Bobby', receiving the response 'No, I'm Bryan, you're Bobby.' It has never been quite so much fun since Bobby Robson was boss of England. But at least he stumbled to a World Cup semi-final proving there is nothing better than a lucky manager. Gullit was not a lucky manager at St James's Park. He was severely criticised for the quality of his signings. Yet at Wembley, the last Gullit signing made, created a huge impression on the nation. Twenty-year-old Kieron Dyer was indeed as Keegan suggested a revelation. Dyer was brought down for the penalty for Shearer's first goal, and Dyer's magnificent run and low cross enabled Shearer to collect his hat-trick with a tap-in. However the focus was firmly on Shearer and his twenty-two-minute hat-trick. He later said, 'If I get the chances I'll put them away. I've always said there are no easy games, but you have got to stick the ball in the back of the net and that's what I've done . . . and I don't have to answer to anyone.' In fact all week on international duty Shearer didn't answer to anyone. He opted out of media interviews, he didn't face any questions. He's from the old school of doing his talking on the pitch. He knew it was the time for action not words. A hat-trick was a powerful way to win the Wembley crowd over, and naturally it succeeded. Fans waited patiently an hour after the game, one group with a banner reading 'We still love you Alan.' Robson had also joined the case for the preservation of Shearer's status. 'It is important for everyone to understand that I am the manager. I will explain to the players that what the club needs right now is strong leadership. A person who can run the club intelligently and sensibly. In the case of Alan Shearer I see him as a strong personality at this club and obviously he is the captain. I understand and respect that.' He later added: 'Everyone at Newcastle wants to see him get back on the goal trail and we've got to get him absolutely focused on that situation. I am a believer in dealing with different players in different ways . . . But there has to be one thing which is consistent. The players must have and show respect for the manager . . . This is a new dawn, a new future, I'm a new manager, I'm a Geordie. We're in three cups, we're in Europe, anything is possible.'

It is tempting to say there have been too many false dawns for the Toon Army in recent years. Only a year earlier the fans turned out in dreadlock wigs and planted one on the Jackie Milburn statue in honour of Ruud Gullit.

Gullit's first eight months were certainly eventful. Ruthless dismantling of the Kenny Dalglish era was inevitable.

The man who put the style back into Stamford Bridge, and coined the phrase 'sexy football' was on a mission at Newcastle. 'I built a team at Chelsea, but I'm still looking to build another at Newcastle,' he said shortly after his appointment. Much later he observed: 'I never thought we would reach a Cup final because, when I arrived, there were so many things to be done, so many things that I wanted to change.'

Expectations were immense when Gullit replaced Dalglish. Freddy Shepherd explained the rationale in appointing Gullit: 'The lucky thing for us was that he was available. Here was a man who had done superbly at Chelsea, a man steeped in European football, a magical name in the game. I'm a firm believer that Newcastle United have to have a top name as manager, and here was one of football's very top names not only available but more than happy to take on the challenge we were offering him. He had turned down many offers from clubs in this country and abroad after leaving Chelsea seven months earlier, but he didn't turn us down. He was very pleased that we asked him to come to Tyneside and he took to the job very quickly.'

Construction of the new stand, bringing the capacity to 51,000, was on schedule for the start of season 2000–01. To keep pace with the digital TV explosion, there were plans for Newcastle's own TV station. Ambitious plans for Gullit's first full season included an expanded transfer budget for him to bring in top class talent as he increasingly convinced the board to invest in new players.

Gullit's idiosyncrasies are far too often mistaken for arrogance, or aloofness. The real Ruud is complex, an intoxicating mixture of a sophisticated style icon with an ordinary bloke happy to hang out rubbing shoulders with the people around the fashionable quayside district of Newcastle. When my daughter accompanied me to interview Ruud with prepared questions for her university newspaper article, one of world football's most recognisable characters simply smiled when asked for the five dinner guests that would top his most wanted list: 'Nelson Mandela, Martin Luther King, Hitler, Jesus, and of course Estelle [his girlfriend].' So, why Hitler? 'Well,' reflected Ruud, leaning back in his chair in my room at the quayside hotel, 'I would ask him "Why?".' Gullit placed an importance on his family life, but he believed he could absorb that into his work. He explained: 'I don't take my baggage home with me. That's a big bonus and means I can do the job better.'

After replacing Dalglish two games into the season, he had shipped out an entire team. Not exactly what you would term a tentative sort of start; sold for a total of around £15 million were David Batty, Stephane Guivarc'h, Steve Watson and Keith Gillespie. John Barnes and Bjarni Gudjonsson left while Alessandro Pistone, Philippe Albert, Carl Serrant, Paul Dalglish and Des Hamilton were loaned out. In came Duncan Ferguson, Didier Domi and Silvio Maric.

Then came a multitude of problems, criticisms and question marks over the board's choice. Shepherd responded: 'We told Ruud what a big task he had on his hands and he's a bright man, he only had to watch us play in his first match in charge against Liverpool at St James's Park to understand the size of that task. This man is nobody's fool and he would know just from watching us play, and then from working with the players, that we weren't the best. Some people have said he's a bit aloof, but they don't know him like I know him. I find him to be an honest man, sometimes brutally honest, but I can live with that. He can put his finger on what is wrong and, more importantly, he knows how to put it right. He's very bright tactically and he works hard on the training ground to make sure that the players understand fully what he wants from them. I speak to him every day so I know how shrewd this man is.

'The rest is rubbish put about by the media that we were unhappy with Ruud having a home base in Amsterdam. It has never been an issue and it certainly wasn't an issue that he spent Christmas Day with his loved ones in Amsterdam. That's where he should have been – a family man wants to be with his family. What was being written about him was just getting out of hand. We knew he had no more time off than any other manager we had employed, but every time you picked up a paper he was supposed to be in Holland when he should have been here. I spoke up because Ruud Gullit was being criticised unfairly by people with a 'little Englander' mentality. It was just ridiculous and it had to stop. We're delighted to have a manager who knows the European scene as well as Ruud does, and in simple travelling terms he can fly from here to Amsterdam and back so quickly and conveniently that it's just stupid to talk about it. Ruud Gullit is here on Tyneside when we need him to be here on Tyneside, which is most of the time. We're more than happy to have him as our manager.'

Gullit inherited what he believed was little more than the previous season's relegation battlers and it took months of tough decisions and persuasion to turn it all around. During that time Alan Shearer was a central character. One of the first major decisions concerned Shearer's which had to be done at the time to raise funds for purchases. The chairman said: In an ideal world, Steve Watson would still be here. Ruud said at the time that the lad had done nothing wrong. But sometimes you have to make sacrifices if you want to change something and Ruud did want to take a certain course of action. We got an offer from Aston Villa and Steve left with our thanks for all he had done for Newcastle United and with our best wishes for the future. Ruud explained what he wanted to do and we backed him all the way, but as I say, ideally I'd have loved Steve Watson, a Geordie boy through and through, to have stayed.

Gullit was happy with his first season at the helm. 'I look back over our season, and I think the turning point came when we lost 3-0 at Arsenal last October. We lost badly and I was able to shout out that I needed some recruits before I could do a job here.' The result was that manager and directors came out displaying a united front and the restructuring really began. Ironically talks opned prior to the FA Cup final on extending Gullit's contract.

Shepherd had every confidence Gullit would remain at St James's Park to fulfil the second season of his two-year contract, and even to take up the option of a third, despite all the hurtful accusations of his being a part-time manager. Shepherd believed Gullit had now become part of the North East fabric of life. He said: 'I honestly believe Ruud Gullit feels more comfortable in the North East of England with every passing day. This city, these great fans of ours, have gone out of their way to make him feel welcome and I know that he very much appreciated the way they chanted his name during the quarter-final Cup win over Everton. I know because he told me so, he was touched by the way our supporters rose to him. It was second nature for our supporters to chant Kevin Keegan's name, and for them to do the same for Ruud really showed him how much they recognise what he is doing for their club. Our fans aren't daft, they knew from day one what a big job he took on and they know how well he's doing that job.

'Can we keep him here? I certainly hope so, because the longer he's here the better we'll get. But managers are like anybody else, it's all down to how happy and comfortable they feel with their employer and how much job satisfaction they're getting. Ruud knows what we think about him and I really don't think our fans could be doing more to show him that they want him to stay. I'm not concerned that he has only one more year to run on his contract – let's face it, he won't have been here a year until the end of August, so he's hardly at the end of that contract. He knows how huge the job is, but he also knows just how huge a club this can be and how ambitious we are. The important thing is that he very much believes he can do the job, and he really wants to do it.'

The last prize Newcastle had won was the Fairs Cup in 1969, when Gullit was six. He was now Newcastle's nineteenth manager since the Championship trophy was last seen at St James's Park seventy-one years before. Newcastle had spent £97 million on players in just over six years under Kevin Keegan and Dalglish – although, of course, much was recouped by sales over the years – but Gullit's challenge was that not once, in nearly three generations, had Newcastle proved equal to their aspirations or lived up to their potential. Gullit spent £28 million, bringing the total to £125 million between the last three managers. Eighteen clubs have won the title since Newcastle last did. Gullit, naturally, was bent on making history rather than surrendering to it but the odds were stacked against him from the moment of his arrival. Joe Harvey managed Newcastle for thirteen years (1962–75) and Keegan promised the earth for five (1992–97) but, for the most part, the club have permitted their chief steward about a couple of years.

Gullit felt the club looked back too much to the romanticism of the past. He argued: 'Don't live in the past, that's what I try to say at Newcastle. It doesn't matter how good or bad that past was, the point is you didn't win anything. People get very romantic about the past. Big mistake. The only time you can romanticise is when you win things. Real Madrid always had style, but they lived on their European victories in the Sixties and Seventies. And Liverpool, they played all that great one-touch football, but people remember them for winning the cups. In the end, it's the one question that matters: what did you win?

'So they have an affection for Keegan, a great affection. Well, why not? That's the way it has to be. For him, it was good to realise the Newcastle crowd don't forget him. And I'll tell you, in ten years' time they won't forget him. If that made me jealous, then I would be very stupid. People appreciate Kevin Keegan here. That's a great thing for him. When I go to Milan, people appreciate what I did for them there. I like that. And, you know, players notice things like that and they think, "If I do my job well here, maybe one day they will do that for me." I understand that. If I didn't, I would be really pathetic.'

Gullit, it has often been suggested, didn't have a great deal of time for his employers at Stamford Bridge, but he said: 'When I came here, I was surprised at how well-organised the club is and how dedicated Freddy Shepherd and Freddie Fletcher are.' Was he surprised? 'Well, I read in the newspapers about what happened in Marbella with Shepherd. But since I've worked with him, I've made up my own mind. I now take a totally different view. He's very dedicated, he works every day very hard. The media tell the public incredible things. Me, I am very grateful Shepherd gave me the chance to come here.'

When he arrived, Gullit had to assess fifty-odd players, sell as many as he could, improve and motivate others, decide on his best team, settle on an attacking format which suited them and bring in new names as and when they and money became available. On top of all that, there was Alan Shearer, whose £15 million fee Gullit had described as 'a waste of money' two years before. He was not going to be allowed to forget it!

1

The first managerial casualty of the season – after TWO games!

Ruud Gullit's first success was to reignite the passion of the St James's Park crowd, whose roar had been neutered by the turgid displays of Kenny Dalglish's teams. The former Liverpool and Blackburn manager had been warned by the hierarchy when he arrived that he could not afford to alienate the fans, who had been used to a warm and emotional manager in Kevin Keegan, whose teams produced stunning football and who was prepared to face them to answer criticism if necessary. Dalglish was one of the few managers with a reputation big enough to satisfy the Geordie fans following the club's decision to part with Keegan. Now Newcastle had little choice but to go for another big-name manager. Gullit had rejected more than a dozen offers from around the world since his bizarre sacking by Chelsea, but he always wanted to return to the Premiership and prove something to Ken Bates and the Stamford Bridge hierarchy.

Dalglish was the opposite of Keegan, the man he replaced as a Liverpool icon during his playing days. His coldness in front of the media is legendary but he committed a major crime in the eyes of the fans by closing some training sessions, normally attended by thousands of them to watch their heroes. His fate as Newcastle manager may well have been decided on a train from King's Cross to Newcastle on a Sunday morning in May. It was the day after the FA Cup final at Wembley. Newcastle's 2-0 defeat by Double winners Arsenal had highlighted many of the failings of Dalglish's brief reign. Two of the passengers on the 3½ hour journey that day were Freddie

9

Fletcher, Newcastle's chief executive, and Russell Jones, one of the Newcastle board of directors. Having stayed in London overnight for their FA Cup final banquet, the club's executives had booked a private railway carriage for the journey home. But they were immediately spotted on the train by Newcastle fans returning from London and, private or not, their carriage was soon flooded with complaining Geordies, some of whom were in a spectacularly relaxed condition.

For most of the journey Fletcher and Jones were harangued and ridiculed by the Geordie supporters. Their complaint? In a word – Dalglish. He had dismantled a stylish team built by Keegan and replaced it with anonymous players and a functional style. Had it been a team capable of winning, the fans would have forgiven him. But not only was it a team boring to watch, it didn't win matches either. If Fletcher and Jones were unaware of the depth of the feeling against Dalglish before they got on that train, they certainly weren't by the time they got off at Newcastle. They reported the anti-Dalglish feeling to the boardroom.

Forced to step down because of newspaper allegations about comments made in a Marbella brothel, Shepherd, the club chairman, and Douglas Hall, his deputy and the major shareholder, had originally sacked Keegan and appointed Dalglish. Now that performance in the FA Cup final had raised the question of Dalglish's future. The next match, the first competitive game of the new season, settled the issue. Newcastle were jeered off St James's Park by disgruntled fans after a goalless draw with ten-man Charlton. Dalglish didn't know it, but his time was up.

It is rare indeed for the opening match of a season not to be accompanied by hope, hype and expectation. The late summer sun has a habit of softening the inbred fatalism of many supporters; a flourish of the manager's chequebook in the preceding weeks can fool even the most cynical of observers into the odd dream of trophies come May.

Newcastle United were expected to thrash their newly promoted opponents. Not all is won or lost on the first Saturday of a new campaign, of course. Newcastle's 2-1 victory over Sheffield Wednesday twelve months earlier had hardly led to a championship assault and neither, necessarily, would defeating Charlton. In fact, the idea of claiming Arsenal's crown was a mere fantasy for most Newcastle fans, but a vast improvement on the thirteenth-place finish of the previous season most certainly was not. Failure to beat Alan Curbishley's team seemed inconceivable. Such an outcome would mean more than just mild humiliation. Since their play-off final win on penalties over Sunderland in May, Charlton had invested around £2 million on new players and were heavily backed to make a swift return whence they came. Kenny Dalglish, after splashing out £15 million on nine acquisitions, knew the pressure was on if his side failed to gel quickly.

Dalglish entered his thirtieth year in the game fired up for the new season. But his message seemed more about stability than going for glory. He said: 'We just want to be positive and achieve a better league position than last time. We did well in the Champions' League, we reached the FA Cup final and we had a very good run in the Coca-Cola. There are no ghosts to be overcome there. But we are not going to make any predictions.'

Robert Lee would have happy memories when Newcastle lined up against Charlton as he was at the London club for ten years until Kevin Keegan snapped him up for £650,000. He proved a bargain buy and now captained the Magpies, wanting Newcastle to be Premiership title material: 'We can compete with the big four. Newcastle have come a long way in a short space of time. But our early strides were so great we couldn't keep going.'

A caller to *Six-O-Six* demanded the sacking of Kenny Dalglish barely 100 minutes after Newcastle's opening game.

When one reporter enquired 'how disappointed' Dalglish happened to be after the match, he was merely posing the kind of question the disgruntled footsoldiers of the Toon Army would have liked to put to the Newcastle manager as they left, their boos ringing round the ground. But when it came to facing the press Dalglish had the unhappy knack of treating even the most innocent of queries as a verbal dagger. He asked his inquisitor to 'spit out your dummy and re-phrase the question'.

'I'm not having that,' the affronted journalist retorted and followed up with a frank counter-attack which left a slightly chastened Dalglish obliged to answer his original question – up to a characteristically obtuse point.

'We're disappointed not to come away with the three points,' he said, 'but we're level on points with Manchester United and we're one ahead of Chelsea. If we finish the season like that, we'll all be happy.' On this showing, Newcastle would be struggling to finish level with Charlton! They had looked the part in pre-season, but in the Premiership, against the debutants from London SE7, they looked like the same team that fell apart after beating Barcelona last season.

Of the £15 million invested by Dalglish in the close season, there was little palpable return. Only two of his nine new players began the match and while Dietmar Hamann, the German international, and Laurent Charvet, the Frenchman, could be reasonably satisfied with their own performances, there was nothing to suggest any real creativity, no sign of a team. The Newcastle left side, in the shape of Speed and Pistone, combined to produce barely a single pass worthy of the name. Dalglish signed Guivarc'h to partner Shearer even though he had his critics at France 98 – including Premiership pundits working for TV. But there was no doubting his club scoring record – thirty-two last season – and his self-belief. He said: 'Going to Newcastle as a World Cup winner will be a big boost to my confidence. The fact that I didn't score in the World Cup doesn't really matter and the fact that I missed some chances won't affect me. In my time at Auxerre I took plenty of chances and I'm sure I'll do the same when I get to Newcastle.' Judgement would be reserved on the partnership of Guivarc'h and Shearer, bearing in mind the minimal impact of previous striking imports like Jon Dahl Tomasson and Andreas Andersson.

Steve Wraith, editor of the influential *Number Nine* fanzine, said: 'Kenny has got to start winning matches quickly because I don't think the board will stand for another season like the last one. But I don't think Kenny has been given time yet. He has got to be allowed time to get everything in the place he wants it. We were running before we could walk under Keegan. Those were incredible days but it had to slow down. That has happened under Kenny, who has taken time to take stock of the situation.' The return of Freddy Shepherd and Douglas Hall to the fold upset some fans but people inside the club knew they had big ambitions and would be ruthless to fulfil them.

Dalglish's demise ran far deeper than the result on the opening day; behind the scenes there was a simmering row. It happened before the season started over claims that Keith Gillespie's career was threatened by injury. The showdown was with United's chief executive Freddie Fletcher after a local paper claimed an ankle ligament problem could leave the twenty-three-year-old on the scrapheap – a claim vigorously denied by the player. Dalglish publicly exonerated the journalist and publication concerned and said: 'If there is someone employed by the club sending stories like that they don't deserve to be here.'

Chairman Freddy Shepherd was called in to mediate between the two senior United figures. Dalglish was seething when reporters asked him about Gillespie being finished. Gillespie's medical from the aborted Boro deal showed an ankle problem, but Dalglish was adamant it wasn't career-threatening. Fletcher claimed the story appeared as a result of a misunderstanding. But it needed the intervention of Shepherd to calm it down. It was later claimed that Dalglish had threatened to resign during the outburst.

But would his latest acquisition offer Dalglish's side some much-needed flair? Over 9,000 fans turned out for a reserve game at St James's Park to see new signing Nolberto Solano score a superb goal on his first appearance in a Magpies shirt against Stockport.

The game kicked off fifteen minutes late to allow a crowd of 9,047 in to watch the Peruvian international. Solano, the twenty-three-year-old captain of the Peruvian national side, was signed by Dalglish from Argentinian giants Boca Juniors for £2.5 million and was pressed into immediate action.

Said 'Nol Sol': 'I know all about the problems Tino Asprilla had at Newcastle not so long ago regarding his long flights home. I will be making sure that the same thing does not happen to me.' Dalglish's patience with the Colombian striker had been severely tested when he went missing after international matches in South America. The controversial star, signed by Kevin Keegan, was sold back to Italians Parma for £6 million. Wing-back Solano became the first ever Peruvian to try his luck in England. 'I have already spoken to our national coach, Juan Carlo Oblitas. And the arrangement now is that I will only go back home for very important games. I will not have to go back until June, when we play the Copa America.'

Robert Lee was pulled out of Glenn Hoddle's England get-together. The Newcastle skipper was withdrawn by Dalglish after injuring his toe against Charlton. Shearer joined the squad, along with the Geordies' defender Carl Serrant, who was not even a sub on Saturday. But ex-England star John Barnes faced weeks out with hamstring trouble.

Despite the squad problems, Gary Speed insisted Newcastle's lack-lustre start to the Premiership was a blip not to be repeated. Another poor result at Stamford Bridge would surely see the knives starting to be sharpened for Dalglish. While Newcastle's confidence had taken a backward step, Speed believed it was far too early for pessimism.

He said: 'We just didn't get into the right positions when dominating the possession and pressing forward. We must get better crosses into Alan Shearer and the rest of the forwards, but we're working hard to rectify this.' Shearer was a frustrated figure last season – quality ball into the box for him to feed off was at times non-existent – and Dalglish had to improve this aspect to get the best out of the club's top goal-getter. During the summer, Dalglish signed a quartet of players he wanted to deliver quality crosses. Speed admitted: 'Pre-season matches are a useful exercise but it's when you start playing Premier League games that the real business starts. That's why we were all so disappointed with our performance against Charlton, although we never underestimated them. Now all we want to do is get into Saturday's match at Stamford Bridge.'

Gillespie was heading for showdown talks; he wanted to know why the club had said his career could be over because of an ankle injury. His £3.5 million move to Middlesbrough had fallen through two weeks earlier because of the injury, sustained in a defeat at Tottenham in April. Gilly insisted his career was far from over and was back in full training. His solicitor considered legal action against the club.

At a routine press conference in the build-up to his second match of the season at Stamford Bridge, Dalglish said Newcastle and Chelsea were both under immediate pressure to put behind them disappointing starts to the season.

Dalglish could comfortably field a side of players from nine different footballing nations. Chelsea, likewise, fielded only two Englishmen. Shearer, always immensely proud of his working-class Tyneside roots, insisted: 'There's a lot of foreigners in our game, but it can work both ways. There are a lot of top class players in our League and that can only help. But I believe that too many average ones pouring in will hinder it . . . It would be nice if every team was full of English players. But you're never going to see that, it's just not the case.'

One of Dalglish's many imports was Laurent Charvet, the French defender who had played for Chelsea. Dalglish was impressed with Charvet in a game against the Geordies at the end of the season, and agreed the £450,000 asking price, and the unflappable Frenchman was in the heart of the defence at the expense of the more experienced Belgian international Philippe Albert. Dalglish joked: 'In these days of ridiculous fees I call him my Asda signing. I don't think, though, that he is the sort of player who believes he has a point to prove. We're delighted with him.'

The evidence of the Gullit era at Stamford Bridge was on view as Newcastle fans looked on enviously at Dennis Wise showing off the Cup Winners' Cup and the Coca-Cola Cup on the pitch before kick-off. In contrast to silverware, Dalglish discussed the virtues of sweat.

Commitment, workrate and those old-fashioned British attributes were 'the least people who support the club deserve', he argued after two points from two hard-fought draws.

With so much talent on show from every part of the globe, it was depressing to discuss sweat rather than polished football. But it was that sort of match. Apart from a superb interchange of passes between Zola and Poyet that led to Babayaro's goal, there was more perspiration than inspiration.

The most disappointing aspect of the Chelsea performance was the lack of goals from a team that managed more than a hundred in the previous season, two-thirds of which Gullit had been in charge. Under Gullit there were the trademark defensive blunders, but the forwards usually outscored their opponents. Vialli said: 'Every manager wants to win games and trophies, and of course my ideas are quite the same as Ruudi's ideas. Some things have changed but nothing strange.'

Referee Uriah Rennie booked two Italians for diving. First Pistone after eighteen minutes when he fell after a challenge from Di Matteo and then in the last minute Casiraghi for trying to win a penalty. Frank Leboeuf was furious not to be awarded a penalty – his French pal Laurent Charvet made the tackle. 'He was lucky.' Leboeuf was sorry to see him leave the Bridge, 'but I am happy for him, he deserves to play in a good team like Newcastle. Shearer hit the post but didn't play so well because we did a good job. So it is difficult for me to say whether defence is our priority – as I play at the back!'

Dalglish said: 'I think we deserved a point because we came here and got a result against a team many people think can win the title. We kept battling away and, judging by Charlton's result today (5-0 at home to Southampton), our result last week wasn't too bad! The players should be commended for their hard work and anyone who says players like Alan Shearer, Dietmar Hamann and Nolberto Solano haven't got flair are watching a different team.'

2

The arrival of Ruud Gullit

Newcastle directors secretly travelled to Amsterdam for talks with Ruud Gullit on Monday, August 24. Whether they used false names or not, they had the perfect cover – the media touting Gullit for the job at White Hart Lane! Tottenham's crisis and inevitable link with Gullit as a replacement for Christian Gross was a more than useful smokescreen but it also added urgency to the top secret mission.

I rang Ruud on his mobile for a comment about being the fans' choice for the Spurs job. He was in a good mood, laughing and joking, and clearly he was in company as the laughter of his friends was easily heard. He gave me his usual welcome: 'Hello, lovely boy.' He was fascinated to hear how much the Spurs fans wanted him and when I asked him for a comment, he remarked: 'That is very flattering, but I have heard nothing from Tottenham.' Comments had been attributed to him recently that he wouldn't want to come back to England after the way he had been treated at Chelsea. 'Oh no, it's not so, I loved my time in England and I would come back to the Premiership . . . we shall have to wait and see.' Ruud never let on to me about any other Premiership club, and nor did I ask him; no one had an inkling.

Only later that evening came my tip that major events were afoot, though my contact was extremely cagey about the details. When I guessed that it was Dalglish out and Gullit in, there was silence. That was all I needed to know.

Later still, in a private conversation with someone in the know at Spurs, I was informed that the North London club had been told the previous day that if they had any lingering interest in Gullit then they had better get a move on, because he would be going elsewhere 'within forty-eight hours'. The Spurs board felt Ruud had the charisma and would attract players, but might not be the best man for a difficult job in the longer term. They had not changed their minds since the week of Gullit's removal from Chelsea. There had been initial interest then, but having decided to stick with Gross and after hearing all the anti-Gullit rumours emanating from Stamford Bridge, they were put off him, and had not changed their minds.

The *Sun* newspaper's poll of Spurs candidates put Gullit well out on top. 'Fans clearly believe Dutch superstar Gullit would bring the style and quality players Spurs need to end years of depression,' said the paper, adding: 'Gullit is definitely being discussed inside the club as chairman Alan Sugar and his directors decide when best to part company with Gross . . . Spurs know that if they turned to Gullit, they would have to allow him to do the job his way. In return, they would get a huge surge in interest plus the prospect of attracting top foreign stars to the club.'

I broke the story of Gullit's impending appointment at Newcastle on the morning of Thursday, August 27. The news landed on rival newspaper desks between 10.30pm and 10.35pm the previous night in the *Mirror*'s first editions, and was immediately picked up by PA, Reuters and BBC Radio 5 Live just before midnight. You have to admire radio's gall, as they rang me at midnight and then strongly questioned whether the story was right!

The Times reported next morning: 'A degree of confusion last night surrounded the future of the Newcastle United manager Kenny Dalglish, amid reports that the former Chelsea coach, Ruud Gullit, is set to be unveiled as the Scotsman's successor at St James's Park later today. While a director of the club described the claims as "absolute nonsense" last night, other well-placed sources refused to dismiss the rumours out of hand. Certainly, gossip has been circulating on Tyneside for several weeks that Dalglish's sometimes unhappy nineteen-month spell at the United helm might be coming to a close. The name of Gullit, the former Holland international, has been prominently mentioned.'

I arrived at Heathrow to travel to Monte Carlo with Chelsea for the Super Cup against Real Madrid. Gullit left Amsterdam on an early flight, arriving at Heathrow just as Vialli and the Chelsea squad departed for Nice. From a public phone in the departure lounge I conducted a succession of interviews, one a live BBC Breakfast TV interview billed as 'The Battle of the Tabloids' as the *Sun* had run a story linking Gullit to Spurs.

For hours no one was sure as there was a media black-out from St James's Park. But the Stock Exchange was told at 3.50pm, in accordance with City rules for listed companies, that Gullit would replace Dalglish. Gullit had agreed a two-year contract, with an additional one-year option.

I rang Ruud on his mobile that afternoon from my Nice hotel. He told me that he was drawn to St James's Park by an everlasting memory of the Geordies' passion for their football. He had turned down numerous job offers but chose Newcastle because he could not get out of his mind just how fanatical their supporters were. He felt they were the right club at the right time. Gullit's pattern was to select a challenge with a fallen giant and build it to the very top again. Even AC Milan had become a mid-table nonentity when he arrived.

Gullit said: 'I'm very proud that I have been given this job, it is a great opportunity. My only target is to make Newcastle the greatest and overtake Arsenal and Manchester United. I want to win. I must win. I have won things all my life and I am going to Newcastle to be successful. I'm glad to come back to English football because the game is very exciting here. My reasons for choosing Newcastle are that it is a great opportunity for me and they are a club that matches my ambition – a great club, with enormous potential – and one of the memories I took back to Holland with me after my time at Chelsea was the passion of their crowd. They are a great crowd, a noisy crowd and that's what I like, nothing better. That is for me. I want more of it and just think what that ground will be like, the atmosphere inside that stadium in the year 2000, when they have 50,000 people in there.'

There were many who had thought Gullit would never return. That had seemed to be the case when he received and did not accept two firm offers from Premiership clubs, one from the Premier League in Scotland, and was approached by two consortiums who wanted him to be part of takeovers in English football. Add to that half a dozen offers from around the world, including the opportunity to coach Nigeria or South Africa in the World Cup, and it seemed he was happy with his self-imposed exile – but again that was another misconception. Gullit said: 'I turned down a lot of things, I didn't even speak to the clubs that wanted me. I just didn't want to get involved because I needed some rest and time to think things over. But Newcastle came along at precisely the right time and I felt they were the right club for me. A club with a lot of ambition and a club that wants to go forward. There was no heavy negotiation with Newcastle. They wanted me, I wanted them. I did not put a gun to their head. There was no crazy money talk.

The only discussion we had was that I be allowed to do the job my way. I had to have that assurance.'

Gullit refused to apportion blame to his predecessor Dalglish or Keegan for failing to turn the passion of the fans into tangible success. He said: 'The person I feel sorry for is Kenny Dalglish. It is the only part of this I do not like. A few months ago I was Kenny, dismissed and out of a club. It happened to me. Now it is different for me. I am in the other chair. That is a part of football that I don't like, but you just have to accept it. As a player, one day you could be here, one day you could be there. Kevin Keegan and Kenny Dalglish did a very good job, and I'll try to continue that, and even try to do something more. The most important thing for me in taking the job is that I think I can do well.'

In his typical manner, Gullit added: 'There's a saying in Holland and also in Italy: "He who is in a hurry goes slowly". And you can apply that to what happens at football clubs like Newcastle. Everybody wants to go quick, quick, quick, but instead they go backwards. My intention is to take it a step at a time.' The Dutchman would blow away the pragmatism of Dalglish, but had learned not to neglect his defence.

For his first game in charge, Gullit left team selection to Dalglish's coaches for the only time. He said: 'I want to see them on Sunday, to see how they play. I'll be in the dressing room to say some words but that is all.' He would also be bringing in his own number two: 'This time I want my own people around me. I do not want a repeat of what happened when I was at Chelsea.' Gullit clearly felt he was let down by some of the backroom staff at Stamford Bridge. He added: 'My own staff will be with me now. All I ask from the Newcastle fans is to be patient.'

He had just won a first-class return trip to Singapore at a golf tournament when the call from Newcastle took him in a different direction. 'I was not ready to come back,' said Gullit as he sipped champagne after completing final negotiations with Newcastle's chief executive Freddie Fletcher and chairman Freddy Shepherd. 'I was enjoying the rest and playing golf with friends. I was enjoying my family. I was beginning to feel guilty at not saying "Yes" to anyone. Then the call came from Newcastle. It was as if I had been waiting for the right call, the right club. I knew this was the moment. Newcastle are a club that attracts me because of their size, their ambition, their style and, of course, their fans. Ruud Gullit is going to do everything inside him to give those fans and the club what they want. Those fans know me. They saw me play, they know I like style. I like my teams to play the kind of football that I enjoyed playing. When I am sitting in the stand or on the bench as coach, I am like the supporter. I want to be entertained. I want to win playing good, attractive football. I want to get on my feet and cheer and sing!'

Chelsea were now out of his system. 'The great thing about Ruud Gullit is that he has nothing to prove, nothing to prove to anyone. There was a lot of things said and accusations made when I left Chelsea. I would like to say this: I have read that I will be earning £1 million a year. It is nowhere near that.

'It could not have been so bad at Chelsea because already I have had phone calls from Monaco, where Chelsea play the Super Cup against Real Madrid. The players are wishing me well and that is good. It makes me glad to be back in English football. I am delighted to be back. The difference now is that before one chairman did not want me, a new one does. That is football. That is change.'

Gullit's agent joked that Ruud had accepted the job as a queue-jumping exercise. Jon Smith said: 'It is a thirty-five-year wait to get a season ticket for Newcastle and Ruud was advised that this was the only way he was going to get his early. Over the last six months it has been very difficult for Ruud because of some of the comments of Chelsea chairman Ken Bates. It was a question of waiting for the right opportunity. He turned down five jobs, and this is the right one. Negotiations lasted about a minute. They made us an offer, we said, "yes", and that was it.'

Shepherd said: 'In welcoming Ruud to Newcastle, we believe we have the ideal person to succeed Kenny and continue the club's development. We have made clear our determination to take the club to the highest level and to play entertaining and attractive football in the process.'

The row over Dalglish's departure simmered – sacking or resignation? The club claimed they had been advised by Dalglish on August 18 that he wished to resign as team manager as soon as possible.

Gullit loves talking sexy football. He was at it again as he lorded it over St James's Park at his public unveiling the next day. He said: 'You can't create something that is not there. OK, I'd like a sexy team but how they perform, and the ability of the players individually, is what I must spot – and what position is the best for certain players. From there you build. And if you win games, confidence comes and then you play better football. I'm the manager here – that's all, even if I take part in training sessions. I've been a lazy bum for six months so it's time I did something!'

It was only nineteen months earlier that Dalglish had been paraded, albeit less flamboyantly, before the Newcastle fans while Keegan slipped out anonymously. This time, as Gullit basked in the near-overwhelming adulation of 5,000 expectant supporters, Dalglish quietly drove away, to a meeting with his solicitors. Contrary to Newcastle's claims that he had offered to resign, Dalglish insisted he had been sacked. In a statement, he said: 'The truth is that I did not resign. They terminated my contract without notice or any prior warning to me. I received first news of Newcastle United's decision through the press. No offer of compensation has been made. I have appointed legal advisers and will defend the interests of myself and my family vigorously.'

Inside the ground the contrasting mood could not have been more obvious. The joy of the fans was reflected in the smile which stretched across the face of the man chosen as their latest Messiah.

Even the club chefs stood in line to greet the dreadlocked Dutchman as, dressed in the black and white regimental uniform of the Toon Army, he climbed into the Gallowgate Stand and gripped the hands of the fans which stretched out to him. Gullit made it plain that he had joined the Magpies as manager only – his playing days were over.

Gullit would not look back on his reign at Chelsea, nor compare the merits of Keegan's exciting side against the less extravagant Dalglish era. He said: 'If I enthuse about Kevin's team it would seem I have nothing good to say about Kenny's. Both did very well here and did some things which were for the good of the club. I want to continue what they began in some areas. I met the players for fifteen minutes after training and it was OK. It is very difficult for players because naturally some had a special bond with Kenny and some did with Kevin. I told them I understood this. It is not easy but we have to continue – and they have to think about their careers. We have to try to be successful.'

He confirmed that the speculation linking him with Spurs had been a useful diversion. 'Tottenham never approached me and all of the speculation linking me with them was a smokescreen.'

He had a clear understanding of his priorities. 'First, we have to be in the right shape as a team, and I have to see what system the team are happy playing. It would be difficult for me on Sunday to be on the bench for my first match. I want to see what the players' talents are and what their movements are like. That's why I want to sit in the stand.'

Gullit also refuted suggestions he would try to fill the team with foreign imports. 'At Chelsea I brought youngsters into the team and

I'd like to do that at Newcastle.'

At the end of an amazing day, Chelsea collected their fourth major cup in sixteen months. So much was built on Gullit's foundations.

Mark Lawrenson observed in his *Mirror* column how Dalglish had floundered in trying to satisfy a demanding public. He observed: 'It's different in Newcastle – they just want to go and be entertained by their team every week. When you are a labourer and you pull in maybe £200 a week and spend £20 to go and watch the Magpies, you don't want to see a team strangling the play and scraping out a 1-0 win over Wimbledon. You want to see stylish, exciting football. You want to see goals, you want to see passion and you want to win 4-3. That was the one fact that Kenny Dalglish was never able to get to grips with, and that is the one thing that brought him down. And now Kenny is gone and Ruud Gullit has been brought in to replace him. That is a move that will go down wonderfully with the Geordie fans. His philosophies are almost identical to those of Kevin Keegan: attack, attack, attack . . . or as he put it himself, sexy football. What's more, perhaps in Gullit English football has finally found a man who will be able to draw star European players to the north of England. So far only the big London clubs have been able to do that, but if Ruud can change that I think that will be a good thing not only for Newcastle but also for the Premiership. But, speaking as somebody who lives in Newcastle, the thought of combining such a great club with Ruud Gullit – who no doubt feels he has something to prove, not least to Ken Bates – will already have the fans tingling with anticipation.'

None of the players had a clue what was going on until Dalglish met them on Friday morning. Shay Given said: 'We had heard the bulletins on the radio and seen TV broadcasts. But it wasn't until Kenny came in to say his goodbyes that we knew it was for real. The situation took us all by surprise and it's taken us a few days to get over it.'

Gullit watched Sunday's match against Liverpool from the directors' box in disgust. He rushed down to dish out a half time lecture and to stem the flood of goals. The game finished a humiliating defeat.

Gullit was in open conflict with his old club over the appointment of his chosen number two, Steve Clarke. Chelsea were seeking a six-figure transfer fee for their longest-serving player and Gullit had always suspected that it was going to be tricky to prise away any player or member of staff from the Bridge after his own acrimonious departure.

Clarke was in his final season as a player in the final year of his contract, after eleven years' service. He was appointed player-coach by

Gianluca Vialli, who didn't want to lose him but wouldn't stand in his way. Newcastle dispensed with Terry McDermott as well as Dalglish, and Gullit wanted Clarke to join him as quickly as possible, particularly after the manner of the defeat against Liverpool. Ruud had planned to sit through the entire match in the stands with his large pad, assessing the team. But as soon as the half time whistle sounded, he shot out of his seat and headed for the dressing room.

The laid-back Dutchman was anything but relaxed. He was angry and it showed. He stormed into the dressing room where coach Alan Irvine was standing by the blackboard chalk in hand. Gullit took the chalk and changed the tactics, switching from three at the back to four. He was astonished at the freedom being afforded to Michael Owen and Steve McManaman, and Gullit's switch of systems at least stemmed the avalanche of goals being conceded. He told the players to have pride in themselves and have pride in the name of Newcastle United, and was dismayed by the displays of so many experienced internationals. He spent many hours after the game discussing events, and was up early on Bank Holiday Monday.

For someone with a supposed aversion to the training ground, Gullit was certainly preaching the work ethic. He was out of his Newcastle hotel at 8.30am to be one of the first to the training ground half an hour later ready to sort out his team. Gullit had clear ideas about what was needed and had identified the problems, but he drove out of the training ground without uttering a word to waiting journalists.

Speculation was rife that Gullit's priority was to be assured that Alan Shearer would be part of the new era. Very much associated with Dalglish, there was even unrest about Shearer's performance against Liverpool. If Shearer showed any inclination not to be ready to pull his weight and wanted to go, then Gullit was big enough to sell him. The money – at first £18 million was talked about – he could raise by selling Shearer would be used to buy star quality from abroad.

Shearer, Stuart Pearce and Robert Lee met Gullit to discuss the future and the direction things would go. Gullit's arrival threw Shearer's contract talks into renewed doubt; he was already stalling on negotiations with Dalglish. After all, when Gullit was in charge at Chelsea, he had suggested Shearer was a 'waste of money' at £15 million. But Shearer said: 'I'm happy. The Newcastle change has had no effect on me.'

3

Shearer's future immediately on the agenda

It was Ruud's thirty-sixth birthday bash on September 1 in Amsterdam and with a couple of days' break for the team pre-arranged by his predecessor, he relaxed with close friends and family. When I rang him to pass on my best wishes, he was clearly enjoying his day.

There was a chance meeting with a fellow Dutchman who had been on strike since the start of the season at Nottingham Forest. Ruud told Pierre van Hooijdonk it would be in his best interests to return to his club. Eventually Pierre took his advice, albeit weeks later.

Ruud said: 'I bumped into him when I was in Amsterdam and I told him what I thought about the whole affair. We spoke about his situation.' When Pierre was persuaded to return by Forest's director of football Irving Scholar, Ruud added: 'It was an impossible situation before, because neither Nottingham Forest nor Pierre could come out of it as winners. They were both losing. I encouraged him to at least take the initiative and talk to them. I am very pleased for him because we were just talking one evening and I had to tell him what I thought about the situation. I'm happy he listened. There is now an opening for him to say what he has to say to the club, the players and the fans.'

Gullit remembered the first time he encountered his new coaching partner, Steve Clarke. Not because he particularly stood out for St Mirren in a UEFA Cup first round tie against Feyenoord but because of the hatred at Love Street that September evening in 1983. It was directed specifically towards the Dutchman. It was his first experience of racial abuse in a football ground, on his first appearance in a European club competition. And he made an instant mark. As

24

Feyenoord's young number nine, he upstaged even the national treasure wearing the number fourteen shirt: the original Dutch master, Johan Cruyff. Gullit produced a virtuoso performance and a stunning goal, the only one of the game.

'Even back then it was clear Ruud was an immense talent,' Clarke recalled. 'He played on the right wing for the first hour, then dropped back to sweeper. I marked him in the second leg out in Rotterdam. We lost 2-0 but I think I acquitted myself quite well.'

It now fell to Clarke to direct the unseen work that desperately needed to be done on the training ground. He brought to his task not just the perceptive playing brain that allowed him to fit seamlessly into the cosmopolitan Chelsea set in his latter years at Stamford Bridge, but also the natural resolve that pulled him through the dark days of relegation and personal demotion. Clarke did not hit the same heights as Gullit in his playing career but he made it to international level, deserving much more as an accomplished right-back or central defender than the six caps he won for Scotland. At thirty-five, a year younger than his boss, he had hung up his boots to help Gullit on Tyneside.

'It was a condition of the move,' Clarke explained. 'But this would have been my last season as a player anyway and I didn't expect to get into the Chelsea team that often. It was a job opportunity I just couldn't turn down.' The reserved, soft-spoken Scot and the flamboyant Dutchman seemed a unlikely couple. But Gullit was determined he wouldn't make the same mistake he had at the Bridge. He wanted his own man as his assistant.

Their friendship is obvious, incontrovertible evidence of the maxim that opposites attract. Clarke cannot explain it: 'It's a difficult one. All I know is that we do get on well. We are opposite characters. I am quite quiet and more reserved than Ruud. He enjoys being in the public eye, I'd rather stay in the background. I think he respected me as a player, I think he respected the job I did for the team. I wasn't one of the superstars at Chelsea, I wasn't one of the big names, but I think he respected the way I went about my business. The way I looked after myself, the way I was prepared to do a job for the team. I didn't really go out of my way to make myself look a good player. I was always happiest if the team won and somewhere along the line that's made an impression on him.

'The only time in twelve years that I came close to leaving Chelsea was a six-month spell in 1989-90. I was being asked to play full-back, but was told I couldn't go forward. It was a compromise of my principles, so I thought it would be better to move.'

Those principles unite Clarke and Gullit: 'When it comes down to football, Ruud and I have similar ideas. We both believe in pass and move. We want players who are comfortable on the ball and players who understand why they make a run – not just people who make runs for the sake of it. Clever players.'

Now Clarke's working days extended far beyond lunchtime. Along with Gullit, he took training, then returned to his office to watch videos of prospective opponents or possible new players. The advantage he has over other assistant managers is the fact that he had played against the vast majority of Premiership players recently.

Ruud himself had concerns away from the training ground. A style offensive was underway, with an at-home photo shoot for *Hello!* The front page featured Ruud, Estelle and their new baby Joelle. Despite all the high profile stars coming and going from St James's Park in recent years Ruud was the first to merit a twelve-page spread in the magazine for worldwide celebrities.

He talked about his lovely apartment, his lovely girlfriend, and his lovely new club. The apartment was in Amsterdam, not Tyneside. Geordie fans raised an eyebrow at that, as well as his description of the job as 'very good work experience for me' and his view that 'Newcastle hasn't won anything yet, so it's the perfect place for me.' About Estelle Ruud said: 'I want to enjoy Estelle and that comes in steps. If you have something really special, you don't want to have it all at once. It's like food; you take your time over it, savour it. To me, Estelle is the starter, the main course and the ice cream with whipped cream on top.'

So much for the new wave nutrition.

Heather Rabbatts, chief executive of the London borough of Lambeth, was featured on the Ego page of *The Director* magazine. When asked which chief executive she most admired, she named Ruud Gullit. Her reasons: 'He's incredibly sexy, speaks five languages and has introduced a softer approach to the motivation and management of a team.'

One man who seemed happier was Keith Gillespie who proved his fitness with Northern Ireland in their 3-0 defeat in Turkey – even if he was hit by a bottle and had his underpants stolen along with a £4,000 watch and silver bracelet! Lawrie McMenemy planned to tell Gullit that Gillespie was back to fitness, after his first match since he ripped ankle ligaments against Spurs in April. Gillespie admitted: 'The Northern Ireland manager has asked me if it is okay for him to send a message to Ruud Gullit about me. There's no problem with that, and

I really feel I proved a lot of people wrong out here in Istanbul. I didn't have to play myself in, there was no problem with the ankle. In fact, I didn't even think about it.'

The first speculation regarding Shearer's future arose just eleven days after Gullit's arrival on Tyneside. The club denied reports that Serie A side Parma had made a £14 million bid for Shearer, after the Italians were said to be interested in reuniting him with his former club-mate Tino Asprilla. Italian sports newspaper *Gazzetta dello Sport* reported that Parma had made a 40 billion lire offer, but Newcastle continued to insist Shearer was not for sale at any price and that, anyway, they had not received any bid. Freddie Fletcher said: 'Alan Shearer is not for sale. He is going nowhere. Anyone who thinks differently is wasting their time.'

Gullit assured Shearer he had a future at Newcastle. The pair met for talks at the club's training ground. The following day Gullit picked his first Newcastle team, for the midweek game at Aston Villa. He said: 'Everyone is enthusiastic. Obviously all the players want to show their best side to me and I am looking forward to this game. If we get a good result then the confidence will come. Already among the fans I have noticed the same sort of passion which exists in Italian football.'

Ruud also warned he would have to buy: 'There will be a time of assessment but you have to be interested if the best players come on to the market. It also depends on the board but I'm not afraid to spend money on good players. Games like this will tell us if we have a good squad. At the moment, I don't really know. It's always difficult to organise things so quickly. I will take it one step at a time and try to introduce things to the players gradually, like I've done in the past. We need a result to restore some confidence and we have to be disciplined.'

Gullit took his new team to Villa anxious to provide the best service possible for Shearer to end his nine-game Premiership run without scoring, and demanded an improvement on the shambles of the defeat by Liverpool. He was relying on Stephen Glass to supply the service for Shearer. Glass would be on the wing from the start, as Gullit said: 'I don't usually talk about individuals but Alan Shearer is one of the best strikers around. He is like the Guns of Navarone. But he must be given the ammunition from other people. He can't do it all on his own. The team has not been working well and it is up to me to find the right people for the right positions. I believe that this team still needs some players adding to it and I know my priorities. It's also like a watch. If you have a nice watch and there's nothing inside it, then it doesn't work. A watch is about its mechanism as much as the way it looks.

'For the last couple of months, Alan has probably not been the gun or the watch he used to be. Whether he's been happy or not, I don't know. But I don't talk about individuals, it's all about the team. I have David Batty filling in the holes, and that's just as important to me. I don't care if Alan scores twenty goals this season. If he does then I'll be happy, but I'll be just as happy if David Batty scores twenty.'

The Villa boss John Gregory still rated Shearer as the best in the business, but he was also confident the prospect of facing England's captain would not worry his emerging young defender Gareth Barry, who had played only four senior games so far, but impressed against Nicolas Anelka of Arsenal and Everton's Duncan Ferguson. 'I wish Alan Shearer was playing for us,' said Gregory. 'He's as good as ever, and I regard him as England's number nine. But Gareth will just get on with it. Nothing perturbs him, he's just a laid-back kind of kid who will treat this as just another game.'

Villa had failed to beat Newcastle since the Geordies were promoted in 1993. Their last ten meetings had seen Villa collect just two points. This was Ruud's opening team (4-4-2): Given; Watson, Charvet, Albert, Pearce; Solano (Guivarc'h, 70), Lee, Glass, Speed; Shearer, Andersson (Ketsbaia, 59). Substitutes not used: Barton, Pistone; Perez. Guivarc'h was dropped despite his scoring debut against Liverpool, but Serrant was the only defender left out – perhaps surprisingly given the way Owen ran amok – while the back three became a four.

The new management team: Gullit, Armani-suited and standing upright, arms folded; the more diminutive Clarke tracksuited and leaning forward on the hoarding in front of the dugout. Clarke stood to the left but as Gullit's right-hand man wrote every observation of importance in his notepad. On the pitch, Newcastle mirrored their new management team: static. They only fleetingly sprang to life when Gullit sent on his number fourteen, Temuri Ketsbaia, to inject a little pace and passion. At the final whistle, Gullit straightened his tie and strode nonchalantly back to the dressing-rooms. He stressed he was 'no magician' after watching Newcastle crash again. England Under-21 star Lee Hendrie's sixty-second-minute penalty deservedly gave Villa the points, after Pearce was punished for wrestling Julian Joachim to the ground. Shearer was isolated but Gullit managed to detect a saving grace as his side's late rally was expertly repelled by joint leaders

Villa. He said: 'I've only had the team two days and in the case of some players, one day. I'm not a magician but as a team they played well. What I saw tonight pleased me. I will give the team a compliment because it was hard for Villa.'

The bemused faces in the press room were a giveaway. 'I have the feeling, if I may say so, that you do not agree,' he continued. 'I must have seen a different game.' As one member of the press corps muttered after Gullit had performed his disappearing trick: 'Not a magician? He can certainly see things the rest of us can't.'

Harsh as the penalty award may have been, Gullit surprised many when he pronounced himself 'happy' with the performance. Villa would not have been flattered if a volley by their Geordie exile, Alan Thompson, had gone in rather than clipping the crossbar in the later stages. Gullit's change of system could not cover up some alarming deficiencies, with Joachim's darting runs exposing Newcastle's defensive squareness much as Owen had done. The only difference was that whereas the Anfield prodigy was ruthlessness personified, Villa squandered a hat-trick of openings in the space of seven minutes early on.

'Of course we have to bring some players,' Gullit said, holding court in Villa Park's interview room. 'We knew that already.' What he and Clarke did not know, perhaps, was that they needed to bring in quite so many.

Indeed, Shearer's agents were caught arriving at Highbury the very next day, fuelling more speculation about his future. The England captain's representatives, Tony Stephens and Jon Holmes, slipped into the stadium for discussions with their new associate, Robert Gutowski from Marquee UK. When confronted as they entered the ground, one of the trio tried to hide the group's identity by claiming they were 'from the caterers'. Holmes later denied that he and his new partners were discussing an imminent Shearer deal. He insisted: 'We were at Arsenal to talk about our merger within the Marquee Group and the stadium problems at Highbury.' Aston Villa admitted they would be in the market for the player if he became available, while Arsene Wenger needed a top-flight striker following Arsenal's poor scoring start to the season. But there had been no official approach.

Meanwhile, Gullit was reported to have lined up his first major signing, Fiorentina's £6.5 million Rui Costa. The Portuguese goal-scoring midfielder was expected to sign a five-year contract but optimism that a deal was 'done' proved ill-founded. Everton, Nottingham Forest, Derby, Southampton and Newcastle's north-east neighbours Middlesbrough were all linked with Steve Watson.

Kevin Keegan suggested that Dalglish 'lost the plot' while he was in charge, and that Gullit was a better choice because Dalglish under-estimated the fans' desire for entertainment. Keegan, whose Toon team entertained but never won a trophy, said: 'I think Gullit can take the club forward. The fans want football with a certain style and I think that's where Kenny, if you like, lost the plot. I respect Kenny very much, and consider him a friend. He was not just a great player, he's proven to be a great manager. But maybe the fact I had two years playing there, and the fact my father was born up there, helped me.'

Keegan, who was now in charge at Fulham, added: 'Ruud has now got to quickly find out what the club is all about and what the supporters want. He's got to get them playing football the Geordies will enjoy. Ruud is a tremendous coach but I don't think he will enjoy it as much as I did. When I was there it was the right time, with the right people in the right place.' Keegan added: 'Fulham is a much better run club than Newcastle ever was. That's not a criticism of Newcastle – it's a credit to Fulham.'

Benfica coach Graeme Souness claimed his former Liverpool team-mate Dalglish had been made a 'scapegoat' by the Newcastle board. He said: 'The people who made the decision were under pressure themselves. They have tried to take the heat off that but the problem will not go away. Kenny never really had a chance and, without a doubt, I think he was made a scapegoat. We used to laugh at Continentals when they sacked their coaches after two or three games. You give someone that amount of money to spend and then, within two games, you are removing them. It cannot be an entirely football decision.'

The question of who would be in the side for Gullit's own second game in charge of team selection, at home to Southampton, was already the subject of much speculation. Gullit's initial attempt to explain his rotation system and how it would even involve Shearer, was sure to backfire with the kind of headlines he would rather have avoided. 'Gullit ready to axe Shearer.' Gullit actually made no reference to dropping Shearer, merely to resting him if it was necessary. He said: 'I am still swapping things around to see who fits where because, for me, this is very much like a pre-season. I could rest Alan, because it is important that he can give his best for the team. If I thought resting him would be best for both the club and Alan Shearer, then I would do it. If there's a game when I don't need him, I will do it also for the good of Newcastle and Alan. That does not need to be misinterpreted. Some players like it like that, but I know that others want to play in every game. If, in Alan's case, he has an injury, it means I can release him for a more important game.'

If it was a piece of kidology, it worked a treat. Shearer awoke to headlines that his new manager wouldn't be afraid to leave him out, and his two goals provided Gullit with his first win as Newcastle coach, also the club's first win of the season. Gullit said: 'We have not invented the wheel today. We have taken another step forward and it was pleasing that we have made some progress. I'm pleased for Alan and especially for the team.' Gullit was emphatic about Shearer's future. 'Alan is just not for sale,' insisted his new boss. 'I want him to be part of it at Newcastle, and he knows that. He's staying for sure and I have the final decision. I don't know if he wants to be a part of it. But he is in my plans. Clubs may be sniffing. But even if a big bid comes in, he is not for sale.'

So what was Shearer's state of mind after his first Premiership goals in ten attempts? 'I'm happy because we won, but I have always said that scoring is the greatest feeling in the world.' Since his comeback in January, Shearer had scored only one goal in open play from nineteen Premiership starts. He ended his 822-minute Premiership goal drought after an eighth-minute blunder by Saints keeper Paul Jones. The Welsh international should have held Ketsbaia's twenty-yarder, but fumbled the ball straight into Shearer's path. His second came from the spot after thirty-seven minutes.

There were suggestions that Shearer had ignored Gullit at the final whistle but Shearer denied this, saying: 'I didn't see him – I don't know where he was.'

But the Sunday papers were determined to make the most of any hint of a rift. Shearer was linked this time with a £20 million move to Inter Milan to partner Ronaldo, with Nwankwo Kanu (who eventually ended up at Arsenal later in the season) offered in part exchange. The *Mail on Sunday* reported: 'Shearer is about to become the most famous fall guy in the clearout being instigated by Newcastle's new manager, Ruud Gullit . . . His advisers are aware of Inter's initiative.' Rumours that Shearer was being touted around to assess interest were confirmed by Parma team manager Giorgio Bottaro, who said: 'Newcastle, or someone closely connected to them, have offered Shearer to us recently.' The same paper reported that Gullit wanted Dion Dublin, that Batty was on his way, and that despite denials of a bid for Portuguese midfielder Rui Costa, faxes had indeed been exchanged. The article was accompanied by a comment from Gullit. 'I already know what I have to do, but it needs time. Everybody is very helpful, the board, the staff, everyone. But everybody understands also that there have to be certain changes.'

There had been constant speculation about Shearer's future on Tyneside since Gullit took over from Dalglish. Bookies had stopped taking bets on him leaving St James's Park. More speculation, as Sony were reported to be involved in a £220 million takeover bid, 'attracted by the global pulling power of Gullit and Shearer'. A Sony spokesman said: 'We are considering moving into the football sector, and Newcastle are a club we are interested in.' Granada, who own Tyne Tees TV, were also linked to the club. Shares rose, and it was thought that club chairman Freddy Shepherd and majority shareholder Douglas Hall, who between them owned more than 65 per cent of the shares, would seriously consider any bid higher than the club's £193 million flotation value.

The challenge of the Cup-Winners' Cup – a first-round tie against Partizan Belgrade on Thursday September 17 – was a poignant one for the new management. For Gullit, it was a chance to settle a little unfinished business. His first managerial venture into Europe had been abruptly halted by his enforced departure from Stamford Bridge in February, when he was preparing his squad for the quarter-finals of the Cup-Winners' Cup. Clarke had actually helped Chelsea to win it. He played in defence the night Zola's goal beat Vfb Stuttgart in Stockholm. 'Yes, it will be a bit strange when Thursday comes round,' he mused. 'The Cup-Winners' Cup was a wonderful competition for Chelsea last season. It was great to go right through and win it. It would be nice to think we could do the same at Newcastle.' In reality, Newcastle were simply no longer a big force on the domestic front, let alone on the continental scene. It promised to be a hard slog. But supporters hoped Partizan Belgrade might be the first to suffer from the team's new mood. Partizan were adept and well-equipped, if a little inexperienced. They beat Dinamo Batumi, of Georgia, in the qualifying stage and, in Sasa Ilic, the attacking midfield player, possessed an outstanding talent.

'Europe still excites me. It's always different,' said Gullit. 'Partizan are a very young team, but technically they're very good. It's important that we play at our pace, because it's a big night for them.'

But first he needed to find out more about his players. Ruud closed off the training ground on Tuesday for his first real opportunity to assess a mammoth squad of would-be first-teamers. Second Division

York City provided the opposition as he put his players through a sixty-minute workout. But the club denied that a list of available players had already been circulated – at least officially! Gullit's own pursuit of Coventry skipper Dion Dublin was hotting up. He was prepared to pay £7 million for the ideal strike partner for Shearer. He also wanted the rebel De Boer twins to sign on loan, although it was a long shot to capture Frank and Ronald until the end of the season.

While in Holland, Gullit had taken the opportunity to sound out the possibilities. The twenty-eight-year-old twins were on strike in Amsterdam, refusing to play for Ajax after a Dutch FA tribunal ruled against their appeal for their lengthy contracts to be overturned. Arsene Wenger had tried to sign midfielder Ronald for Arsenal in the summer, but withdrew his offer before the case went to tribunal. The brothers wanted a move to Barcelona, coached by former Dutch World Cup boss Louis van Gaal. Ajax, though, were adamant they would not be allowed to get their own way. Gullit tried unsuccessfuly to break the deadlock by offering the brothers nine months of top-level competition in the Premiership while Ajax retained their registration.

Freddy Shepherd, meanwhile, told Leeds boss George Graham that David Batty was not for sale. Graham wanted to spend £4 million to take Batty back to Elland Road where he started his career. Shepherd felt Batty was one of the few players guaranteed a future under Gullit, who had tried to sign him when he was manager at Chelsea. Shepherd said: 'Like Alan Shearer, Batty is going nowhere. It's as simple as that.'

John Gregory was reported to have set up talks with Tony Stephens, Shearer's adviser, to be held after Villa's Uefa Cup first round match against Stromsgodset of Norway, at Villa Park. Gregory seemed undeterred by Gullit's public comments that Shearer was not for sale. The Villa boss said: 'We are obviously in a stronger position to get the top players right now. This is the optimum time to buy when you are doing well, because players are more interested in joining you.'

Shearer released an official statement, prepared by Stephens, designed to damp down the transfer speculation, but it only heightened interest because Shearer did not state categorically that he wanted to remain at Newcastle. But he reaffirmed his future with Newcastle after talks with Gullit. The Independent Newcastle United Supporters' Association pleaded for Shearer to make it clear he was staying at St James's Park.

'If I comment on speculation every time it is written, I would be in the press all the time and I would rather concentrate on preparing for my football,' Shearer said. 'However, because the fans have specifically asked, I can say that I've spoken with the chairman and the manager and they have told me that they see me as an important part of Newcastle's future. The manager feels that my strength is scoring goals, but he realises that I am the type of striker who needs service. I am sure the club's ambition matches mine. I have no doubt that the manager came here to win things, just as I did.'

Gullit was delighted by Shearer's comments, but Steve Wraith, editor of the *Number Nine* fanzine, insisted Shearer's remarks were not helpful. Wraith said: 'He has said nothing. It would have been much better if he had just said whether he wants to stay or not.'

Steve Howey wanted talks with the new boss about his future at the club as his contract expired in the summer. He said: 'I want to know if I have a future here.' Georgiadis, who had yet to play since his summer move from Panathinaikos, was also unsettled. He said: 'I came here to play Premiership football but I am nowhere near achieving that dream. I'm waiting to prove myself to the new manager. It's been very difficult and disappointing for me because I have settled so well in the area.'

Gullit was seething the following evening despite a win against Partizan Belgrade in his first ever Euro evening on Tyneside. A minute before Nikos Dabizas climbed high to head home a seventy-first-minute winner, Laurent Charvet felled striker Menad Bjekovic to concede a penalty and a damaging away goal, as Vuk Rasovic tucked away the penalty to the left of Shay Given. Charvet's initial challenge was clearly outside the area, although Dutch referee Dick Jol did not see it that way.

'I thought it was outside,' said Gullit, 'although the challenge was unnecessary in the first place. It was just a shame to give that goal away. It was sloppy and it was down to a momentary lapse of concentration. It was sad because we created a lot of chances.'

Exactly a year ago, Newcastle had enjoyed one of their greatest ever nights with a stunning 3-2 victory over Barcelona, when Tino Asprilla stole the show with a glorious hat-trick. This display fell well short of that. For Gullit, though, it was a second successive win and he added: 'Now we have beaten Southampton and won in Europe. You have to take positive things out of that. European games are played at a different tempo, and you have to be patient. We created a lot of chances and that was pleasing.'

Shearer's twelfth-minute opening goal was superbly taken. But it was his all-round display that spoke volumes – even if the carefully worded statement on his own future twenty-four hours earlier had not. He looked hungry throughout and took his chance with all the clinical style of a world-class striker. Gary Speed began the move with a surging run into the Partizan half before setting Pearce away. The veteran defender then put Shearer away with a neat flick and he did the rest, drawing keeper Nikola Damjanac and calmly slotting the ball over his diving body into the far corner. The goal came at a time when the Geordies were just starting to gain the upper hand. Partizan had looked slick and technically sound in the opening minutes, but they were knocked out of their stride by the home side's aggression.

However, the lead was a slender one. Gullit added: 'From my point of view, we will go into the second leg at 0-0. I won't be looking at it as 2-1, because I would rather keep my feet on the ground. We go there disappointed to have conceded a goal. But we are confident after two good displays.' Twice a European Cup winner with Milan in his playing days, Gullit had yet to taste defeat in continental club competition as a manager, but now his record would be put to the sternest test.

Speed believed Gullit's vast European experience would be the key. 'Ruud knows what we have got to do over there and we will all weigh in to make sure we get the result we need.'

One area of speculation about Shearer's future was soon squashed as Arsene Wenger effectively ruled out an Arsenal bid for him, to protect Nicolas Anelka's status at Highbury. He said: 'Shearer is a great player, but I think at the moment it's important to keep the door open for Anelka as first choice, because he is only nineteen years old and that would nearly close the door for him, and I don't want that. I believe that Nicolas will be a great striker and I have to give him a chance to play. I am not close to signing anybody and not at all close to signing Shearer.'

The club were going to test Shearer's resolve to stay by offering him a contract that would keep him at Newcastle for life, and he indicated he was ready to sit down and talk. Shearer, twenty-eight, had three years of his existing £30,000-a-week contract to run. A new contract would tie him down for a further two years, increasing his wages to £40,000. Shepherd knew it would be a public relations disaster to lose the club's biggest hero. In the short term, a new contract would bury rumours that Shearer was leaving. In the long term, Shepherd envisaged Shearer becoming Newcastle manager.

Guivarc'h was out because Gullit felt he was too similar to Shearer. Guivarc'h admitted his Newcastle days were numbered. Only two months after moving to St James's Park, he wanted out. He said: 'It's difficult to know how long to wait. I'd like to play alongside Alan Shearer but it was not good for me when Kenny Dalglish left. I may have to change clubs to play.' Gullit had told the Newcastle board he wanted Dublin, the Coventry skipper, as his first major signing. United were due to face Coventry the very next day and Shay Given did not want reminding of his howler last season against the Sky Blues when he allowed Dion Dublin to creep up on him, snatch the ball and score. Highfield Road presented the ideal opportunity to open negotiations at director level.

The memory of Given's embarrassment was wiped out as the Magpies stormed to a 5–1 win. More than sexy football, this was the Full Monty. Gullit enthused that his team 'played with a smile on their faces'. He was particularly pleased as Newcastle had played a European game only two days before. 'It showed me the kind of football I want,' he said. 'Shearer played well because the team played well. It's not just about one man. When I arrived everyone's confidence was very low, not just Alan Shearer's but the whole team. Now I believe it is much better. It won't always be like this, of course, but at the moment everyone is happy.'

If ever there was a sideswipe at the dour days of Dalglish, that was it. But Gullit was becoming fed up with the constant media questioning on whether Shearer would go or stay.

One journalist asked: 'Ruud, there has been a lot of speculation about Alan's future.'

'These questions, all the time the same, just to keep the story going, inventing all sorts of things. Things keep coming out that do not make sense. If Shearer was not happy, would he be scoring?'

The interviewer continued: 'Yes, but Ruud, would you not agree that there has been a whispering campaign surrounding Shearer?'

'The whispering campaign is what you do, not what I do,' he said, and with that he turned on his heels, refusing to say another word.

Shearer's performance, like Newcastle's, flattered to deceive. He scored twice – both exemplary goals in the best tradition of the English centre forward.

But his first meaningful contribution was an own goal later credited to Noel Whelan and his second was a mis-kick at the other end, after which he ended up on his backside in an undignified heap. Dabizas's equaliser came out of the blue but Shearer's first and Newcastle's second turned the game. After Speed added a third minutes before the break, the game was up for Coventry. Glass and Shearer embellished the scoreline in the second half but nobody was fooled.

Given a second chance to impress Gullit, Guivarc'h made his finishing against Brazil in the World Cup final look positively explosive by comparison with what he managed here. One particularly embarrassing effort barely had sufficient oomph to reach Coventry keeper Magnus Hedman from twenty yards!

Tactically Gullit appeared to have got it completely wrong when he chose three players who are essentially wingers: Gillespie, Solano and Glass. But at least he rectified matters by bringing on Speed for the puzzled Peruvian after twenty minutes. At that stage the game was delicately poised.

'I changed tactics very quickly because we were not effective enough. Then we began playing much better. It's my job to get everyone performing, and playing with confidence. I was very pleased with our defence, because we have been a bit sloppy in the past, but we were very disciplined this time and that is why it was so hard for Coventry.'

But on Sunday, more Shearer headlines. The *Sunday Mirror* reported that Juventus were joining the Shearer chase, while the *People* reported Gullit had targeted Tore Andre Flo for £9 million. Gullit had signed Flo for Chelsea and rated him so highly he told the directors his signing was a priority. Flo's agent Gunnar Martin Kjenner said Gullit had the all-clear to make a bid if Chelsea were willing to sell.

In his *News of the World* column, Shearer said: 'I want to stay here, but I want to win things. If I'm honest, we are not as far forward as a football club as I thought we would be when I joined Newcastle. I told the manager and the chairman this when I met them this week. The situation at Newcastle at the moment is not the dream which was sold to me by Kevin Keegan in the summer of 1996. At that time I had eight of the world's biggest clubs chasing me. I chose Newcastle – not just because I love the club, the city and the Geordie people. I came back home because I genuinely felt they would give me the best opportunity of winning things.

'I would still love to see Kevin's dream come true. It was shared by Kenny Dalglish as well. I want to be part of it. Kevin told me he intended to build a new stadium and wanted to challenge Manchester United's dominance of English football. He said they would build a new training ground, an academy of excellence and a sporting club to rival that of Barcelona. But the most important thing of all was that they wanted a successful football team. I shared that dream with both

Kevin and Kenny and it's still there today.

'My motto in life has always been: "First is first – second is nowhere." All I've got to show for ten years as a footballer is that Championship medal I won at Blackburn. I treasure it – but it's not enough. I've got dozens of individual awards and I'm proud of those as well, but I'd swap them all for major club honours. In football nothing means as much as your team being number one and that's what I want Newcastle to be. I remain as ambitious as I have ever been – probably more so now that I'm twenty-eight because it means I've only got a few more years at the top.'

Shearer discussed with Gullit his role in the team. 'I explained to the boss that I am the sort of striker who needs a good service from the flanks. The boss said he would prefer to see me playing right up front where I can cause most damage to the opposition, not wandering out to the wings or dropping too deep. It seems to have worked so far because I have scored three goals in his first three games. But I made the point to him that I did not want people to think that my work rate had dropped and I was not contributing to the team in other areas. I accept that it is going to take the new boss time to get things done his way. I have been impressed with what I've seen from him so far. There's an aura about him which makes it difficult for you to ignore him or what he says. He's a different kind of personality from either Kevin or Kenny.

'If I have to compare their personalities to Ruud Gullit's, he is closer to Kevin because he's an individualist with his own particular way of doing things. If you look back on his career he's played with some of the greatest players in the world and been up there among them. I get the impression he's the same as me and won't accept second best. He's come to Newcastle to win things, and I like that. Obviously his ambitions are just as powerful now as they've always been. We both have a burning desire to be successful.'

Gullit needed to raise £30 million for the five world-class stars he wanted to buy. He targeted eleven players in Newcastle's first-team pool who didn't fit into his plans. He would try to offload them in a bid to finance his restructuring. One of the first out could be Batty, back to Leeds. Others were Guivarc'h, Barnes, Albert, Watson, Hamilton and Andersson. The Swede, who cost Dalglish £3.6 million from AC Milan, had started five games this season but been subbed in all five.

Guivarc'h, however, said he believed he was good enough to partner Shearer in every game – and even to outshine him! A remarkable assessment after making only his second appearance at Coventry and failing to score. Despite being the French league's top marksman for the last two seasons, Guivarc'h had had a wretched France 98. But he hit a debut goal in the home defeat by Liverpool, and won praise from his Dutch boss for helping create two at Coventry.

In an interview with *France Soir*, he said: 'I have proved I am capable of playing alongside the England captain. Gullit has told me that Shearer is his first choice and I am his second. My aim is to turn that the other way round. I am not interested in playing just one game in two. I have not joined Newcastle just to spend my life on the bench. It seems that Gullit prefers to use out-and-out wingers. My absolute objective is to get back into the French national side. If I am unable to do that, I will have to find a solution.'

Guivarc'h insisted his form had suffered from a far from ideal start to the season. 'The Coventry game was physically tough. I am lacking pace – but that is understandable when you spend most of the time on the subs bench. A sprained ankle disrupted my build up to the season, and then Dalglish – the man who'd signed me – got the sack.'

He was sounded out by Celtic, Middlesbrough, French champions Lens and Metz. But a return to his homeland would also mean something like a 50 per cent cut in wages. 'It would be a shame. I like being at Newcastle – life is peaceful, I've found a house in the countryside and the local people are charming. It's a bit like back home in Brittany.'

In midweek Batty was back for the first time since his infamous World Cup penalty miss, with a crowd of around 200 there to welcome him. Finally free from the shackles of a six-match ban, he played for Gullit's reserves at Rotherham. Despite speculation over a move, Batty was only concerned with forcing his way back into the first team while cleaning up his act. He had finished last season with the unenviable record of picking up more disciplinary points than any other Premiership player. 'Indiscipline has been a problem for me in the Premiership,' said the player who was sent off three times last season. 'I have had too many suspensions. But the fact remains that whether I am playing in a World Cup or for the reserves, I always believe I can win the ball.'

Stephen Glass had his transfer fee decided by an independent tribunal in Glasgow. Dalglish had snapped up the youngster from Aberdeen, offering a mere £100,000. The Scots wanted more like £1 million. Aberdeen could not conceal their disappointment after the tribunal ruled Newcastle must pay £650,000.

Gullit refused to get carried away after eleven goals in the last three matches in a week. There was still a lot of work to be done.

Alessandro Pistone was one of the first casualties of Gullit's reign. He had cost Dalglish £4.5 million when he snapped him up from Inter Milan just over a year ago. But he had yet to take to the pitch under Gullit and that alerted a string of Italian clubs including Sampdoria, Fiorentina and Parma. Pistone, totally out in the cold after featuring in the first two games of the season when Dalglish was still in charge, was told he could leave.

Dalglish's son Paul was wanted by Wigan, who were prepared to pay £500,000 for the twenty-one-year-old striker. Recently called up for the Scottish Under-21 side, he was anxious to break through at Newcastle. 'I was scared about the future after Dad went,' he said. 'I didn't know what was going to happen to me. But I am no different to anyone else. When a manager goes and another one comes in, everyone feels less secure. When Dad left he just told me to keep going. Obviously he thinks I am a good player, or he wouldn't have involved me with the first team. All I can do is my best for Newcastle and myself. Hopefully that will be enough, because I want to make the grade here.'

Kenny Dalglish clashed with angry Geordie fans after watching his son in the reserve game at Rotherham. An eyewitness from the club said that there was a scuffle as Dalglish spotted a few fans having a go at his car outside the Millmoor ground. Dalglish left early but apparently the handful of fans were waiting for him outside. They turned on Kenny as he walked to his car after watching Newcastle Reserves win 4-0. As he left the ground the fans confronted him in the car park and hurled a tirade of foul-mouthed abuse before kicking out at his £55,000 Jaguar XK8. It was claimed punches were thrown, but that was later retracted by both Newcastle and Rotherham. Dalglish also denied he was involved in a punch-up. As son Paul scored, Dalglish watched from the directors' box and signed autographs for young football fans throughout the evening.

Rotherham commercial manager Dave Nicholls said: 'After the match, I was told a number of Newcastle fans had been waiting outside for Kenny. He was having none of it and apparently made a dash for his car and made off at speed. I had seen him inside the ground and there was no bother. It seems this was something to do with just a small group of Newcastle fans. It is well known that there is bad feeling in the North East over Dalglish and some fans obviously took the opportunity to start some aggro.'

Clubcall – the official voice of the Magpies – confirmed the fracas.

It reported: 'Kenny Dalglish left early, fans from Newcastle United were waiting for him and there was a fracas, with unsubstantiated reports that his car was kicked. It is a very sad state of affairs that an ex-manager of this club has to endure this sort of treatment after simply watching his son play football. These fans should be thoroughly ashamed of themselves.' An earlier broadcast referred to a punch-up but that was quickly removed.

Feelings were happier in the dressing room. Ruud's heart-to-heart with the players had turned Newcastle around. Gullit explained: 'Among a number of the players there was great disbelief when Dalglish left, not just Alan Shearer. There were other players, too, who were buddies of Dalglish. I told them: "I can understand that you look strangely at this new situation, but you must think about your own career. You and I have to work together, you and I have to go for glory". After a week the ice broke and we had the first good talks with those players. I really made it clear to Alan what I was going to expect from him and what he could expect from me. I told him about my ideas and my plans, it was great to see that he's scored five goals in the three games after the chat we had. I first had to get through to the different characters within the squad and now I'm trying to get the best out of them. Shearer wanted to know what the future was. I think I spelt it out to him. I will keep the details of our conversation private, but the fact is I now have a totally different Alan Shearer at Newcastle.'

Gullit, speaking in an interview in Dutch magazine *Sportweek*, added: 'A big part of my coaching is based on a good atmosphere within the squad. I can see now that players are willing to come forward and express their feelings or their frustrations.'

But now it was the turn of Middlesbrough to stir up speculation. Bryan Robson, a huge Shearer fan, was in the frame for his signature.

Even so, Shearer's 'suck it and see' policy meant he was prepared to stick around to see how the club developed under Gullit. He was on record saying that he was certain Gullit's ambitions matched his own.

Gullit meanwhile dropped any notion of trying to sign Flo. 'I won't be moving for Tore,' Gullit said. 'But then I won't be trying to sign any other player from Chelsea either. It's just my own principle. I don't want to give anyone a reason to say I demolished the team I built at Chelsea. I won't go to Chelsea. If a player says he wants to come and play for me, that's a different thing. But I'm not going to do it myself. People have used this to push up Tore's market price. I won't be approaching them, I don't think it's correct. I took Flo there and I made that team. I don't want to be accused of demolishing it.'

Gullit laughed off suggestions that his long-term aim was to produce sexy football on Tyneside. 'Once, in the past, I used the phrase "sexy football",' he said, 'and it just seems to have stuck. What I really want is effective football, and that's different. I've never said I want to play sexy football at Newcastle – all I've said is that I want us to be effective, play well and win. I don't mind people reminding me of it, but I like to see elegant players and I want an effective team so you can get by even if four players are not performing properly. That's how you win titles.'

Shearer still did not have a regular strike partner; Dublin fitted the bill and Gary Speed was linked as a possible makeweight in a swap deal. But Ruud's Revolution was being frustrated because the players he wanted to sell were refusing to move. New signings had to be subsidised by sales. The problem was that Newcastle are a big club who pay well – so there was no rush for the exit. Speed, for example, didn't want to be involved in a swap for Dublin.

Batty had become a target for several clubs but he only considered a move back to Leeds. Watson refused to move to the south coast, where Southampton were prepared to pay a club record £3 million for him, while £3.5 million Guivarc'h was unwilling to return to France because a move to Lens or Metz would mean cutting his wages by half.

Stuart Pearce was looking forward to playing against Nottingham Forest, the club he used to manage. The thirty-six-year-old, playing in the heart of Gullit's defence, was out to get the better of a club he played for more than 450 times before temporarily stepping into the hot seat. 'I have a huge affection for Forest. But anyone who knows me knows that I'll be going flat out to beat them at our place. If there are two wins I want more than any other this season, then it's Forest home and away.'

And Pearce got exactly what he wanted. Shearer gave Newcastle their 100th Premiership win in typical style against Forest, taking his tally to seven goals in his last four games after a nine-game Premiership run without even the hint of one.

Newcastle had already been caught offside six times in the opening ten minutes but Shearer is always ready to play the percentage game. When Given booted the ball forward, he beat the offside trap to round Beasant and slip the ball left-footed into the net from a narrow angle. Gullit had now seen his side win four games in a row, three of them in the Premiership.

In an attempt to break down the stubborn Forest defence, Gullit had sent on Paul Dalglish for the disappointing Ketsbaia. And it had worked as Dalglish certainly freshened them up. Shearer and Dalglish. Two world-famous names from two different footballing eras. It had a magical ring to it.

Dalglish made his debut operating alongside Shearer for the last thirty-two minutes, emerging from the dugout to rapturous applause. He drew more chants of 'Dalglish, Dalglish' than his father ever managed in nineteen months!

Dalglish junior looks and moves like his old man. He smiles just like him too, although any recollections on that score tend to be a little on the hazy side. 'At least you can understand me,' he laughed after giving an eloquent account of both his home debut and life under the man who replaced his sacked dad. 'I don't want to leave this club. It was ironic that Ruud Gullit was the man to hand me my debut after my dad brought me here and involved me with the first team. But Ruud has put his neck on the line for me and I will always be grateful for that.'

Gullit, too, was full of praise for the youngster, but he knew his team had been lucky to beat Forest. Shearer's first half strike – he did look suspiciously offside before rounding Beasant – set United on their way. But Forest were desperately unlucky not to grab two or three of their own. Only the brilliance of Given denied them on a day when their enterprising play deserved at least a point.

Still, it was a third successive Premiership win and he hadn't bought or sold a single player.

'If Alan Shearer is worth £15 million, then Tore Andre must be worth £25 million,' said Ken Bates, the Chelsea chairman, indicating one of Gullit's problems. 'Newcastle haven't got the money, and of all clubs, would we sell him to them?'

Gullit's next target was Ipswich wonderkid Kieron Dyer, but the First Division club wanted £8 million for their nineteen-year-old forward. Proposed sales of Watson to Everton and Guivarc'h to Paris St Germain collapsed, scuppering any immediate plans of swooping for Benfica's £8 million-rated forward Joao Pinto. Sources in Portugal insisted a deal had been on the cards – but that Everton's failure to snap up Watson had put it on hold. PSG had hoped to take Guivarc'h for a knockdown £2 million.

Batty suggested he did not want to quit Tyneside. 'I recently signed a new five-year contract and I've never for a minute regretted coming here. We had a bad season last time around, but the confidence is back in the dressing room now and I have a good feeling about the future. Ruud Gullit has come here to win things and that suits me just fine.'

★

In Belgrade for the return leg against Partizan, Ruud's courteous smile hid a feeling of utter bewilder-ment. He had just been besieged by a frantic Yugoslav media, whose first question was as bizarre as it was direct.

'Miss Yugoslavia is in the same hotel, will you be seeing her?' enquired the interviewer as Newcastle's players went through their final paces in the JNA stadium. A bemused shake of those famous dreadlocks was Gullit's answer, along with a gesture towards the nearby Shearer – as if to say he was the only person who commanded his undivided attention.

Nowhere was the new mood of optimism which Gullit had swiftly engendered in post-Dalglish Newcastle more apparent than in the sparky demeanour of the England captain. Any antagonism he might have felt seemed to have dissipated with the clutch of goals which saw him forge ahead as the Premiership's leading scorer.

Batty, who played the last two minutes in the victory against Forest, was to provide an abrasive midfield presence alongside Lee. Gillespie hoped his ability to counter-attack would win him the vote over Glass, as he said: 'Pace could be the key in this game and I can provide that. I'd love to be involved. I'm fit and those who were writing me off, saying my career was finished, have been proved wrong.'

Watson, whose future at the club was in the balance, missed the tie after suffering a dead leg against Forest; he trained gingerly and apart from his team-mates in the JNA Stadium, a stronghold in which Partizan had a 100 per cent record this season in all competitions. Partizan, a team who also wear black and white stripes, had won eight successive games to lead the Yugoslavian league by four points. Gullit said: 'I'll be happy with any result, as long as we go through.'

He didn't expect the Newcastle players to fear anyone. 'It will be an intimidating atmosphere in Belgrade. But that should be what you want as a player. It should bring the best out in you. I know it did that for me. The crowd might be hostile, but they can't do anything. They cannot come onto the pitch. You have to stay calm in situations like these. I know how it will be. You have to absorb the crowd and be disciplined in what you do. I love such atmospheres.'

Gullit was sure to learn a great deal about his players as they tried to cope with the cauldron inside the Partizan stadium. He said: 'It is about quietening their fans' hostility early on; after all, they will have no direct bearing on the match. But I know through experience that passionate crowds can affect players.'

Shearer was in the goalscoring groove. 'Alan is doing really well,' said Gullit. 'He has taken on more responsibility and he is scoring goals. Other individuals are performing better too, but Alan is the one who catches the eye and therefore the one I am always asked about. We feel as though we can score against anyone, and in any given situation. Playing in Europe is exciting, but it is also a big part of a player's education.'

The game took place only fifty miles from the epicentre of an earthquake which measured 5.7 on the Richter Scale late on Tuesday night. There were the inevitable jokes that Ruud must have dropped his wallet. And another about Newcastle playing 'a flat back four'. Ironically, Partizan are known as 'The Undertakers'.

September had been a good month, on the field and off it. Ruud's arrival had had an electrifying effect on the share price. Newcastle were the Stock Market's best performers in this month, rising by over 67 per cent to 103p.

The happy atmosphere began to dissipate shortly before the match when a row broke out over the appearance of David Batty in a saucy newspaper advertisement promoting Channel 5's TV coverage of the tie. Batty's head was superimposed on the image of a male model dressed in stockings and suspenders, with the headline: See Ruud Gullit's 'Sexy Football'.

The advertisement, published in several national newspapers to plug the game, was attacked by Batty's agent Hayden Evans who said it was unauthorised. Channel 5 hit back, claiming Newcastle United had given full permission for the picture to be used and that Batty was happy to co-operate. The television station confirmed a sum of money had changed hands but they would not disclose how much.

A furious Evans said: 'I am not happy about it at all. This was arranged by Newcastle United outside the normal commercial routes. It stinks. I have represented David since he was seventeen and this is the type of cheap advertising we have kept him clear of. David is a private person, it is his image that concerns me, not the money. David has a contract with Puma and he does the promotional work approved through the club. David is not a kid, he is an established England international and he doesn't need this. I am not worried about him getting stick from his team-mates, because he can deal with that. I also don't blame Channel 5 at all. I would have had them on a lot tighter rein, but it is a funny advertisement. But there is no price that could have been worth paying for this advertisement.'

Channel 5 maintained they acted in the right way, with negotiations conducted directly with Newcastle United. Spokesman Gary Double said: 'This advertisement is what our coverage is all about – making an impact and grabbing the headlines. The idea was to capture Ruud Gullit's "sexy football" idea in a picture. Newcastle and David Batty gave their full approval for the advertisement to be used.'

It was not a happy night for Batty. He was booked, conceded a vital penalty, and Newcastle went out. His trip on Vladimir Ivic eight minutes after the break proved crucial. Until then, the Geordies had looked reasonably comfortable. But Partizan, with a crucial away goal already in the bag, suddenly had the advantage. The spot kick swept them into the second round to leave Gullit with only domestic competitions to consider.

The defeat left a nasty taste for Gullit, who was far from convinced that Batty had actually fouled Ivic. 'I warned the players beforehand that Partizan men would dive if they could,' he said. 'I think we've been unfortunate because over the two games we have gone out to two dodgy penalties. The one they got at Newcastle was a foul outside the box.'

Ketsbaia pulled a first half effort wide before squandering the best chance of the game three minutes after the break. The Georgian skipped past two lunging challenges, drew keeper Nikola Damjanac and seemed hell bent on finishing the job off himself. But the striker opted to play in Shearer, his pass was dreadfully mistimed and the chance was gone.

United's other best chances both fell to Batty who only started because skipper Lee was forced to miss out because of a thigh injury. But he steered his first well wide and then just failed to lob the keeper with a fine left-foot effort.

But Gullit remained philosophical: 'You have to take your chances in cup football and although we created enough, we just didn't do it,' he said. 'We had a lot of chances to score whereas most of their pressure came from corners. We've scored a lot of goals recently but we were lacking tonight – although I don't blame any individual for the defeat.'

The Magpies were out of Europe at the first hurdle for the first time in their history. But Gullit said: 'It's all part of life. You can't have everything, you have to be content with what you have. If you are not grumpy for two days after a defeat they say you don't care, but I put my mind on something else like reading a book or watching a funny TV show to deflect the bad feeling.'

His all-time favourite funny TV show is – *It Ain't Half Hot Mum*. Borrowing a catchphrase from the show's Windsor Davies character, he would refer to his players at Chelsea as 'luverley boys'. No change at St James's Park.

He laughs uninhibitedly at a show some might consider racist. 'Look, I'm black myself and there were so many shows that were racist when I was a boy, but you must see the humour in things.'

Ruud laughed off the controversial Batty ad for Channel 5 and stressed that he was not intending to sell him: 'We need players like him. He wins balls, keeps everything together and is vital to our plans.'

The main question still centred on Shearer.

'I can understand Alan's frustrations because I have been there. I have gone to places where I thought you could win something. For a fan, that's very difficult to understand. Of course, I don't want him to leave, but if he doesn't win anything here and still wants to leave, I can understand his point of view.'

Gullit had coaxed the goals back into Shearer. 'I've asked Alan to be more selfish,' he explained. 'He thought he could help the team by playing out on the right or out on the left and working very hard. But I don't get the best out of him in those positions. He should be in the box frightening the opposition.' The new manager had hauled the team from near the bottom of the league to fifth, averaging more goals per game than any other Premiership side.

'I do want to win things,' he insisted. 'Very badly, but let's see what happens. If it comes, it comes. If it doesn't, it doesn't.'

'It's easier to sack the coach than the players. I know that if I don't win, I'm out. Even at Chelsea, where I was successful, I was out. If you are successful in this game there's a lot of jealousy. You get a lot of stick which you just have to cope with. Danger comes from unexpected quarters. The one thing I always say to myself is, your enemy never sleeps.'

Shearer was named Carling Player of the Month. His seven goals had taken him to the top of the Premiership goalscoring charts. He said: 'Of course, it's nice for me to receive another individual award, but you can't do that without having the team around you. It's also a credit to the new management team here because when they came a month ago we were near the bottom, and now we are fifth from top. The service has been there for me, we have been creating chances, and fortunately I've been putting them away.'

Now another big test loomed, away at Arsenal. Shearer admitted: 'Going to Arsenal and facing the champions will be very hard. But then it is Arsenal that we are trying to catch. If we want to build here then we must emulate them because of what they have achieved in the last twelve months.'

Gullit returned to London desperate to keep his side in touch with the early pace-setters. The Newcastle boss would have joined Shearer among the awards but for the scintillating run of form by Aston Villa, led by the new manager of the month John Gregory. Said Gullit: 'It's not my goal to be coach of the month, but I would just like to put something down at the end of the year. I've been here a month now and the team still needs improving. I know I need new players and so it's hard to say at the moment exactly how far we can go.'

Watson talked with Everton, as Shepherd explained: 'Managers must be allowed to manage and we will back Ruud over whoever he buys and whoever he sells. Of course, as directors we are also fans and we have our favourites, too. But it's up to the manager what he does.'

Rob Lee was back for the game at Highbury following the bout of flu that had forced him out of the defeat in Yugoslavia. Another boost was the inclusion in the Scotland squad of young winger Stephen Glass. 'I'm very happy for him and very proud,' said Gullit. 'He's made incredible progress. He was technically very good already, but tactically he has learned a lot. And now, the more experience he can get at a higher level, the better he will become.'

Gullit did not intend to concentrate his team talk on fellow countrymen Dennis Bergkamp and Marc Overmars. Dalglish had disastrously reshaped his FA Cup final side, switching Pistone to right-back to mark Overmars, and the new boss didn't want to fall into the same trap. He wanted to mark his return to London with a positive outlook.

Gullit wasn't surprised that Bergkamp had found it difficult to keep his form going. He said: 'I think everyone who played in the World Cup will have suffered a little bit this season. It would have been a shock if Bergkamp's form hadn't dipped after the standards he set earlier in the year. We are fortunate that Alan Shearer has quickly rediscovered his scoring touch and I'm very pleased with his form.'

A European reprieve? It sounded far fetched, more clutching at straws . . . but there were suggestions that Newcastle would sneak back into the Cup-Winners' Cup as Yugoslavia were in danger of expulsion because of the Kosovo crisis. Shepherd said: 'We've heard strong rumours that we could get back in. We have yet to make an official enquiry, but we will.'

Gullit was being linked to the post of coach to World Cup hosts

Japan, who wanted him to spearhead their historic 2002 campaign and could offer £3.5 million for a two-year contract. According to a couple of reports top Japanese officials had already sounded out Gullit before he accepted the Newcastle job, and the fact that he would only commit himself to a two-year contract at Newcastle greatly encouraged Japanese officials. Their new coach, Philippe Troussier, was himself only on a two-year contract . . .

Meanwhile on Sunday a smiling Ruud, wearing the Geordie tracksuit top, signed autographs for the fans and shook hands with Arsene Wenger before the kick-off. But the ineptitude of his team made him want to spit – and he did.

Gullit's team were unable to get off the blocks, still suffering a hangover from their Cup Winners' Cup exit. Referee Mike Reed was forced to change his striped shirt after complaints from Shearer and Batty. Both had fired their best two passes of the day straight to the Birmingham official.

Bergkamp celebrated his first goal since the World Cup. It seemed there were no half measures with Newcastle under Gullit, it was either a spectacular success or, as in this case, a devastating defeat. He despatched young Dalglish for the start of the second half in place of the ineffective Ketsbaia and if nothing else, the youngsters in Gullit's line-up put in the effort. Shearer looked a forlorn figure leading the Newcastle attack, with little service from Solano to his liking. The only time David Seaman was tested came in the fifty-eighth minute when Dalglish's trickery at least confused the Arsenal defence long enough for Shearer's deflected effort to reach the Peruvian, whose own deflected shot was flipped over by the England keeper.

It went from bad to worse for Gullit when Dabizas brought down Overmars from behind in the penalty area and was shown his second yellow card. Gullit looked away as Dabizas walked slowly past him, the Newcastle coach concentrating on the penalty which Bergkamp put away for his second goal.

Gullit spat on the ground in disgust.

With the result virtually a foregone conclusion after the second goal in just on half an hour, the latter stages were most notable for the fans' lively exchange of views. 'Shearer, Shearer, what's the score?' was a touch predictable but the Arsenal contingent livened it up with, 'There's only one England captain.' This clear reference to Tony Adams' belief that he should lead the England team brought a response from the Newcastle fans: 'There's only one alcoholic!'

A few minutes from the end, substitute Philippe Albert was shown the yellow card for bringing down Bergkamp just at the point he was about to complete his hat-trick. It seemed just a matter of time as Bergkamp got up to take the penalty, but Given denied him with a smart dive to his right to deny Bergkamp the match ball.

Bergkamp had been allowed to score his first goals in ten matches this season, Newcastle hardly managed a shot and Shearer was marked out of the contest by his England team-mates Adams and Keown.

Newcastle's recent run had only papered over the cracks. The gulf between these two clubs, as evident in the Cup final when Arsenal completed the double, was emphasised once again. And on Sky TV, it appeared as if Gullit was challenging Newcastle to come up with cash for new signings. Was he on a collision course with his directors, little more than a month after taking charge?

Gullit said: 'We have to improve on a hell of a lot of things and now it is up to the board to do something about it. To improve we must have new signings. I am knocking on their door every day. They are being co-operative, but now it is up to them to do what we have to do. I knew when I came here that big changes had to be made. The wins we had before were just hiding things, masking our mistakes. I have the players I want ready to come in – they are in the fridge waiting to be brought out. We need to buy certain players with a certain type of character.'

Some £18 million was wiped off the value of the club's shares during trading on Monday, as the City apparently reacted badly to Gullit's TV plea for cash. Shareholders feared another boardroom clash and by the end of trading, Newcastle's share price had dived 13 per cent to just 84p, its lowest for weeks.

'Somebody should have the courtesy to tell Ruud that he's working for a public company, not a football club,' said NatWest Stockbrokers analyst Jeremy Batstone.

The club's profits were forecast to slump by over 50 per cent to just £2.5 million over the next year, while revenues from football accounted for just 60 per cent of the club's income – the rest coming from lucrative commercial spin-offs. Batstone added: 'The board is under pressure, and pretty much obliged to spend any cash there is on things where they can pretty much guarantee a return on investment. You can't do that with players. Ruud seemed to think he could pop along to the board, ask for £10 million and wander off with a cheque. Not in a public company, you can't.'

Newcastle directors told Gullit he had to present the board with a business plan, detailing any suggested expenditure and what long-term value it would bring to the club. 'Ruud's a footballing man. How long he can put up with this, or the City can put up with comments that cost £18 million, remains to be seen,' said Batstone.

Having seen one or two potential deals collapse, the board shared Gullit's worry that too many players would have to be sold for less than they cost. Guivarc'h held further talks with Paris St Germain and remained a target for Celtic. PSV Eindhoven were the latest to ask about the striker. Steve Watson's proposed £4.5 million move to Everton fell through, while Gullit was keen for Parma to make an official move for Pistone and IFK Gothenburg to step in for their former striker Andersson.

Gullit wanted rid of several big money buys. Gary Speed, who had missed an expensive sitter in Europe, was reputedly on that list, with Lee and Barton as the saleable propositions. Batty would have to be sold if the others didn't bring in enough cash to give Gullit the money he needed.

Freddy Shepherd made it clear Gullit must sell before he could buy. He insisted: 'Ruud knew the score before he came here. There are no spare lockers left at St James's Park and there's no room left on the team bus. We have brought a lot of players in, but it's not up to me to say whether they have been good buys or bad buys. It doesn't surprise me to hear that he wants money for new players. In fact, it pleases us. He has come out fighting and that just shows what enthusiasm he has for the job here. He wants to be a success and, make no mistake, he is the man to get it right. He is a Kevin Keegan type of manager. Keegan was never away from our door asking for money, and neither was Kenny Dalglish. Ruud is no different to any other manager in the country. They all want money to spend. We never talk about how much we have to spend. But what we will say is that we will give Ruud all the support we can.'

The pledge appeased Gullit. Naturally, Shepherd refused to knock out his players at bargain basement prices. He said: 'If other clubs think they can come in for easy pickings, then they can forget it. We know what our players are worth and we will stick to our valuations. We have already been offered £2 million below what we think one of our players is worth and, in another case, it was a million. There's no way that is going to be acceptable.'

Fresh from the first England training session at Bisham Abbey, Alan Shearer was one of ten players on interview duty in the build-up to the Euro 2000 ties with Bulgaria and Luxembourg. He gave the biggest hint yet that he was considering his future, saying: 'I've already made a statement that I'm happy to stay at Newcastle but I want to win things. Read into that what you want.'

There was only one way to read it. But he added: 'My job is to play, it's Ruud Gullit's job to manage the football, and he will decide that, not me. I don't know whether they have to sell before they can give him money or not. That has nothing to do with me. That's up to the manager. But if he decides to sell me or anybody else, it is his decision.'

His comments reverberated all the way back to Tyneside. It sounded like an ultimatum to deliver the trophies, the reason he signed in the first place. He refused to give a time scale, but it was doubtful whether Shearer's patience for the big prizes extended beyond the season.

After the crushing Arsenal setback, Shearer knew precisely the time when he realised Newcastle were not good enough. There was a handshake with his England team mate David Seaman and the usual after-match polite congratulations. Shearer thought about it for a second and immediately told the England keeper that he didn't deserve any accolades. Newcastle had been that appalling, they were that bad, they hadn't given Seaman a thing to do.

Shearer said: 'I said well done, then I thought about it and pulled him back and told him, "I don't know what I said that for, you didn't do anything!" It was painful.'

Shearer nailed the lie that he didn't get on with Gullit because of his affiliation and affection for the deposed Dalglish. He said: 'It's been put in there that I don't get on with him. I don't have a problem with him and he doesn't have a problem with me, and I hope my performances suggest that. He's got on very well with everybody. He's got good ideas and everybody has enjoyed his coaching. He's different to Kenny. They are totally different individuals, but they both know the good things about the game.

'Ruud has come in to coach and he is very good, he has a laugh and joke with the lads, and also we work extremely hard. But you don't realise you are working so hard because you enjoy it so much. The last three games before Arsenal went extremely well and the confidence was extremely high.

'He had sat us all down, not just myself, and told the players to be themselves. He told me he wanted me to play more up front rather than out searching for the ball. He wanted me up front to do a job, and it suggests it has been working well, with seven goals in the last however many games. I'm not the type of striker to beat three or four and stick it in myself, I need people to create for me. But it's not just about me, and I'm not standing here criticising the team, I'd rather criticise myself.'

The dream move back to his roots had promised so much for Shearer when he was signed by Keegan. That was so far unfulfilled. 'It's just that it's not gone as well as I'd hoped. Who is to blame, I don't know. Maybe myself, I'm part of that side. Perhaps we haven't had the luck, we've had our injuries and selling Les Ferdinand didn't help. There are a whole lot of things that haven't gone right. I'm sure the manager is aware of it and will be putting it right.'

And that would decide Shearer's future . . . whether Gullit could put it right.

Gullit quickly moved to quash suggestions of a rift with the directors over cash to buy new players. In a statement, he said: 'Having read the reports of my comments made following the game at Arsenal, I am disturbed to see that a lot of people are assuming that there is a rift between myself and the board of directors at Newcastle United. That could not be further from the truth.

'When I spoke on Sunday I was not being critical of anyone. I was not criticising the board. My job is to make decisions. The directors recognise this and they are doing their hardest to make funds available. But we need to move quickly. It is still early in the season and there is still time to achieve some success, and that's what everyone at this football club is aiming for.'

Apparent rifts with players seemed harder to resolve. Gillespie, having fully recovered from his ankle problem, was in Belfast for Northern Ireland's Euro 2000 qualifier against Finland. His contract expired at the end of the season when he could then move for free under the Bosman ruling, and he dropped the broadest hint that he would switch to another Premiership club come the summer.

'I felt I was surplus to requirements at Newcastle, that's why I went to speak to Middlesbrough. They are an up and coming club and they had a lot to offer me. I was happy to go there and I didn't ask for the transfer. It maybe had a lot to do with the fact that I can go for free at the end of the year. The club maybe feared they might lose me for nothing, which might still happen.'

Batty was again linked with his old club Leeds United, currently managerless, as well as Villa, but his agent Hayden Evans said: 'Leeds have not put their money where their mouth is. David will always be connected with them because he comes from Leeds and is a Leeds fan.'

The latest story linking Shearer with a move brought a groan of resignation from St James's Park. It was reported that Shearer's agent Tony Stephens had been holding secret talks with Serie A champions Juventus. Before that had time to die down next it was Lazio ready to launch a bid – offering Alen Boksic plus £10 million in cash.

With no league programme on the second weekend of October there was time for reflection. I shared the TV hot seat with Warren Barton for Channel 5. Sitting in the 'green room' over a cookie and coffee, it was an illuminating conversation about Ruud. Barton often stays in his native London whenever there is a break in the domestic programme and he keeps in touch with the scene in the capital. He's as knowledgeable as anyone at St James's Park about Ruud's reputation at Stamford Bridge – being branded a part time coach more interested in making pizza adverts than spending time on the training pitch coaching.

Barton was mystified by that. He told me: 'Ruud Gullit has been on the training pitch every day. In fact he's the first one there at nine o'clock and he's the last one to go. We heard all the stories that at Chelsea he didn't do a lot of training sessions, but that's not the case here. He has some interesting ideas on the game and I like the way he points players in the right direction. Because of his stature, personality and being charismatic, he has the respect of all the players. If you have anything to say, then he encourages you to say it.'

Barton believed that only someone of the stature of Gullit could have appeased the fans and held the respect of the players in the wake of the traumatic dismissal of Dalglish. Just as he had given Chelsea their first piece of silverware in a quarter of a century, he felt he was the right man to make the breakthrough for Newcastle.

Barton had been named in the paper that day as one of ten players Gullit was ready to offload to finance his massive spending spree. But he wanted to stay and had not held any discussions with the new boss to lead him to believe the rumours were true.

There was no Premiership programme on the Saturday following the Arsenal defeat as England were playing a vital Euro 2000 qualifier. Shearer and Lee were in the England team booed off after the sterile draw with Bulgaria at Wembley. On the eve of the game, Lee said: 'I prefer staying out of the limelight. I don't push the publicity. I enjoy what I do, captaining Newcastle and playing for England, but I don't bother if people don't write about me. As long as Ruud Gullit and Glenn Hoddle are happy with me, then that's fine by me.'

The following day the *Mail on Sunday* reported that Newcastle were involved in £150 million takeover talks with a media-based company.

Since BSkyB's £623 million bid to buy Manchester United a month earlier, speculation was rife that other top clubs would become targets for media conglomerates. Newcastle denied they had been approached by the Japanese electrical company Sony. But the paper added: 'The conviction now on Tyneside is that a deal to buy control of Newcastle from Douglas Hall, who owns a majority stake in the plc, is imminent.'

The feeling that changes were afoot at the club seemed to be confirmed as Steve Watson finally became Gullit's first sale for £4 million to Aston Villa, and his departure meant Shearer was now the only Geordie on Newcastle's books. Yet Sir John Hall once spoke about his dream of seeing eleven local-born lads wearing the first-team colours.

Watson said: 'Gullit is having a clear-out and I had to make way to bring in some money. I couldn't tell you what the atmosphere is like there now, I don't understand half the players because they are foreign. Now I'm at Villa, I'm the one with the funny accent. It is certainly a big wrench for me to leave Newcastle, because I first joined United at the age of ten and made my senior debut as a sixteen-year-old. But Ruud Gullit gave me no option about moving. I was told the transfer fee had been agreed with Villa, so I realized the writing was on the wall. After working under five managers at Newcastle, perhaps the switch will do me good. Villa are six points clear at the top, and after missing out with Newcastle in 1995, it will be nice to take another serious crack at the title.'

His new manager, John Gregory, expressed delight with his latest acquisition – and said he was also surprised Gullit had allowed Watson to leave. 'I still can't believe Newcastle have sold him. Steve is just the sort anyone would want. He's the right age, performs well in several positions and possesses courage and ambition in equal measures.'

Sheffield United boss Steve Bruce lined up the loan signing of £1.5 million misfit Des Hamilton. Hamilton, signed by Dalglish eighteen months before, was told he had no future at St James's Park. He made only twelve appearances last season, five as a substitute.

But Shepherd issued a hands off warning over Batty, insisting: 'There's no chance of him moving.'

Gullit turned tough. 'The fans must trust me on this because I am taking responsibility for the situation and it's important we get the right sort of players in as quickly as possible. If Newcastle want to be where they should be, there have to be a lot of changes. It's not going to be a nice time here. But I have told players that they will be leaving and that from now on I will be like a battering ram breaking down the gates. I have players in the first team who have already been told they will be leaving and so it could be difficult motivating some of them. But in the meantime, the fans are just going to have to trust me. We cannot continue winning games by playing badly.'

As Newcastle prepared to face Derby, desperate for a home win having lost the last two games to Partizan Belgrade and Arsenal, the odds were the majority of the players on duty would find themselves surplus to Gullit's requirements sooner or later.

Ruud sped away from the Chester-le-Street training ground in his Mercedes only for Stephane Guivarc'h to reverse right into his path, causing the United boss to slam the brakes on. Fellow Frenchman Lionel Perez could barely stifle his laughter. No doubt Stephane was trying to speed up his move!

Around 10pm on the night before the meeting with Derby, I was just finishing my pizza at Uno's at the Quayside with my daughter Jordanna and her two university friends, when my mobile rang. It was the office. They wanted me to contact Glenn Hoddle about a story in the *Sun* concerning a dressing room row with Shearer after the Luxembourg match.

An hour later, back at the Copthorne Hotel, I contacted Hoddle. He denied that Shearer had blamed him. Hoddle added that he supported Shearer when he had a row with a journalist outside the dressing room over his future at Newcastle and his attitude to playing against the part-timers of Luxembourg. Hoddle pointed out: 'Rather than me having a row with Alan Shearer, Alan Shearer had a row with a journalist and I was very supportive towards him.'

That story consumed the London editions the next morning.

In the North East, only the *Sun* and *Mail* carried the Hoddle-Shearer row, otherwise the headlines centred on Guivarc'h, who accused Gullit of a lack of respect while his agent said Gullit had 'put a curse' on the World Cup-winning striker. 'Humiliated' was the back page banner headline in the *Express*. Guivarc'h said he was astonished when Gullit ordered him to train with the reserves. 'It has been humiliating for me,' explained Guivarc'h. 'I have had to train with the juniors twice because the club clearly do not want me. It has happened twice, but it will not happen a third time. I must leave here. I don't want to play for Newcastle. It was bad for me when Kenny Dalglish left, and it has just become worse ever since.

'If he told me to do it again I would refuse. There is no way to dislodge Alan Shearer and as Gullit wants to play two men wide, I cannot hope to get into the team,' he said. Guivarc'h, who chose a move to Newcastle over other better-paid offers from Arsenal and Glasgow Rangers because he was impressed by Dalglish, was still talking to Paris St Germain and was also considering a renewed offer from the Scottish giants. His agent Frederic Dobraje ruled out letting his client move quickly just to please Newcastle. 'Gullit has put a curse on Stephane, but that doesn't mean he should move because that is what is wanted by the coach,' Dobraje said. 'We have to take time to assess all the offers and I feel a move to Scotland would not help his chances of getting back into the French side.'

Gullit would not discuss any possible move for Guivarc'h, saying the matter was being discussed by the board. Ironically, Dalglish's son Paul became one of Guivarc'h's main rivals for a place in the team, and would make his first start against Derby.

Gullit felt the overall display in the 2-1 win over Derby at St James's Park was the best since he took over, and praise was forthcoming for so many players. In particular, he couldn't praise Shearer enough.

Not for another of his famous goals, since Shearer went empty-handed as Glass produced a spectacular strike and Dabizas a typical towering header.

Not for the power of his shooting. He didn't manage one attempt on goal.

Not for any of his bullet headers. There weren't any.

Not for forcing the keeper into any blinding saves. He didn't test Russell Hoult once.

For time wasting? You'd better believe it . . . time wasting. Shearer deliberately ran down the clock as Newcastle sought to hang on to three valuable points.

Not exactly sexy to watch, but effective, as Gullit said: 'Alan knew he had to go to the angles and took the ball there. It is not only about scoring goals. It wastes time, takes that pressure off and the time is ticking away, that's what can win games. It helps youngsters like Glass and Griffin, they say to themselves, "Hey, he is keeping the ball." They see him doing it and they can learn how important that can be.'

Gullit stressed Robert Lee's future was assured, saying: 'He is not leaving. He has been assured he will not go, and he shows that on the pitch. He was already outstanding before this game, so I don't think he is undervalued, although I don't know the answer to that because I didn't follow him when I was at Chelsea. But now he is excellent and he played very well against Bulgaria.'

The same definitive comments were made about Shearer's future. The significant difference was that while Lee would want to stay, the same couldn't be said with such certainty about Shearer.

Shearer whizzed past waiting reporters so quickly that one quipped, 'That's the fastest he's moved all day.' However, accuracy wasn't exactly a strong suit this weekend after the contorted, misinterpreted and exaggerated versions of the Shearer-Hoddle dressing room 'discussion', designed to further discredit the England coach.

Gullit's first after-match question was whether he was happy with 'the two points'! When the hysterical laughter subsided, Gullit playfully threatened to walk out!

As much out of sorts with his club as he was with England, at least Shearer was motivated. He deserted the central positions, where he was guilty of stagnation, and worked down the channels, delivering one dangerous cross. And there were plenty of aerial flick-ons that might, in the future, be better read by young Dalglish. Shearer didn't exactly excel but pleased Gullit for the way he kept trying right until the end, and for a vital participation in The Team, the new work ethic that Gullit had focused on from his extensive Dutch coaching course. Gullit was a much improved coach from earning that badge. How many coaches in English football are equally qualified? The reality is a surprising few.

This was a different Gullit to the model that began his coaching experience at Chelsea. A touch more pragmatic than the sexy football image would have everyone believe. More the middle ground between Keegan's gung-ho approach and Dalglish's cautious football. An effusive Gullit was just as appreciative of the industrious, no-frills Lee and Batty, working their stockings off, as he was of the isolated incident where Shearer showed he was just as much a part of The Team.

Newcastle fretted, then dominated, could have scored a bundle, then panicked when Derby stole back in with a scrambled goal from sub Deon Burton and might have surrendered the win that took them again to the fringe of the title hunt.

The knowing Gullit smile couldn't disguise that he felt he had done much better than he envisaged with the players he inherited. 'Slowly, slowly making progress with this impressive performance,' was Gullit's reaction.

Gullit would never be totally happy, no matter how many players he brought in. 'If you have a team that makes you happy, a month later you want to improve it, that is always the case. That's what it is like at a big club, it is always your goal to improve the team, you are never satisfied. That is why I wasn't satisfied when we won four on the trot, because I knew we didn't play so well and against Arsenal we got what we deserved, but it was good because it made everyone look in the mirror. The timing of it was the good thing. It showed everyone our position and that we could be criticised. It made us aware that we would make sure we didn't feel or think we were good enough.'

This was not Stamford Bridge transported to the North East. There were some similarities with how he transformed Chelsea, but also some startling differences. Gullit has a reputation for buying world foreign stars, but it's easily forgotten the influence that he had on the young players at the Bridge. Gullit was not afraid to put his faith in the kids.

Gullit afforded Master Dalglish a congratulatory handshake when he came off late in the game, while his dad was still awaiting his golden handshake. The warmth of the new manager toward the deposed boss's son was thoroughly genuine as he enthused: 'Paul is happy to be part of the team and he worked very hard to give himself a chance and every young player here knows that.' Dalglish senior watched his boy and would have been proud of his endeavours, while Gullit had equally encouraging comments for Andy Griffin, in the light of the sale of the popular local hero Watson. 'I was very pleased with his performance, too, and the players know if they perform well, they will play. It doesn't matter who they are, or what they have done in the past. It's the team that counts, if they do it for the team, then they will play.'

As for trying to recreate Chelsea, there was no sweeper, no three at the back, no wing backs. Instead, a more traditional 4-4-2 to accommodate Lee and Batty. Ruud said: 'I don't have the same type of player. At Chelsea I had a diamond in midfield because I had Di Matteo going forward all the time. I don't have that, but I do have Lee and Batty as 'sitting' players in a more flat midfield. If I don't have the players, I don't try to play a system that won't work for them. The club brought me here because they wanted changes, so they must want me to do it 'My Way', otherwise they would have brought another coach.

'It is important the crowd try to understand what we are trying to do when we go forward and then come back again. If we go forward and there is no room and we lose the ball, we are open to the counter-attack.' Gullit's teams keep possession, go backwards to go forward, and the Dutchman wanted to re-educate the Geordie crowd to appreciate thoughtful, probing, patient football. If they could see the results, they would be less anxious for the hoof straight down the middle.

Nolberto Solano, the man dubbed 'Little Maestro' by Diego Maradona during his days with Boca Juniors in Argentina, gave defender Darryl Powell a torrid afternoon as he foraged down the Newcastle right, providing the crosses for both goals. 'Nobby,' as he is known to his new and less poetic team-mates, turned in his best display, but the winger passed up three glorious chances to open his own Premiership account. Gullit, however, was delighted with his performance, especially considering that the South American had played at left full-back for his country in midweek. 'For me, it's important that you get there, that you create your chances. If you don't get there, you can't do anything. The goals will come.'

Stuart Pearce was warmly applauded by his team-mates when he walked into the dressing room at lunchtime – he was a father at last, at the age of thirty-six. On the Thursday night, his wife Liz delivered a girl in a Nottingham hospital and Ruud had given him paternity leave to be with her. Pearce said: 'The baby is a month early and I thought it was OK to leave Liz on Thursday and drive up to Chester-le-Street for training. But at Scotch Corner she called me to say I'd better head home and because it was a Caesarean birth, the doctors were able to wait until I got there. People think because I'm thirty-six that I must already have a family, but this is our first and we are delighted. My contract at Newcastle is up at the end of the season and I will definitely be aiming for a new one now there is an extra mouth to feed.'

Later that evening, I bumped into Shearer in the Copthorne Hotel, where he was staying overnight with his wife. We had a private chat, and he was still seething about the story in the *Sun* as he explained that he had been contacted at 11.30 the night before an important game and he was none too pleased about the disruption to his match preparation. The content of the call didn't help his demeanour much. Shearer was taking legal advice over the Hoddle story, which intensified when Danny Baker claimed on Talk Radio that a player had made a tape of the row.

I told Glenn I was on the same floor of the Copthorne as Alan – the top one. 'No coincidences in life,' Hoddle told me enigmatically. I wish I could remember the name of the book he was reading about the force of coincidences.

Ruud was still clearly enjoying the afterglow of his success, smiling as he strolled along the quayside the next day, chatting away. Later he gave serious thoughts to his rebuilding plans. AC Milan's German left-back Christian Ziege was targeted more realistically now, after the sale of Watson. And Newcastle had offers from Lazio and Roma for Pistone, while Marseille wanted Guivarc'h. If Gullit could continue to sell, there would be no need to cash in on Shearer. But he was running out of time for the twenty-five-year-old Ziege, as the Italian transfer market closed down at the end of the month. Ziege wanted to join his former Bayern Munich team-mate Didi Hamann at St James's Park.

Former Newcastle skipper Glenn Roeder said: 'Ziege is a Ruud Gullit-type signing, and as a Newcastle fan I hope he pulls this one off. I saw Ziege play for Germany in the World Cup finals in the summer and he is the sort of player United fans would love. He attacks for fun and he would be just the player to get in the crosses which Alan Shearer thrives on. Ruud knows Europe well and he will know that Ziege is a big fish over there. He will also know that if Newcastle are going to win trophies, he will need eleven big fish.'

To catch the big fish Gullit would need the bait of big money, but there was mixed news on the financial front. On Monday the club announced a 10 per cent decline in merchandise sales from £9.02 million to £8.1 million, despite a 20 per cent increase in turnover. The preliminary results of the plc nevertheless showed an operating profit before net transfer fees and associated costs up 33 per cent to £10.8 million.

The fall in the sale of branded products, including replica shirts, coincided with the storm over comments made by Shepherd and Hall in March (the duo claimed then that the club were selling shirts for £40 which cost £5 to produce). In his statement, plc chairman Denis Cassidy blamed poor weather, disappointing results on the field and a general decline in sportswear sales for the slump. Cassidy said: 'Most informed observers recognise that they (the fans) top the premier league of supporters because of their unswerving loyalty and affection for the great club, measured by sell-out crowds at most home games. For the first time in thirty years, St James's Park welcomed more than one million spectators last season.'

John Regan, secretary of the Independent Newcastle United Supporters' Association, called for a fairer merchandising deal for fans: 'If the club come out and produce quality merchandise, with decent designs and at a reasonable price and the team play the way they did on Saturday, then I'm sure the merchandise sales will go up again in the future. I think there are several factors to take into account for the drop in merchandising income. One is, in my view, that the current home strip hasn't sold as many as the old one because of the design. Fewer people are buying the away strip because it changes every year now whereas it used to be every two years. Obviously, the business with Hall and Shepherd will have put people off buying strips as well. During the period talked about in this report, we had some of the worst football seen at Newcastle for six or seven years under Kenny Dalglish. So morale was down among the fans and people were not buying because of that.'

Cassidy described 1997-98 as 'disappointing' even though Newcastle reached the FA Cup final and took part in the Champions' League. But he said: 'Our record over the past five years as a whole is strong and on this evidence we rank highly. Similarly, in turnover terms we are the second most successful club in the UK. The difficulties in one year should not be allowed to diminish our bright prospects for the future.' Matchday takings were up 21 per cent, TV revenue by 35 per cent and sponsorship 39 per cent. Cassidy, the man charged with the task of safeguarding the club's financial future, welcomed satisfactory results, but pointed to the devastating loss of Shearer through a horrendous ankle injury before the Premiership campaign had even kicked off the previous season as a major blow. 'Reshaping and increasing the size of the playing squad in the prevailing post-Bosman climate and in the shadow of relegation throughout the second half of last season increased operating costs,' he said. 'In the event, the pre-season injury to Alan Shearer turned out to be a serious blow to our FA Premier League ambitions.'

Shares jumped 10p, valuing the company now at £143 million. A £40 million development plan would raise ground capacity from 37,000 to 51,000 in two years – good news for the 10,000 fans on the season ticket waiting list.

Steve Howey was despatched to Wales for a two-week fitness course. The centre-back, whose career had been blighted by groin and calf injuries for the past two years, attended a specialist clinic. And his frustration was not to be over for many months.

4

Dalglish . . . Paul and Kenny

Kenny Dalglish's shadow remained at St James's Park long after his acrimonious departure. Ruud Gullit taking over from the former Liverpool idol discovered that the ex-Blackburn boss still had influence within the North-East club.

However, Gullit's version of events would contrast most vividly with the sort of propaganda that was part of the village gossip that the Dutchman loathed. Gullit felt that because of the one-town, one-club scenario, every piece of gossip spread across Newcastle like wildfire, picking up all sorts of misinformation, until it reached the media completely distorted. It was the snowball effect, as Gullit would call it.

The theory that Gullit took revenge on Paul Dalglish for the actions of his father is treated with a mixture of disdain and anger by the Dutch coach. He felt it was a perfect example of the snowball effect of gossip from so-called club insiders. The most popularly held theory circulating on Tyneside, and the one widely repeated in the national press when Gullit resigned, was that the reason behind the players' dislike for their coach was his handling of Dalglish junior and a number of other popular players such as Robert Lee. But it was the triangular relationship between Gullit, Dalglish and Dalglish junior that fascinated the village gossips. There was a suspicion that Alan Shearer was still in touch with Dalglish, among many of the old guard left at Newcastle – it was naturally assumed that Dalglish senior was upset by the treatment of his son, and that Shearer sympathised. Dalglish junior, according to the anti-Gullit grapevine, was summoned to the coach's office and told he had to go because his father was

63

making life difficult for Gullit. That is the theory put forward as the catalyst for the dressing room split between the English players led by Shearer and Lee, and Gullit's foreign imports.

However, there is a great deal of evidence to support Gullit's alternative view that he did not treat Dalglish junior any differently to the other players, and that Gullit did not single him out because of a fear of the Dalglish connection. Gullit's argument is that he gave Paul a chance, encouraged him, and wanted him to do well. Gullit saw some raw talent in the boy and was disappointed that he did not fulfil all of his early promise and had to be first loaned to Norwich and then sold. Gullit would roar 'nonsense' at any suggestion that Dalglish junior was victimised by concerns over his father's access to sensitive information at St James's Park.

It is true that Gullit was angered by and was suspicious of Dalglish senior. However this did not influence the coach's view of his player. Gullit, in fact, was desperately seeking alternatives to Shearer at this stage, and would dearly have wanted a striker to come forward to increase his options in attack. If Gullit was seeking to discover if there was a 'spy' in the camp, Dalglish junior was not the obvious focus. Detailed analysis of every staff member's mobile phone calls is made periodically. However, a special search was made of one of the backroom staff's calls who was suspected of being in constant touch with Dalglish. Whether it was paranoia about Kenny Dalglish, or whether it was connected to the legal action the departed coach had instigated over his acrimonious exit, the club appeared to be seeking out those from within who were in contact with the former manager. The club was fully entitled to take such action as they saw fit; Gullit clearly had no objections and was interested to know the outcome.

In the immediate aftermath of Dalglish's departure, most of the players and members of staff had been in contact with Dalglish. That was only to be expected. However, one person in particular engaged in excessively lengthy dialogue with Dalglish. It was discovered that there were more than one hundred calls made to Dalglish from one mobile number. Action was taken against the individual who was not a member of the playing or coaching staff.

If there was any suspicion of Kenny Dalglish being involved in any of Newcastle United's business regarding the players, then Gullit dealt with it personally – and confronted him directly. Gullit rang Kenny to protest at his suspected involvement as far as Steve Howey was concerned. It is believed that Kenny Dalglish was asked for an opinion of Howey as a prospective Liverpool signing, and having been his manager at St James's Park with access to his personal telephone numbers, had passed on such information to his old Anfield club. Dalglish's alleged involvement in helping Liverpool in this manner couldn't have come at a more sensitive time. Howey was negotiating a new long term contract with Newcastle. He was in a strong negotiating position as his contract expired at the end of the season. Liverpool and Arsenal's interest had been reported in the national press, but Newcastle were confident of securing a new deal. As a mere coincidence, Howey was represented by the same agent who looked after Gullit – the Smith brothers at First Artist Management.

Gullit told me that he phoned Kenny Dalglish, who protested strongly he had done nothing wrong. Gullit was told by Dalglish that Liverpool had asked him for his help. Kenny felt he had acted in the right way in helping out his old club and possibly aiding Howey. Gullit was not impressed, and told Dalglish so. The job was hard enough as it was for Gullit; Howey was a key player for Newcastle. It was Howey's return that had enabled Gullit's team to edge towards Wembley, and it was the big centre-half's injury in the semi-final that was a massive blow to Gullit's aspirations of outwitting Alex Ferguson at the Wembley final. Gullit understandably felt that Kenny had undermined Newcastle's chances of persuading Howey to stay. In the event, however, Howey signed a new contract with Newcastle.

Gullit feels the village gossip, not party to the full facts, assumed that Paul Dalglish was in some way caught in the crossfire of something that was going on that involved his father – but that no-one was too clear precisely what it was about. Had anyone known the full facts about the confrontation between Gullit and Kenny Dalglish, then surely much more would have been made of Paul's demise at Newcastle.

But in October 1998 there was no hint of Paul leaving Newcastle. In fact he was tipped to become Scotland's answer to Michael Owen. Scotland boss Craig Brown said: 'I don't want to build him up and put him under any pressure, but he could be our Michael Owen. We are taking a look at a lot of young players, and Paul is at the top of the list.'

Gullit was promising to bring only the best to St James's Park, although recent results had given him a little breathing space. He had had a shopping list drawn up for some time, but he ruled out a move for Danish international Brian Laudrup, whose widely publicised bust-up with Gianluca Vialli at Chelsea over the club's squad system had alerted managers all over Europe at the weekend.

Stephane Guivarc'h was now being tracked by German club Hertha

Berlin. Celtic had withdrawn their interest, while Paris St Germain's offer of £2.5 million was not acceptable to Newcastle.

Greek side PAOK Salonika, however, were ready to end George Georgiadis' nightmare. The Greek international forward signed by Dalglish in the summer for £500,000 had yet to kick a ball for the club. He begged Gullit to either back him or sell him. Salonika were preparing to give the Geordies their money back when the Greek transfer window opened in mid-December. 'I wanted this move to Newcastle so much, but it has become a nightmare for me,' revealed Georgiadis. He had also lost his place in the national side following his switch to Tyneside from Panathinaikos.

David Ginola was the central character in the run-up to the Magpies' game with Spurs as he prepared to face his old club. He had been sold by Newcastle after a fall-out with Dalglish, and Gullit was an admirer. Yet he was confident he already had an appropriate replacement for Ginola in Stephen Glass.

Ginola had been given a vote of confidence by new Tottenham boss George Graham and invited to show he could adapt his star quality to the new manager's work ethic. The flamboyant but temperamental Frenchman and the tough, demanding Scot were seen as incompatible in the Spurs set-up, which Graham pledged to imbue with fierce commitment, hard graft and dedicated direction. But as both Ginola and Les Ferdinand prepared to face their former club in Graham's first home match in charge, the Spurs boss revealed: 'David has shown a great attitude in the two weeks I have been here. He hasn't missed a single training session, and I have been surprised by just how very fit he is.'

Dabizas was suspended after being sent off during Newcastle's last trip to North London, the 3-0 defeat by Arsenal. Hamann was back in training after suffering knee ligament damage in the opening week of the season, and Andersson was recovering from glandular fever.

Guivarc'h found himself on standby for the injured Shearer as in a surprise twist, Gullit named the unhappy Frenchman in his seventeen-strong squad. 'Alan has a pain in his foot and we have given him two days' rest,' Gullit explained. 'It is nothing particular. We will wait and see.' Both Shearer and Pearce, who had a broken toe, were determined to play through the pain. Gullit did not encourage them to do anything foolish, with two games in a week approaching against Tranmere in the Worthington Cup and West Ham.

Gullit called up eighteen-year-old defender Aaron Hughes, who had represented Northern Ireland twice this season while managing only two reserve games for Newcastle. But Carl Serrant, twenty-three, would step up to join young Griffin. Albert was struggling with a hamstring, joining Howey and Pistone on the injured list. Barnes was making progress, Gullit said: 'He is trying to get his fitness back, he is training hard.'

It would be a terrific test for Gullit against Graham, the boss who gave Ruud's Chelsea side a mauling or two while at Leeds. The public perception of the two managers couldn't have been more different, with Gullit stuck with a 'sexy football' tag and Graham still labelled 'boring' from his days at Arsenal. Gullit insisted they were both soccer brothers under the skin. 'It would be boring if we were all the same,' he said. 'It's good to be different, but we share one major goal – to be winners. I respect and admire George. He did a hell of a job at Arsenal. His teams have always been hard to beat. He builds from the back and so do I. We have a lot in common. We both know what it takes to win. I admire winners like him and Alex Ferguson.'

Graham's reputation is as a disciplinarian, but Gullit was tough with his players, too. Gullit said: 'They are always playing for their futures, that is normal. It is important that players are on their toes. Some players need comfort, some need a stick behind the door.' Gullit ducked the question when asked if he would have kept Ginola at Newcastle. 'He's not here, end of story,' he said.

Laurent Charvet was ready for Ginola. 'We were pals in London when I played for Chelsea,' he said. He is very tricky and we will have to watch him. But we are improving and hopefully we can do better than we did against Arsenal on our last visit to London.'

Gullit was still waiting for a breakthrough in the transfer market. 'There are bids on the table,' he said. 'It could take days, weeks or hours. I'm not frustrated, I'm philosophical. I'm prepared to wait for the men I want.' But he denied he had bid for Zinedine Zidane. He said: 'No. Everybody throws in a whole lot of names, maybe they will suss it out. But I'm not interested in Zidane, not because I don't think he is a great player but because I don't see him coming to Newcastle when he is at Juventus going for so much. I've not made enquiries, but he is a great player.'

Gullit, in need of some great players, was experiencing a roller-coaster time. Before the game he had talked about acquiring 'consistency'. But the 2-0 defeat at Tottenham was a real down after the Derby up. Gullit observed: 'I don't want that, of course. But even when one player is out it is hard to get a good back four, especially against a Tottenham attack that was good in the air.'

With Dabizas out, Gullit had switched Pearce to central defence and brought in Serrant to left back. The lack of height was the deciding factor as Gullit said: 'They were winning every ball up front, we couldn't win one header or tackle, and that made it hard for our midfield players to go forward as well as back. That kills you most of the time, you cannot go fifty yards backwards and then fifty yards forward. I knew it would be difficult without Dabizas who is a very strong header.'

Gullit was not impressed with the game. 'Both teams didn't play well, and we gave it away, but not because they were better than us. We knew we would have difficulties in the air, we didn't have tall players without Dabizas, and even the first goal came after a header.'

Gullit was impressed with his young talent, but it became too much for them. He made a double substitution, bringing off youngsters Glass and Dalglish and sending on two experienced internationals, Guivarc'h and Speed. Gullit said: 'The switch caused them problems, Speed got forward a little bit more. The boys have worked very hard and I have had to play some youngsters. But we still showed some very good things, but it didn't go our way. If they had really outplayed us then I would be really worried, but this wasn't like the Arsenal game.'

There was another gibe in the media after the game – this time a *News of the World* snippet that Gullit had upset German legend Andreas Brehme, who branded him 'the biggest idiot in football' after he failed to play in his testimonial. Angry Brehme claimed he chartered a jet for Gullit but he failed to show. Gullit made it clear he was unable to play.

United travelled to Birkenhead on Monday ahead of the midweek Cup tie at Tranmere. Ketsbaia was ill and was left behind. The rift with Guivarc'h had widened. His thirty-five-minute appearance as sub at Tottenham told Ruud everything he needed to know about his attitude. Gullit said: 'Everyone saw his performance and on that performance, he is going to be judged.' Deportivo la Coruña were the latest club linked to a bid.

Gullit warned his players to take nothing for granted in this Worthington Cup tie. First Division Tranmere had plundered four goals in the opening fourteen minutes to cruise to a comprehensive victory at Crewe while Newcastle were losing at Spurs.

The Merseysiders in fact had enjoyed four successive League wins, which followed their worst ever start to a season. 'There is no pressure on us now,' said Aldridge, who called on his players to 'go out and make a name for yourselves' against Newcastle.

United needed no reminder about Rovers' capabilities after facing John Aldridge's side in the fifth round of the FA Cup on their way to the previous year's final. Only Shearer's header separated the sides that day and although United never looked like losing, they were given the sternest of tests by a side determined not to be overrun at St James's Park. Only five of the men who started that game in February – Given, Pearce, Lee, Batty and Shearer – were likely to line up again.

The Magpies went out of this competition at the quarter-final stage the previous season after an extra-time defeat by Liverpool, and Gullit was keen to improve on that performance. He had parted company with Chelsea by the time they defeated Middlesbrough in the 1997–98 League Cup final, and he welcomed a chance to emulate that success. 'I've never been to the final of that competition and I've never won it, but any cup we play in is important to us,' he said. 'It gives you something to play for.'

David Batty was again being linked with Leeds after the newly installed David O'Leary was given the all-clear to sign two players.

Gullit tried to land his own first signing, going for Dion Dublin after Blackburn made a £6.75 million offer and he was alerted to Coventry's willingness to sell. Roy Hodgson was given the go-ahead to talk terms with Dublin, but Gullit wanted to take advantage of the opportunity of a quality player becoming available, even though his priorities were a central defender and a full-back. Newcastle were also vying for Brondby's international defender Soren Colding, along with Spurs, according to the tabloid *Ekstra-Bladet*.

John Barnes was at Buckingham Palace to receive an MBE for services to soccer from the Queen. Now also a TV football pundit, with a striking fashion sense, he was being linked before the Cup game with a return to Watford or a move to Crystal Palace.

While his old club Chelsea, Manchester United and Arsenal had demoted the Worthington Cup to third rate, that was not the case for Gullit. After the 1-0 win against Tranmere he argued: 'This Worthington Cup competition is very important to us and I'm very pleased that we're through to the last sixteen. Pleased, too, to have a home tie against Blackburn Rovers. They will provide us with a different challenge than we encountered at Prenton Park, but we certainly feel that we have a good chance to go through to the quarter-finals. This Cup not only offers the chance to play at Wembley in March, but also qualifies the winners for a place in the UEFA Cup next season. Believe me, we are very interested in winning this Worthington Cup.'

Gullit was indebted as much to Given as to Dalglish, the goal scorer of the night. The goalkeeper made a string of crucial saves.

Newcastle were starved of clear-cut opportunities. The closest they came before Dalglish's decisive strike was Shearer timing his run to the near post to head a Glass cross against the woodwork.

Journalists waited in the tunnel, TV crews jostled for interviews, and Dalglish was happy to oblige and talk them through his first ever goal in professional football. He stopped without hesitation, keeping Gullit and the players waiting on the bus as he faced a barrage of questions. The answers came back with the same quickfire delivery as his dad, peppered with wisecracks. He also had the stone-faced look perfected by Dalglish senior when suspecting he was being led into areas he would rather not discuss. On this occasion it was comparisons with his father; he knew the question was coming and answered firmly to put the record straight. He was Paul Dalglish, aching to succeed in his own right and not on the back of his famous father. He said: 'It's been harder for other people to accept that I am a Dalglish than for myself. It's just hard to know whether I knocked the ball in against Tranmere like my dad. I don't want to be compared with him. He doesn't compare me and I don't compare myself. My dad has been very critical. But every young lad trying to make the grade has a critical dad. Mine is just more critical than most, but then he's done it, hasn't he? I am only learning. And I can learn off everyone.'

'Yes, but you've got a lot of your dad in you.'

Young Dalglish laughed and replied: 'I have got half of my dad in me and half my mum. Have you seen my mum play?'

But Shearer, who knew a lot about both father and son, had noticed one difference: 'I certainly don't remember Kenny having Paul's pace.'

This was confirmed by Tranmere's manager. Aldridge, who played alongside Dalglish senior, remembered: 'He's quicker than his dad. Mind you, Kenny was a bit slow. It's unfair, though, to make comparisons. Paul is his own player. He is making a name for himself at a massive club like Newcastle. He's a lovely lad and a credit to his father. People shouldn't burden him, comparing him with Kenny. But I am sure he's mature enough to ignore that.'

By the end of the week Gullit was resigned to losing out in the chase for Dion Dublin, but wouldn't discuss him. 'We have a saying in Holland, "Don't sell the fur of a bear if you haven't killed him." ' Villa were favourites to sign Dublin, providing minimum disruption to the player and his family.

Gullit was happy to have the pelt of young colt Dalglish on the peg while he waited for a transfer market breakthrough. He said: 'It doesn't matter who his father is, I'm pleased with Paul.' Gullit's praise for Paul Dalglish contrasted sharply with his tight-lipped reaction to questions about Guivarc'h.

Despite a flu scare Gullit expected Rob Lee to play against West Ham, but Hamann had to wait. He was back in full training after a nine-week lay-off but Gullit said: 'It's too soon to think about bringing him back.'

Ruud met Gabby Yorath later that Friday evening to film an interview for ITV's *On The Ball*. The venue was a bar next to Tyne Bridge, in the middle of an impromptu wedding reception.

Gabby discussed with Ruud the irony of the current debate over the rotation system at Chelsea, where Vialli once complained when he was a victim of Gullit's squad rotation. The Dutchman smiled and said: 'Yes, but the difference is, it worked for me!'

When Gabby compared Ruud's departure from the Bridge to an acrimonious divorce, he insisted that, unlike most divorces, he was 'over it'.

In such a public place there were the inevitable well-wishers, and Gabby wrote in her *Sunday Mirror* column: 'It's clear that the love and admiration of the Geordie nation is certainly within his reach, but trophies and championships are going to be a lot harder to come by.' Gabby pointed out how Ruud was so complimentary towards Shearer, admiring his will-to-win attitude – as she put it, even when they were off camera.

Despite all the mitigating circumstances the 3-0 defeat at St James's Park by West Ham was a big setback for Ruud. He wanted to reproduce the form his side showed against Derby in the last home match. It didn't happen.

A Shearer 'goal' was ruled out for pushing, Dalglish had a penalty appeal denied, and Pearce was sent off. Shearer called for video evidence to aid the referee. He argued: 'There is so much at stake financially and in terms of prestige that referees need some help. The technology is available and so is the money to put it in place, so I don't see why it cannot be introduced.' Graham Poll later admitted he had made a mistake with the penalty incident, but Shearer said: 'That's not much good to us, the damage had already been done.' Shearer felt there were three main areas for video technology to be used; whether the ball has crossed the goal-line, penalty decisions for handball and fouls, plus red cards.

The absence of Dabizas was an excuse that stretched only so far as Gullit emphasised the necessity for a big and good enough squad. Once again it was a case of not good enough. Pearce had been sent off for violent conduct, though Shearer and Gullit later agreed that Pearce's attempt to beat Trevor Sinclair to a high ball had not been malicious.

Pearce led with his arm when he raced Sinclair to a 50-50 ball, and referees will not tolerate raised elbows. Gullit said: 'The referee wanted to be spotted. I don't think there was any intent in the challenge. You always have to lean when you go in for a header like that. But I think Mr Poll had too big an influence on the game. I believe he has already sent off seven or eight players this season. The referee made it hard for us. There was no motivation for the sending-off because nothing happened. It did not make any sense. I'm being very polite about what I say because I don't want to be on an FA charge. We were not beaten by a better side, but by a referee's decisions.'

Shearer reckoned that discretion was the better part of valour – then promptly changed his mind. Poll's handling of this bizarre affair left him fuming. 'I would not give the man the satisfaction of seeing his name in the papers,' he pointed out in contemptuous vein. 'I am sure he would enjoy being slated by me. We have a problem with the game of football now. Players' livelihoods are at stake here.'

With only forty-nine minutes on the clock Newcastle were reduced to ten men and very quickly afterwards were in shreds as two-goal Ian Wright inspired the Hammers. 'There are always going to be knocks, kicks and bruises,' explained Shearer. 'And it's quite wrong to take that away from the game. It's a contact sport. But certain decisions turned it into a farce against West Ham. People talk about having professional referees – but how could they improve standards if the same people are going to be involved?'

West Ham boss Harry Redknapp thought Poll was 'quite strong' throughout. 'I'm a big fan of Stuart Pearce,' said Redknapp. 'But I do think he caught Trevor Sinclair in the face with an elbow. I think replays will show that. Sinclair's not the sort who would go down if he hadn't been hit. Alan Shearer had a goal disallowed and I felt that was definitely a push, and the Newcastle fans also shouted loudly for two spot kicks that were never penalties. Newcastle fans shout for everything, but Graham Poll didn't buckle to the pressure.'

Poll himself responded: 'Stuart Pearce was sent off for violent conduct. I had a very clear view of the incident and I was no more than seven metres away. He ran from a distance, led with his forearm and hit the player on the back of the head. I sent him off for violent conduct and that's all I want to say.'

Referee Poll later admitted he was wrong to have refused a penalty. Premier League referees' officer Philip Don said: 'Graham Poll popped in to see me and we had a look at the Newcastle video against West Ham. Graham didn't give a penalty when Paul Dalglish was brought down and now accepts it was a penalty. I think it is superb for him to admit this and it just shows that referees are human.

Gullit declined to comment, but Don stood by Poll's decision to send off Pearce, saying: 'I support Graham on the sending-off of Stuart Pearce for illegal use of the elbow. I don't think there is any argument at all on the sending-off. In the referee's opinion and on the video, Stuart Pearce clearly goes in and catches the opponent on the back of his head with his elbow.' A package containing video evidence plus a statement from the former England skipper was compiled in the hope of saving Pearce from a ban.

Sending-off apart, it had been galling for Newcastle supporters to watch the former Gunner upstage Shearer in his own back yard. At least Paul Dalglish played well again. The kid who cost nothing looked a darned sight more talented than either Andersson or Guivarc'h, who together cost his old man a grand total of £6.5 million.

5

The first signing . . . £8 million Duncan Ferguson

Ruud Gullit's signings at Chelsea had been outstandingly successful. No-one thought his judgement was impaired when he started to sell Dalglish players such as World Cup winner Stephane Guivarc'h. At the beginning of November Guivarc'h finally agreed to sign for Glasgow Rangers. Having turned them down for Newcastle in June before the World Cup, Guivarc'h now joined his compatriot and former Auxerre team-mate, goalkeeper Lionel Charbonnier, at the Scottish club. He said the chance of playing regularly again would help in his bid to reclaim his place in the France team and claimed Shearer had also been close to leaving.

Guivarc'h was furious at his treatment by Gullit. He said: 'Gullit took away all my incentive to do well. But I have always got on well with the other players, particularly Alan Shearer, who almost left as well. I am happy to be leaving Newcastle. It is a huge relief because I will be able to get back on the pitch and compete again. It has been so long. Gullit made it crystal clear that I was not part of his plans. He never gave me a chance and never gave himself the chance to judge me. He said nothing at all to me. He didn't want to have anything to do with me but I never knew what the problem was. Gullit has his choices and his ideas but he could at least talk about them. He put me on the bench once and then totally excluded me. I will keep good memories of Newcastle, but later. When I look back on it, I'm sure I will have a good laugh.'

Gullit knew he would miss out on Dublin, as Dion prepared to tie

74

up a deal with Aston Villa. A rumour had circulated that Ruud was too busy back in Amsterdam to keep an appointment with Dublin for transfer talks. But as the two clubs had not agreed a fee, how could such talks take place? Certainly they could not involve the manager!

Even so Ruud was criticised by Jimmy Greaves in his *Sun* column. Under the headline 'TOON GET A RUUD AWAKENING', Greaves hurt Ruud when he wrote: 'When Ruud Gullit was appointed Newcastle United boss, I dismissed him as just an international playboy. The statement was probably ignored in the euphoria of the dreadlocked one entering the doors of St James's Park just after the departure of the dour Kenny Dalglish. On Wednesday, Coventry striker Dion Dublin had talks with Newcastle as he tried to decide which club would make best use of his services. Surely Gullit, with his undoubted charm and presence, would have helped to sway matters the Toon's way and clinch the Dublin deal. However, the only person there to persuade Dublin was chief executive Freddie Fletcher. And where was Gullit? He was attending a fashion shoot in Holland for his "Ruud" brand of clothing. I hate to say I told you so, but don't be surprised if Newcastle lose out on Dublin and he chooses to go elsewhere.'

An immediate apology had to follow under the headline: 'PARDON ME FOR BEING RUUD.' Greaves backed down unreservedly: 'I have got to hold my hands up this week and admit I got something wrong. In last week's column concerning Ruud Gullit, I said that instead of him being around when trying to get Dion Dublin signed, he was out in Holland promoting his "Ruud" fashion line of clothing. It has been pointed out to me that he was on more personal business in Italy, for which he was fully excused. I'm sorry, Ruud, and realise how upset you were from the telephone call I received from you last Saturday night. In the past I have suggested the Newcastle role is one you are not suited to because it needed a man more in tune with the unique area of the North East. I hope you can prove me wrong again and that come May, I can devote a more sizeable amount of this column to your success at Newcastle. The fans deserve it.'

Would David Batty be part of that, or would he have to go? Batty said: 'As long as Newcastle want me, then I want to stay.'

Freddy Shepherd insisted: 'I have not spoken to Leeds about David Batty. But he is not for sale at any price. End of story. It is rubbish to say that we have put a £7 million price tag on his head, because we want him to stay and he wants to stay. The manager thinks the world of him. And if we were to sell for £7 million, where would we find a replacement of his calibre in today's market?'

Newcastle were ordered to pay £650,000 for Garry Brady from Spurs in a tribunal valuation. Icelandic striker Bjarni Gudjonsson, the teenager signed by Dalglish as a top prospect who made little progress, joined high-flying Belgian side Genk for a knockdown £150,000.

Newcastle's forthcoming clash with Manchester United on Sunday had not exactly worked out according to plan. The Geordies had the fixture put back 24 hours on the assumption they would still be battling it out in Europe. But their early exit left them twiddling their thumbs, while Alex Ferguson was delighted with the extra recovery time following his side's Champions' League clash with Brondby.

Dabizas confirmed he would miss Newcastle's game against Sheffield Wednesday the following weekend in order to play for his country, departing for Greece on November 12, the day after United met Blackburn at St James's Park in the Worthington Cup. Greece faced Albania the following Wednesday.

Dabizas was one of three men likely to miss the Sheffield Wednesday game. Given was on international duty with the Republic of Ireland in Yugoslavia on the same night, while Pearce started a three-match ban. But Northern Ireland players Gillespie and Hughes were available for selection against Wednesday. Lawrie McMenemy's side faced Moldova in a voluntarily rearranged game, and were not allowed to invoke the five-day rule. Gillespie and Hughes would join up with the Irish squad the day after the Owls game.

There were to be heartbreaking casualties along the way of Ruud's Revolution. Philippe Albert's contract expired at the end of the season, and he was moving on. 'It is hurting me to leave Newcastle,' he confirmed. 'When I came here, they were one of the top clubs in the country. And although they are not that now, I believe they can be again. I would like to be a part of that, but I don't think it will happen. I am open to offers and prepared to move almost anywhere – although I would like to stay in England.'

Albert's first club Charleroi were interested, as were Standard Liège. The Belgian said: 'I was dropped after we beat Southampton 4-0 and I went to see the manager, who told me he needed some quick defenders in the side. The situation is quite clear. I accept I'm not the quickest. I've never been that way, even ten years ago, but I feel I have qualities other defenders don't have. I would be sad if I couldn't play for the club. But I didn't leave my family, my country and my friends four and a half years ago to spend too many weeks on the bench. The situation may not improve in the next few weeks and if that is the case,

I will have to play somewhere else. Everyone knows how much I love Newcastle, the city and the club. But although I am training hard, I accept that I might have to move.'

Albert knew it was a vastly different atmosphere at the club, not just because of Gullit but with the gradual disappearance of local stars like Andy Cole, Watson, Robbie Elliott, Lee Clark, Barry Venison, Peter Beardsley and Scott Sellars. 'They made the atmosphere at the club tremendous, on and off the pitch. That is why we had some great times. You can't recreate that same atmosphere when you have so many foreign players. It took me time to get used to the humour of a few of the lads. I settled quickly, but I'm not the same type as say, Temuri Ketsbaia, George Georgiadis or Laurent Charvet, because it has taken them more time.'

As for the confrontation with potentially the best team in Europe, he said: 'We will feel that if we play our football, we can give United problems. Everyone has written us off because United are flying, while we are having our troubles off the field. We are all relishing the game, I promise you. We will be up for it: if not, then we'd be guaranteed a hammering.'

After their early-season scoring flurry Newcastle were without a goal in 253 minutes of Premiership football, with Shearer six League and Cup matches without a goal. His seven goals were still more than twice as many as any other Newcastle player.

Dietmar Hamann, though, was keen to take on Manchester United after playing only half an hour's football in two months. He came through a thirty-minute work-out with the reserves earlier in the week and showed enough in training to force his way into Gullit's plans. 'I am ready to play,' he said. 'I think I have shown the manager my skills in training and I am fighting fit again. I have never played against Manchester United and, at the moment, they are probably the best team in Europe. I would love to get back into the first team straight away – and I have an extra incentive because Germany have a game against Holland on November 18 and I want to be involved in that as well.'

Hamann operated either as a midfield anchor man or as the central attacking player behind the front two. But it was as an attacking midfielder that Gullit would use the German as Batty was still very much the automatic choice for the holding role.

Gullit and Ferguson; they have immense respect for each other. Ruud had even received a call from Fergie shortly after his acrimonious

Chelsea departure, with an invite to United's training ground.

'I couldn't go because I was on a coaching course in Holland,' Gullit said, 'but it was a nice gesture, very nice. I really admire Alex Ferguson, the way he does things and what he has achieved.'

Ferguson's men had capped a stunning string of comprehensive victories with a 5-0 demolition of Brondby in the Champions' League, and while Gullit acknowledged Man United were on top of their game, he was expecting his players to wipe the 3-0 defeat by West Ham from their memories. 'You prepare yourself as a team in exactly the same way,' he said. 'Then it's a case of performing well on the day. The toughest games are against the so-called lower teams.'

Gullit gave late fitness tests to Rob Lee, laid low by a virus, and Hamann. Ketsbaia and Pistone were ruled out by minor injuries. While Manchester United's prolific frontline pairing of Cole and Yorke made scoring goals look like second nature, there were still concerns over Shearer.

No luck with Dublin, unsuccessful offers to Milan for Christian Ziege and to Deportivo La Coruna for Jerome Bonnissel, another left wing-back – and Gullit's wanted list also included Ulf Kirsten of Bayer Leverkusen, Ivan Zamorano of Internazionale and Michael Mols of Utrecht, all strikers, plus Milan's defender Guiseppe Cardone. Ruud was also linked with Kanu, who continued to attract the interest of Arsenal.

Defeat at Old Trafford would direct Gullit's side towards a possible repeat of last season's relegation dogfight. As a manager, Gullit had yet to lose at Old Trafford. But just once in forty-eight years had Newcastle beaten Manchester United away from home; in February 1972, the week after their famous FA Cup humiliation at Hereford. John Tudor and Stuart Barrowclough scored the goals in a 2-0 triumph against a line-up which featured the names Best, Law, Charlton and Kidd.

In the event, both records were intact at the end of the match. After the 0-0 draw, Ferguson applauded Gullit's tactics in stifling his free flowing side, stopping them scoring at Old Trafford for the first time since March. Manchester United had scored thirty goals in their previous nine games, Yorke and Cole had hammered eleven in their six-match stint together. But Gullit ensured a blank day. Ferguson said: 'I thought Newcastle's tactics were terrific. They really pressed the ball and had us on the back foot. They forced us to pass the ball back. For a team that's supposed to be struggling, they did very well. It was a brave selection. I didn't even know two of the players. They deserved the point, even though they didn't really create anything.'

Gullit was delighted to be sharing the spoils. Newcastle should have had a penalty when Dalglish was bundled down in the box by Irwin. But Ruud didn't moan about Bristol referee Steve Dunn. 'The penalty? I wasn't in a position to see the incident, but I didn't have much to complain about today.'

Gullit's young guns left Old Trafford with their heads held high. It was a side including teenagers Griffin and Aaron Hughes – who celebrated his nineteenth birthday – and young twenty-somethings Given, Glass and Dalglish who again looked dangerous.

There was more transfer speculation and frustration the following week. A £3.5 million bid for twenty-three-year-old left-sided Turkish international midfielder Erkan Abdullah was turned down by Trabzonspor, and Bayer Leverkusen rejected a £4 million offer for German international striker Ulf Kirsten. Leverkusen spokesman Reiner Calmund said the club had told Newcastle that Kirsten was not for sale. 'We are honoured by the offer and so is Ulf, but we would not let him go for any money,' he said.

Paul Dalglish was still striving to forge an impressive partnership with Shearer. 'I am just trying my best to make a name for myself as a Premiership player. I am coming up against very experienced defenders, and I am a late developer at this level. In fact, I am probably still growing, and hopefully I will fill out a bit. I am playing against men who are fully developed while I am just a young boy. But I am happy with the way it's going so far.'

Another wanting to carve out a future was Georgiadis, who Gullit had introduced as a replacement for Solano. He had already aimed a broadside at Gullit for not playing him, now he hoped to start afresh.

Gullit took a swipe at Leeds, accusing them of trying to uproot Batty. Ruud had maintained a discreet silence during Leeds' on-going attempts to lure him back, but finally snapped: 'They are trying to say he's unhappy here. It's not nice to say someone is unhappy just because you want him. It's not a nice thing to do, to try and make someone unhappy. He is from that area and maybe his wife wants to go back there or whatever. You try to give the player wrong ideas and then he says, "Yeah, I want to go." But if you want someone, then just come and tell us what you want to do. Don't go through the back door.'

Gullit declared his interest in 'unhappy' players at Elland Road. 'I'm seriously interested in two players – an attacker and a defender. Some Leeds players are unhappy, although that's not something I would normally choose to say. But there, I've said it now. I wouldn't have done so if they hadn't done it first.' His 'targets' were Dutch striker Jimmy Floyd Hasselbaink and Lucas Radebe.

Shearer would face his old club in the Worthington Cup clash with Blackburn, casting one eye towards Wembley. 'Of course we have to take this competition seriously,' said Shearer. 'Europe is the prize for winning this competition, so it is not a tournament we are taking lightly.'

Pearce officially failed in an attempt to have his sending-off against West Ham overturned, as the FA rejected his appeal. But fortunately he was able to play in the Worthington Cup match against Blackburn, although his penalty-taking skills could not save Newcastle.

Shearer missed a penalty for the first time during normal time, and eventually Blackburn booked a quarter-final clash with Leicester by winning a bizarre contest on penalties. Their eighteen-year-old substitute David Dunn tucked away the crucial spot kick after Aaron Hughes missed his penalty by about ten yards. Before that, Johnson, Dailly and Kenna, as well as Shearer and Pearce, converted their penalties. Sherwood and Hamann both hit the woodwork.

Before the shoot-out drama, Shearer missed his spot kick on eighty-seven minutes. Kenna then had the chance to do away with extra-time a couple of minutes later, but his spot kick was saved by Given. 'Glory all depends on nights like that,' reflected Gullit. 'But before the penalties, Blackburn had one shot on goal and scored from it.'

The game was only nine minutes old when Shearer pounced with his first goal in eight games, powering home a near-post header. Blackburn hit back after thirty minutes when Kenna knocked a neat ball into the path of Sherwood, who swept a superb low right-foot drive past Given.

Gullit refused to blame Shearer for his costly penalty miss. 'Alan is only human,' he said. 'I was confident he would put it away but taking a penalty is a 50-50 chance. It could happen to anybody. I have nothing to moan about regarding the players, the effort or the way we played. Blackburn stuck nine men behind the ball. Good luck to them.'

Shearer said: 'That's another chance of honours gone and another chance of playing in Europe.' He pinned his hopes on the FA Cup after writing off Newcastle's title chances. 'I think it's true to say that we are not going to win the League. That only leaves us with one more chance – the FA Cup.' What added to Shearer's hurt was that his penalty miss – his first for Newcastle – ultimately proved decisive.

'You've got to be up there to take it. I took one in the shoot-out and scored. You just have to get on with it.'

Dabizas was ordered to stay on Tyneside the following day while a club versus country row raged. He was meant to travel to Athens at 2pm in preparation for the international with Albania but Newcastle put his departure on hold in a bid to secure his release for Saturday's game with Sheffield Wednesday.

The club were also fighting to have Shay Given available. He was due to link up with the Republic squad for the Euro 2000 clash with Yugoslavia in Belgrade, but Newcastle discovered that the Irish had not followed the proper procedure in invoking the five-day rule.

Steve Harper was on standby, having yet to play a League game, and having spent the previous season on loan at Hartlepool and Huddersfield.

One of Given's predecessors, Pavel Srnicek, relished an amazing return to St James's Park – with Sheffield Wednesday. The fixture list had handed the former Geordie favourite an instant return to the city in which he became a cult hero.

Dalglish had given Srnicek just one start last season and he played only five times under his management, culminating in a huge FA Cup semi-final bust-up at the team's headquarters as Srnicek – who had believed he was going to be in the side – finally blew his top.

'I just hoped I could get back into the Premiership,' he added, 'and then Wednesday came in for me and my first two games will be against Newcastle and Manchester United.' The Geordie faithful would find it extremely difficult not to sing their 'Pavel is a Geordie' anthem, and Srnicek would find it equally difficult not to shed a tear or two. 'I don't know why I was so popular there,' said the keeper who played over 150 games for Newcastle during his eight-season stay. 'Maybe it was because I always tried to give it everything I had, or maybe it was just because they thought I was a nice bloke. Whatever, it will just be a great feeling for me to be back.'

After immense confusion, Dabizas finally flew back to his homeland but Given stayed behind after the Republic's error in not invoking the five-day rule.

Gullit stressed the importance of an immediate antidote to the cup exit. 'We are looking to recover from an indifferent start to the season, and face another group of players who can be very dangerous. Wednesday's situation is similar in many respects to that of Blackburn, in that they have not done as well as they hoped when the season opened and they have also lost players through injuries and suspensions. And, again like Blackburn, they would look upon victory at St James's Park as the perfect way to kick-start their season after a depressing sequence of results. They have their backs to the wall and you can be quite sure that they will seize upon any lack of concentration on our part.

'There's a saying in my country that goes, "If you drive a cat into a corner it can make some very strange jumps." Sheffield Wednesday, you might say, are in just such a situation and we have to be on our toes to make sure that they don't make those jumps at our expense.'

Ruud relied on the fans' support and knew from the moment he arrived the importance of that kind of backing. 'I said when I took this job that I wanted St James's Park to be a formidable stadium for the opposition to play in. We have to make it so again.'

But just three months into his reign and his team were booed off the next day. It hurt.

He was in realistic mood after the 1-1 draw. 'The crowd deserve better, and Newcastle as a club deserve better.

'I know what the people expect from me, but for the way I like to play the game we need different players. I like to play sexy football, but the players who have been brought here were signed to play another kind of football, and changing the style without changing the players is not easy. Getting other people's players to play my way is not easy. The sooner I get some new ones in, the better it will be.'

He likened his preferred style of football to a car with five gears, able to switch from one to another and change the pace. For now, Newcastle were struggling to get out of third.

Truthfully, United were dire. Gullit axed Batty for the first time and then had to throw him into the action after only thirty-two minutes. He felt his side would have more attacking options without him. But they were far more vulnerable in midfield. Given was constantly exposed. His bravery rescued the situation on at least three occasions.

Srnicek explained after an emotional return to Tyneside: 'The Keegan era here was something totally different. I don't think English football had experienced anything like it. I think the club can recover, but it might take four or five years. They play a totally different game now. A few years ago, if this Wednesday side had come here, we would have been hammered. But we weren't, and in the end we could have won it.'

Dalglish's first Premiership goal after only four minutes was a platform on which to build. Gillespie looked lively, but faded, while Hamann had just over half an hour in which to impress before being withdrawn so that Batty could shore up the centre of midfield. To make matters worse, neither Shearer nor Griffin reappeared for the second half. Serrant, a reliable enough full-back, slotted in for Griffin. Andersson was inept.

Wednesday's eighty-first-minute equaliser just about summed up Newcastle. Humphreys' header into the box fell somewhere between statuesque defenders Barton and Charvet, enough to confuse Given and leave the bewildered Irishman rooted to the spot himself. Petter Rudi stepped in to take advantage of the farcical situation and prod the ball home via a deflection off Charvet.

Batty and Lee did provide an engine, while Dalglish, before he, too, was injured, provided some spark. But the partnership with Shearer had yet to produce a flood of goals.

In fact Gullit, physio Derek Wright and club doctor Roddy Macdonald had probably saved Shearer from a lengthy lay-off by persuading him not to emerge for the second half. A club spokesman confirmed: 'Alan wanted to go out for the second half. But in the end, he did what he was told.' Newcastle were quick to quash rumours of a dressing room bust-up between Shearer and Gullit.

Shearer had a scan on his right hamstring, showing a slight tear, and was ruled out of joining up with England for the friendly with the Czech Republic. Griffin had joined Shearer in the treatment room at half-time with a groin strain, while the injured Hughes and Dalglish had had to play on because Gullit had used all his substitutes.

Gullit was now concerned about next Monday's trip to Goodison Park. Shearer and Dalglish were doubts, while Andersson was desperately short of match fitness after six weeks off with glandular fever. And Batty was far from happy at having been axed. His omission from Gullit's ever changing team had only served to remind Leeds that perhaps all was not necessarily lost in their quest to take him back.

Ruud planned to be away from Tyneside all week as he stepped up his search for fresh talent. Newcastle took Norwegian Under-21 international defender Ragnavald Soma on trial. The nineteen-year-old played for Brann.

But there was yet another transfer setback, as a £4 million bid for Kieron Dyer was turned down. Gullit had one or two transfer targets in 'cold storage' even before the departures of Watson and Guivarc'h, but feared the players would not wait for him indefinitely. Spanish international centre-back Miguel Angel Nadal had interested Newcastle a year ago and the 'Beast of Barcelona' now contacted the Geordies to say: 'I would love to play for you and I still have plenty to offer.' However, at thirty-two, Gullit now considered the Barça strongman too old.

Dabizas' on-off season continued as he faced a one-match ban. More annoying for Gullit than the fact that two of his cautions had been for dissent was that the first of them came in the pre-season JD Sports Cup tournament at Middlesbrough. The club awaited confirmation of the one-match suspension after the Greek collected his fifth booking – his fourth in six games – during the Worthington Cup defeat. It would be his second ban of the season following his dismissal for two bookable offences during the defeat at Arsenal. He was not the only player with disciplinary problems. Batty, who missed the first six games of the season, had picked up four yellow cards, as had Lee. Shearer had three cautions, the same as Griffin.

Albert had decided he wanted out, and sooner rather than later. He was wanted by Southampton as well as by several clubs in Belgium.

In contrast, Steve Howey was offered a much-needed lifeline by Gullit. Howey had collected four full caps and was looking forward to Euro 96 when a freak ankle injury ruled him out of the tournament. A string of operations on groin and calf kept the central defender out of the spotlight for more than two years. Gullit adopted an upbeat philosophy: 'When I first came to the club, everyone told me that Steve was one of the best players at Newcastle. It must be right, too – he was just establishing himself as an England international when his injury problems began. The only problem now is that I have not seen him play yet. But he has come back from a special fitness programme and is getting stronger all the time.'

Gullit's reaction delighted Howey, whose league appearances since the summer of 1996 totalled a mere twenty-two. 'I don't want to leave Newcastle. But my contract is up at the end of this season and at the moment I don't know what is going to happen. I'm from the area, my family is settled here and I don't really want to move away. But I suppose that if you have to, then you have to. I have to think of my career.' A fully fit Howey would be a great asset to any club, but his chances of re-establishing himself at St James's Park increased with the announcement that Albert could leave.

Gullit confessed to having had two 'nice surprises' since taking charge: 'Both Andy Griffin and Stephen Glass worked out that way. I did not know much about them until I came here, and I have been very impressed by both of them. It could be the same with Steve Howey.'

On November 20 a crucial meeting between Gullit and Shepherd took place – headlines the next day declared 'crisis' talks. After three months Ruud was anxious to secure a breakthrough in the transfer market and he wanted the fans to understand the precise details of his predicament after suffering the boos from the supporters.

He said: 'I want to put the fans in the picture, and explain why I cannot give them what they want. Kevin Keegan spent £60 million and Kenny Dalglish £38 million, but I've had nothing, and I took over a team that was not functioning at all. That's nearly £100 million and, I'm sorry, with no success at all. Now I'm left with a relegation team. I have £7 million to spend, although there is more to come. We know we need to bring new faces in, but we have to have the right players, not the ones that other clubs don't want. Our fans deserve the best and that's what we are striving to get.' It would take all the cash available for just one important signing. He needed more: 'Seven million pounds is not enough.'

Gullit responded firmly to the club securing a loan of £40 million to finance the redevelopment of the Milburn Stand: 'The board are trying to get money, I know that, but there's a lot of money being invested in the new stand. If we have a nice new stand but the team is not doing well, then what is the point?'

During their meeting, Gullit was reminded by Shepherd of the restraints under which he had agreed to replace Dalglish. Gullit went on: 'I knew what I was getting into. I was getting a relegation team. When the directors asked me to do the job, it was impossible, given the circumstances at the club, to get results immediately. I told them that, and they understood. It will take time to put things right. My job is to pull them out of trouble this season, then buy the right players to improve the team. But you need money to do that. I knew in the beginning that I had to wait for a short time and, of course, money would be available. How long is later? I came here with a mission. I came here to bring this team up, but I can't do it without the tools.' Shepherd understood Gullit's anxiety and admired his enthusiasm for the job.

Ruud stressed that it was not possible to build a second Chelsea. He explained: 'Chelsea was very different. I had better players earlier on, so I could go forward quicker. I took over at the end of the season, so I had all summer to look for players. At this stage it's not so easy to get the right ones – the players you can get are mostly cast-offs. But if I had Dalglish's £38 million, I could get the people I want. I had them lined up from day one, and it would be no problem at all. That's the big difference. At Chelsea I had the money.'

Most of his targets were abroad, but there was some movement in the Premiership. 'You don't get better players abroad, but you do get value for money.'

According to the *Sunday Mirror* headline on November 22, Shearer was now definitely for sale! Gullit diplomatically responded: 'I will not sell Alan Shearer. I will not use him to raise funds. It does depend on the player. But the situation a couple of months ago was that he did not want to leave, and so I am working on that basis.'

Nevertheless the transfer frustrations continued. Fans were mystified that Gullit had just £7 million to spend. Kevin Miles, chairman of the Independent Newcastle United Supporters' Association, said: 'Personally, I can't see that the figures quite add up. We were told that the manager had £5 million to spend when he took over the job, plus whatever he raised from sales. He sold Steve Watson for £4 million and Stephane Guivarc'h for £3.5 million and now he has £7 million to spend. That just does not add up. I think most fans would think it was tragic if we got back to the situation where Newcastle becomes a club which sells players to survive financially, having just got used to the idea of buying for success.'

Miles believed Gullit should be allowed time to sort out his problems, welcoming his intention to build a team around the keystones of Shearer, Batty, Lee and Given. 'If you're trying to be a successful team competing at the highest level, you're unlikely to do that by selling your best players,' he said. 'Every Newcastle manager is always under pressure, but I don't think anyone would feel that Gullit has had the time to prove he can or cannot do it. It's far too early to say.'

There would be no Shearer at Goodison Park on Monday, but Dalglish had recovered from a groin injury to face the team that had been his dad's great rival. 'I don't know what kind of reception I will receive,' commented Dalglish junior on his return to Merseyside.

But in the end Dalglish was hardly the issue as the 1-0 defeat at Goodison was overshadowed by Gullit's announced intention to sign Duncan Ferguson from Everton in an £8 million deal, in his quest for more strength and physical presence. Gullit made an official approach for Everton's skipper, absent from this game through suspension, and expected to complete the swoop for the controversial striker from under the noses of local rivals Middlesbrough and Sunderland. The move came as Gullit delivered a veiled threat to Shearer and discussion afterwards focused on the two absent number nines.

Gullit made no comment about his impending deal for Ferguson after the match but mapped out a picture of the striker when he described the qualities that his team currently lacked. 'We need some power up front. We need someone to get the ball and let our midfield players have something to aim at. We can't get the ball in the air because we can't win it. It just comes back as quick as possible. It's our main problem and we hope we're going to sort it out quickly.'

Ferguson was an idol at Everton but chairman Peter Johnson found the cash hard to refuse. Manager Walter Smith was unhappy to lose one of his stars. Gullit said the same thing about Shearer, but the tone in his voice suggested his staying on Tyneside was not guaranteed. 'For me, Alan Shearer is not for sale. I have already told him, but it is also important that the player wants to stay. If the player does not want to stay for whatever reason, well . . .

'I don't know where these comments come from in all the newspapers. Maybe somebody is talking, maybe somebody is throwing a fish for the sharks. It depends on him, not on me. Every player needs to be happy where he is. If he is unhappy, then what's the point? I would like to hear from him if he is not happy. If he is happy, then he will stay.'

Newcastle fans certainly feared Big Dunc's arrival would spell an early departure for Shearer, and Shearer himself dropped a huge hint that Newcastle would eventually sell him. He said: 'As far as I am concerned I am staying at Newcastle United – but at the moment I really don't know what the board and the manager are thinking.'

Just twenty-four hours earlier Gullit had said that he wanted Shearer to stay – but wasn't sure whether *he* wanted to. That was, in reality, a challenge from Gullit to Shearer for the striker to pledge his future to the club. Shearer's response was virtually a challenge back to Gullit and the board. Behind the scenes, it still looked like a stand-off situation.

The arrival of Ferguson seemed the ideal solution to Shearer's call for more support in attack, but the Scot arrived on a superior contract – a five-and-a-half-year deal worth £7 million – to that of the England captain, adding to Shearer's growing conviction that the ultimate solution was a move, or a new contract.

But Gullit insisted he wanted Alan Shearer to play with Duncan Ferguson. And to reinforce the point, Freddy Shepherd added: 'We have no ulterior motive in signing Duncan Ferguson. Don't forget we are all Geordies, and we want Alan Shearer playing for Newcastle. Whatever happens, no one can accuse this club of lacking ambition.'

The suspended striker watched his team-mates beat his future colleagues before finding himself locked in talks with Gullit. He was close to tears when he left Goodison Park to chants of: 'Don't go,

Duncan.' Ferguson's love for Everton is such that he has the club's crest tattooed on his arm, but he travelled to Tyneside to be officially unveiled as Gullit's first signing the next morning.

Ferguson is the archetypal black and white number nine, a powerful goalscorer in the Jackie Milburn-Malcolm Macdonald mould. More street fighter than fantasy footballer. But at last Gullit had made a significant transfer breakthrough, and typically a spectacular opener.

His new striker had seldom been out of the headlines since he started his career at Dundee United in 1990. He won the first of five Scotland caps in 1992 before leaving for Rangers the following year in a then British record £4 million deal. He scored his first goal for Rangers in a 4-0 win over Raith at Ibrox but in the same match was involved in head-butting incident with Raith's John McStay. Despite a subsequent £4 million move to Everton, the McStay incident led to a court appearance for assault in 1995 and a three-month jail sentence. A twelve-match ban for the attack on McStay was eventually lifted, but he served six weeks of the suspension in Glasgow's Barlinnie Prison. He later decided to retire from international football because of the SFA's treatment of him over the McStay incident, and always maintained a strict silence when it came to the media.

At Goodison on Monday night, news of the deal went round among the fans after Ferguson's father had started the story by tearfully telling fans in the pub across the road that his son was moving. Many stood in the street afterwards to shout at Johnson.

Johnson also angered his manager, Walter Smith, by his handling of the sale. The boss did not want his star player to go and was not consulted until late in the negotiations. Smith considered quitting Everton only five months into the manager's job after not being told about Ferguson's transfer. He actually appeared on television to deny rumours that Ferguson could be joining Sunderland, but an hour later, was informed that the player was being sold.

Ferguson was tipped to set Tyneside alight by one of Newcastle United's most celebrated old boys. Micky Quinn, who won over the Geordie faithful with seventy-one goals in 132 starts between 1989 and 1993, was confident the big Scot could do the same. 'I think it's a great signing for them,' said Quinn. 'He's a player who's coming to the peak of his career and who took on a bit more responsibility with the captain's armband at Everton and revelled in it. He's very enthusiastic, and I hope he sets the place on fire up there.'

Quinn reserved judgement on the new partnership with Shearer. 'They're both out-and-out centre forwards and similar players in many

A grim-looking Alan Shearer walks with manager Kenny Dalglish
(courtesy of Allsport)

Above: The players Ruud Gullit signed in the summer to help build a new Newcastle: Marcelino, Goma, Dumas and Dyer
(courtesy of *The Mirror*)

Left: Happier days... Ruud arrives at Tyneside with Chairman Freddy Shepherd for a press conference
(courtesy of *The Mirror*)

Below: Ruud Gullit and Alex Ferguson patrol the touchline
(courtesy of *The Mirror*)

Right: Captain Alan Shearer on the ball at the FA Cup final... but Gullit questioned Shearer's commitment and involvement at Wembley
(courtesy of Allsport)

Below: Dressed to thrill for the final, but the Armani suits were the only style the Newcastle team showed at Wembley
(courtesy of Armani)

Above: Ruud with Estelle, the beautiful mother of his daughter Joelle, and the niece of Johan Cruyff. His personal life is in turmoil
(courtesy of *The Mirror*)

Below: the final act of defiance for Gullit; the body language tells the story of a night of gloom against Sunderland at a rain-soaked St James's Park
(courtesy of Allsport)

The third 'Messiah' in a year... Bobby Robson hopes to revive Newcastle's ailing fortunes
(courtesy of Allsport)

respects. They're both good target men and good in the air, but I think they're very similar and I don't know how they'll gel as a duo. Not a lot of people give Duncan credit for his touch and his ability on the deck.'

But the fans seemed to have no doubts as Fergie-mania gripped Tyneside: Number twenty and 'Ferguson' became the order of the day for the black and white shirts. Geordies were ecstatic over his arrival and were clamouring to have the striker's name and number on their backs.

'The fans are loving it,' said a delighted Gullit. 'And it is great to see them so happy. As soon as they began to hear that we were signing Duncan, they were coming up to me and asking whether or not it was true. The fans will love him. They will identify with his passion for the game. He will give everyone an extra boost.'

Ferguson's swift arrival came a little too early for most fans, who missed the opportunity to watch his first training session at Chester-le-Street. Little more than two dozen were on hand to see Gullit's first signing for the club meet his new team-mates as he rushed from a press conference to enjoy a late morning session.

Ferguson insisted: 'Of course, I am looking forward to teaming up with Alan and I hope it's going to be a potent partnership. But I don't think I can bring the best out of him as he's already one of the best in Europe and he's proved that he can do the business on his own. He's a proven goalscorer and a world class striker. I think everyone knows that. I am sure we can form a good partnership. I'm also looking forward to scoring a few myself.'

Ferguson often retreated from the limelight to his pigeon loft, but at his unveiling he was transformed. Relaxed, smiling and comfortable. He married into the Parrott family (his wife Jeanne is the sister of snooker star John Parrott's wife) and spent £2,000 on a new pigeon loft (pigeon cree, as they call them in the North East) at his Ormskirk home. 'I'll be bringing the pigeons up to Newcastle with me,' he said. 'But I'll have to bring them up in the car – they're not good enough to find their own way here yet!'

More surprises – he was ready to play for Scotland again. Labelled 'Duncan Disorderly', he even hinted that perhaps it was about time he started speaking to the press. ('About time,' muttered a Merseyside-based scribe. 'He's already said more than he's said in four years with Everton!')

Gullit insisted: 'Yes, I would like to see Duncan playing for Scotland again. I think it is good for everyone's career to play for their country.

I know he has had some difficulties in the past, but they can be overcome. I want him to make a fresh start here and make the most of his talents.'

Fletcher recalled: 'I remember, ages ago, Kevin Keegan asking me to check out Ferguson with the Dundee United manager, Jim McLean. Unfortunately for us, he was not interested in selling at the time. But we have him now. And you don't have to be a rocket scientist to see what type of player the team has been lacking. He can be another in the mould of Milburn, Macdonald, Gallacher and even Cole. They love their centre-forwards here.'

Gullit was no stranger to the Ferguson fan club himself. 'I tried to sign him for Chelsea, but it was difficult at the time. He was just the type of player I was looking for. He was in the picture at the time.'

Ferguson believed he had joined a club whose fans shared his passion for the game. Speaking of the Everton tattoo on his arm, he says: 'It won't be coming off just because I've left. It is something I don't regret, not after the loyalty I showed Everton and the loyalty the fans showed towards me. I can't just switch on and off like that. Would I consider having a Newcastle tattoo beneath it? You never know. If I'm here long enough. It's a five-and-a-half-year contract, but the longer the better. I was loyal to Everton and I will be loyal to Newcastle. Everton decided to sell me. They decided that they no longer wanted me.'

Shearer looked no further ahead than to forging the sharpest of spearheads. 'I think Duncan is a superb player. And together, I would hope that we would be a handful for any defence. I know defenders don't like playing against him because I have heard them say so!'

Things were looking up. Shearer would return for the next match so long as his hamstring injury suffered no reaction. And Gullit no longer necessarily had to sell in order to buy again. By the same token, he was told to reduce the wage bill.

He was given an opportunity almost at once when David Batty put in a written transfer request of one sentence: 'I would like to leave Newcastle and join Leeds.' His agent Hayden Evans confirmed: 'If a player puts in a written transfer request, he doesn't get the rest of his signing-on fee.' Ruud would not stand in the way of any unhappy members of his squad, so Batty's days were numbered and talks with Leeds began. David Batty trained with the reserves.

Ironically, in a Sunday newspaper, Gullit had said not so long before that he was going to build a team around Given, Lee, Shearer and Batty. He had singled Batty out as one of the keystones of his new team but faced losing him just two days after getting his hands on his first signing.

Always one of the first names on the Newcastle team sheet, Batty was upset that Gullit saw him as part of a squad rotation policy. He had been a central figure since Keegan laid out £3.75 million to take him to Tyneside from Blackburn Rovers in March 1996. Now he was a week away from this thirtieth birthday and was devastated to be left out of the starting line-up for the visit of Sheffield Wednesday. Batty was concerned that as a squad member at Newcastle he would lose his place in the England set-up.

Gullit had a contingency plan: Hasselbaink or Radebe as part of the Batty deal. He said: 'It would have been better for him but also for the club if it had happened earlier, because we would have had more possibilities to get players in. At this stage of the competition, you can have the money but maybe you can't spend it because you can't get clubs to let players go as we did with Duncan. But we'll sort something out.'

Batty's impending departure inevitably started tongues wagging again about the future of Shearer, but Gullit was adamant that his apparent difference of opinion with the striker was history. 'Alan wants to stay and I want him to stay. Now the issue is over. There's no issue anymore.' Arsene Wenger had finally admitted he was interested in Shearer – but only at a knock-down price. No more than £8 million.'

With Ferguson in and Batty with one foot back in Leeds, Gullit had finally begun to put his own mark on Newcastle United. Shearer was included in the squad for Saturday but a late decision would be taken on his fitness.

Ruud was upbeat as he prepared his side for what was always a tough test, at home to Wimbledon. 'Everyone was very happy with the signing,' he said. 'It gives us an extra boost. But we are not finished yet. We still have to get players in with certain qualities to work with the players that we still have here.' He was happy that he had the players to complement Shearer and Ferguson.

Batty left training clutching a large cardboard box, his Newcastle career over. Gullit confirmed: 'I haven't accepted an offer from Leeds yet but a move is imminent. Batty is not in the squad for tomorrow but he will be able to train here until he leaves.'

Other less valuable assets were to follow him out. Barnes was linked with a player/manager's job at Blackburn while Andersson would leave as soon as Gullit found a buyer.

Shearer denied reports that Ferguson was his hand-picked choice.

'The senior players at Newcastle have no influence whatsoever on transfers.'

When Keith Gillespie arrived at Newcastle as the makeweight in Andy Cole's £7 million switch to Manchester United, Kevin Keegan hailed him as the best young player in the country. That was almost four years before. Now twenty-three, and in his fifth season with Newcastle, he had hit the crossroads. Gambling, stories of the occasional bar room brawl, and, of course, that infamous clash with Shearer when 'horseplay' led to the Irishman being treated for a head wound in a Dublin hospital, would all tend to suggest that Gillespie was on his way out. But he had been offered a new four-year deal. And, just for the record, there was no problem between him and Shearer. 'It was just a drunken day out that time. Alan would laugh if he thought people believed there was a problem there. We're in the same card school together and we have a laugh together. Anyone who says otherwise is way off the mark.'

The same day Garth Crooks was dispatched to the North East for a special feature on Ruud for BBC's *Football Focus*. Garth suggested that Ruud would not be happy with the results or indeed performances of his team, nor would he be satisified with his own contribution so far. Ruud said: 'I ask that of myself. I've been a winner and yes, I've done nothing here yet.'

Stuart Pearce suggested the players, rather than the manager, should take the blame. 'I don't believe in criticising managers, it's the players who have underachieved.'

Against Wimbledon, though, both the manager and the players had cause for satisfaction as debut Duncan, with a double second-half strike, gave Newcastle their first Premiership victory in six games. Ruud raised a laugh by replying to the enquiry 'Did Duncan give you a lift?' with the deadpan riposte: 'No, I came in my own car . . .' But at last Gullit's team were capable of getting out of first and and second gear.

The debut goals were a delight. Midway through the second half Ferguson met Solano's cross with a volley which bounced past Sullivan. Then a minute from time he headed Gillespie's cross into the corner to complete the 3-1 win. Shearer hadn't played but Ferguson said: 'It's great to be on the winning side on your debut. Scoring two hopefully repaid the tremendous support I got from the fans. Alan Shearer is on his way back to fitness and I am looking forward to linking up with him.'

Ferguson was the hero, and for once not the villain as well. He never looked like losing his rag, yet still maintained an aggressive edge. He was whisked away from the ground by cab with the former world snooker champion John Parrott. They dashed back to Merseyside. 'Everton won as well,' Fergie beamed. 'That makes me very happy.'

There were other reasons for Ruud to be happy, like the return of Howey. Gullit said: 'It was like having a new £5 million player in the team. We sent him to Lilleshall on a two-week programme so that all his problems could be sorted out, but he stayed for three. He has worked very, very hard and looked fit for someone playing his first game of the season.' Howey marked his first start of the season by being captain on the day. Now Gullit was set to come up with a deal that would keep Howey at the club he joined from school. Howey said: 'Coming back into the side and being made captain of Newcastle was the greatest moment of my career. I didn't think they would ever let a lad from Sunderland lead out Newcastle. But they did, and the whole day was magnificent. I don't drink much alcohol these days, but when I went out for a meal on Saturday night I had about fifteen gallons of water. I was so drained, mentally and physically.'

6

Gullit and Shearer in crisis talks

Only three months into Ruud Gullit's reign, and Alan Shearer knew he was expendable.

After weeks of intensive speculation about his future, Shearer made a dramatic TV appearance the day after the Wimbledon match to discuss his situation. Shearer spoke out on Sky TV following a plea from former team-mate Tim Sherwood begging him to return as player-boss at Blackburn.

Shearer did his best to kill off suggestions that he would quit Newcastle at the end of the season. Asked if he thought he would start next season with the club, Shearer left no room for doubt when he replied emphatically: 'Yes I will.' He said he had had talks with Gullit after the manager questioned his commitment to the club: 'I couldn't understand why he said it and we had a chat. I said, "Look, this speculation has got to end. It's got to stop somewhere." I really don't know where the speculation comes from and as far as I'm concerned and the club is concerned, we'd like to put an end to it all. I've told him I want to stay. The chairman says I'm not going, the manager says I'm not for sale, and I say I'm staying. This is the third time this season I have had to come out and say I will be staying. It won't be happening again because I'm not going to do it again. I'm sick of doing it and I shouldn't have to do it. The clear fact is that I am staying at the club. I am looking forward to developing a partnership with Duncan Ferguson.' But behind the scenes, Gullit's disillusionment was growing and Shearer became aware of the possibility of a move at the right price.

Sherwood, worried about the future of managerless Blackburn, had said: 'I would get in Alan as boss. He could also score ten or fifteen goals a season.' But Shearer believed Blackburn had only themselves to blame for their freefall since winning the Premiership title in 1995. Sold to Newcastle a year later, he said: 'We were in a very powerful position. We could have gone out and got the world's best players, but never did.'

The *Sunday Mirror* reported Barcelona preparing an offer of £16 million for Shearer, plus the £2 million rated Miguel Angel Nadal. Newcastle denied it, but the paper insisted Barça had been alerted to his availability. It was clear that talks had taken place with Barcelona at this stage, and had a deal been reached that Shearer would have been sacrificed.

Celtic were the latest club linked to Shearer. Kenny Dalglish, who bought him for a then record £3.3 million at Blackburn, was involved with Simple Minds star Jim Kerr in takeover talks with the Scottish giants in an £80 million deal. The task was that he would bring Shearer with him. Dalglish and Shearer had been at Parkhead together to see Celtic beat Rangers 5-1, intensifying the speculation.

Attention to the Shearer situation was temporarily diverted, however, when chairman Freddy Shepherd and deputy Douglas Hall sparked a fresh row by returning to the board. The pair had resigned from the football club and plc boards after mocking Newcastle fans for paying high prices for replica kits, dubbing Shearer 'Mary Poppins' and branding Tyneside women 'dogs'.

Now they wanted to replace their representatives on the board, John Fender and Tom Fenton. When the move went before a vote of shareholders, Hall's holding, combined with the 8.1 per cent owned by a trust run by Shepherd, meant the pair could easily elect themselves. But their return ran contrary to assurances given to businessman and lifelong fan Dennis Cassidy in July when he took on the role of company chairman. Cameron Hall Developments, a Hall family vehicle that controlled 57 per cent of the Newcastle shares, proposed Shepherd and Hall as directors so long as their own company nominees were not re-elected.

The boardroom manoeuvres coincided with takeover reports but shares fell by around 4 per cent, wiping off most of the gains made on Monday as a result of the successful debut of Ferguson.

With a huge controlling interest in the club, Shepherd and Hall were still working behind the scenes and their public return to the helm came as no surprise. Shepherd, in particular, had been closely involved in Gullit's efforts to bring in new faces, which took a turn for the better with the arrival of Ferguson. With bids of around £220 million for the club expected, Douglas Hall stood on the brink of a personal £125 million fortune, which would make him the richest man in British football. The son of former chairman Sir John Hall had paid only £3 million for his 57.1 per cent stake in the club.

Meanwhile, David Batty was desperate to quit, even accepting a £5,000-a-week pay cut to speed up his return to Elland Road. Batty's agent Hayden Evans waited for the all clear to sort out personal terms and said: 'I will be disappointed if the talks take any longer than half an hour. There has never been any question of him going anywhere other than Leeds. He does not want to join another club, which is why he's made things so easy by handing in a transfer request.' But Shepherd countered: 'We are not giving anybody away in a cut-price deal. Nobody sells us any of their players on the cheap, so why should we?'

Malcolm Macdonald aimed a 'good riddance' gibe at Batty. 'I think my old club will be better off without him. His passing range is abysmal. I know that if I was playing centre-forward in the current Newcastle team, I would be tearing my hair out. He would have killed me. The ball either goes sideways or backwards. There's no penetration. Ruud Gullit dropped him, and good for him. Now perhaps United will buy some vision to go into midfield!'

Gullit was weighing up a move for German international centre-back Thomas Helmer, the Bayern Munich star, as a possible short term solution to his side's defensive problems, and was keen to take him either on a month's loan or until the end of the season. Helmer, thirty-three, was a member of the World Cup squad with sixty-five caps.

Another on his way out was Perez, wanted by Dundee United who had watched him in the reserves. Gullit was also linked to Eyal Berkovic at West Ham, as a replacement for Batty.

There was another vital matter to resolve. Unbeaten with white socks against Wimbledon, Boro and Blackburn, the club were unable to continue wearing them as they couldn't change any part of their kit during the season. Ruud had worn white socks as a player with AC Milan, Sampdoria and Chelsea. Newcastle spokesman Graham Courtney explained: 'Ruud feels happier with the white socks. It's a superstitious thing not a major change, but one which he and the players are all happy about.'

Former captain Bobby Moncur said: 'I don't care if the socks are tartan, as long as they bring success. I'm not going to argue with Ruud

Gullit about the benefits of wearing white socks. The theory that players can pick each other out easier is a new one on me. If it wins things, which I have my doubts about, then go for it. But there are more important changes needed before Newcastle win some trophies.'

Steve Wraith, editor of *Number Nine* fanzine, commented: 'Parents who now have to buy a £12 pair of white socks will not be pleased, but if it brings the success Ruud had at Milan and Chelsea, I'll be happy. If he messes with the black and white shirts there will be protests.'

But Batty had not yet been sold. David O'Leary demanded Newcastle lower their price: 'There's no way we can meet their £6 millon valuation. That takes him out of the market as far as we are concerned.'

Gullit said: 'Nothing is decided yet. The clubs are still negotiating. That's how it is with negotiations. If we can't reach an agreement, then it's going to be difficult for him. It's not difficult for me. The player made the decision. He distanced himself from the team. If a player does not want to stay for family or private reasons, then it's important that I think ahead to what I am going to do without him. I don't think he will ever play for Newcastle again. He cut the line. He will not be in the squad for Middlesbrough because I don't want a player who doesn't want to play. I don't want to sound nasty or negative. But I have to be realistic. It's a risk he took by putting in a transfer request, although I accept it's a difficult situation.'

Shearer's 'best man' had been Middlesbrough's Neil Maddison. Now the North East lads were preparing to go head-to-head at the Riverside.

The two joined Southampton as youngsters, becoming firm friends as they rose through the ranks. Maddison was sure Shearer and Duncan Ferguson would be a goalscoring machine. He said: 'I would say that it's going to be a formidable duo at Newcastle. It will be their first appearance together against us – I just hope they don't click too quickly.'

Paul Gascoigne was back in training following a knee injury, and would start against his hometown club. But Shearer was still battling to shake off the hamstring injury, and that suited Boro boss Bryan Robson just fine. 'All the hype has been about Shearer and Ferguson,' he said. 'And at £23 million for the pair, you would expect them to produce the goods. But I'm happy to let them get all the pre-match attention. We too can score goals and in Hamilton Ricard we have a player who has hit twelve already this season.'

Robson had been desperate to land Ferguson before the big target man made the move to Tyneside. 'They were asking too much for our liking. I did want him, but it was an expensive package. In the end I went for Brian Deane at £3 million, and that suited our club much better at our stage.'

It was Gullit's first Tyne-Tees derby and he did not know quite what to expect. 'Derbies are always special. I've played in a couple of them and it's always a special atmosphere. I haven't yet tasted the derby atmosphere in town. In Milan they were already talking about the game three weeks before. For me, I suppose, it's just another game, but for the local people and some players who come from the region, it's something special. It's about winning and surviving, and being king of the region. There are a lot of emotions, especially for the boys who come from here.'

Boro were four places above Newcastle in seventh, but Newcastle had completed a double over the Teessiders during their last season in the top flight, and also came out on top in a penalty shoot-out during the pre-season tournament.

And the match proved characteristically hard-fought, ending with honours even at 2-2. Gullit was pleased with his side's approach and character in twice coming from a goal down to secure a point, despite no return for Shearer.

The new-look Gazza turned the other cheek, shunning the attentions of a topless Santa and a helper wearing nothing but a G-string. Chased around the pitch by the near-naked festive duo, the Geordie boy kept his cool. His delightful left-wing corner created the first goal for skipper Andy Townsend after 13 minutes.

It was not the most pulsating of North East derbies but Gullit's side deserved their point. He said: 'This was another step forward for us. Two weeks ago, we would not have come back from being 2-1 down. I was pleased with the way we played. You could tell from the reaction of the crowd and their coaches that they weren't happy.' Robson and Gullit both singled out Harper, who pulled off three superb saves on his full debut in the Premiership.

Dabizas had returned from suspension only to find himself on the bench. But he emerged for the last nine minutes, salvaging a point with his first touch. It was his fourth goal of the season, all headers. 'I am scoring more goals in England because the style of play and the quality of the crossing is better over here. Now I am hoping to win back my place in the team. It hurt me to be left out, but I am a professional and therefore had to accept it.'

Gullit had more good news a few days later as he emerged the winner in the boardroom turmoil. His pursuit of new players was enhanced by the comeback of Shepherd and Hall, even if the share price dropped as three directors and the club's stockbrokers resigned in protest. Gullit's hand was strengthened because the two major shareholders were back in total control. Guaranteed £4.4 million to spend following the sale of Batty, he made Ajax's Richard Witschge a target.

Hall and Shepherd, directors of the football club, previously needed to consult the plc before sanctioning deals. Now they didn't need an answer from the plc boardroom.

As the team prepared for another crunch game against Blackburn, Gullit banned a stereo from the dressing-room. He wanted his players to talk more to build up team spirit.

He declined to add to the constant speculation of more signings. 'All I can say is that we have our targets, they have not changed, but we'll leave you all to do the guessing.'

Howey's future was on the point of being settled and he was to lead out the team again in the absence of Shearer and Lee. Howey said: 'I have spoken to the chairman and made him aware that I want to stay at the club. He has offered me a new deal and I'm now very hopeful things will be sorted. This is an important stage of my career. I'm aiming to get myself really fit and stay that way. I have never wanted to leave the club and the fact they seem to want me to stay makes my decision easy.'

Gullit refused to be rattled by the continued absence of Shearer, although the striker was back in light training. 'I am not disappointed that Duncan and Alan are still not together, because I know what it is like when you are trying to come back from an injury. What is important right now are the other players in the team. I do not talk about individuals, that's not my main thing. It's about the eighteen or twenty people who make up the squad. I like to talk about Newcastle as a group and following our draw at Middlesbrough last weekend, I think we have now given ourselves a yardstick for the rest of the season.'

Gullit believed his side were no longer pushovers. 'We showed great character to get a point at Middlesbrough and I was pleased with our mental strength. It hasn't been easy for the players adapting to new methods here. But now they are much better and we are going along the right lines.'

Also missing would be former Blackburn keeper Given and Gillespie who had a broken toe. Pearce was available again after suspension, but Gullit kept faith with young Hughes.

Kenny Dalglish came to the game and watched his old clubs bore each other to death! Gullit solemnly said after a depressing 0-0 draw: 'It was a bad game. I was not happy with our performance. What made me so unhappy was that after looking as though we could control the game early on, the players just disappeared. It wasn't until close to the end that we started to play again, and I can't be happy with that. We are best when we pass the ball around, but too often we were just playing sloppy long balls.

'It's disappointing and not good enough to see my players disappearing. They only played the first twenty minutes and the last fifteen. What did they do in between? I can't be happy with a point. There are a whole lot of things that are wrong. I can pinpoint the problems, but that's something for the locker rooms.'

Mr Cool had lost patience with his team. He conducted his after-match press conference standing up, clearly agitated.

Indeed, Newcastle had been lucky to get a point. Harper had pulled off an astonishing save from Davies, who had also hit the bar, and Jeff Kenna had hit the post from the penalty spot.

The performance again showed how badly the team needed new blood and Gullit was ready to splash out £8 million on Frenchmen Ibrahim Ba and Didier Domi. The bleached-haired Ba asked for a move from AC Milan and was told that the club would not stand in his way. Domi was happy at Paris St Germain, but might still be tempted by a move to the Premiership.

Gullit, with only Ferguson on board, was beginning to lose patience with his squad. The dour draw at Blackburn served to emphasise certain weaknesses, and he needed to act sooner rather than later. To add to his problems, Shearer was out until the New Year. And Ferguson had not posed too much of a threat since scoring twice on his debut.

At least there was one change as Gillespie was sold to Blackburn for £2.35 million. Gullit explained: 'It was not difficult for me to part with him. We had offered him a new deal, he waited quite a while and then in the end he refused to sign it. It was not a difficult decision to make when he was going to be on a free transfer at the end of the season.'

Gillespie launched a bitter attack on Freddie Fletcher. He could not hide his contempt for the people who had written off his career. 'As a young player it was the last thing I wanted to hear. It was wrong for him to come out with such a statement and your guess is as good as mine about what possessed him to do it. When it came out, I set out straight away to prove these people wrong above everything else. I knew it wasn't true but people obviously believe things when they are said publicly. If that's what he thought then fair enough, but I knew it was far from true and that was the only thing that counted.'

There was confirmation that a prospective buyer for the club had made an approach. Sony insisted it was not them, but Newcastle's announcement set the rumour machine into overdrive. Still, nothing would be concluded until the Monopolies and Mergers Commission had ruled on BSkyB's £623 million bid for Manchester United.

The club had been floated at 135p per share in April 1997, although a series of public relations disasters and poor results on the pitch saw the price drop. The share price now stood at just 96p, but rose to 116p as the news emerged, and further rises were likely if, as expected, a bidding war ensued. Sports Minister Tony Banks said Trade and Industry Secretary Peter Mandelson, whose Hartlepool constituency is a little more than thirty miles south of St James's Park, was keeping a watchful eye on the situation. 'The Government will study this particular takeover bid, if it materialises, just like we are still studying the BSkyB bid for Manchester United. I don't envy Peter Mandelson in his decision-making process but I have always said, as a football fan as well as sports minister, that I don't really believe that football can be treated like any other economic product on the market to be bought and sold like motor cars or refrigerators or hi-fis. There's more passion involved in it. Peter knows my feelings very well and he knows the feelings of football supporters. But of course, he has to put himself in a position where he's looking at the commercial involvement, because we are also talking about publicly quoted companies. This is what happened, of course, when football decided to go down the plc road.'

Nearly 10,000 fans would be out of pocket by £400 each if the club agreed a takeover. The board were ready to grab just 110 pence a share for the club, leaving 8,500 die-hard Newcastle fans holding four million shares in the company between them, putchased at 135p a share.

At the time, 75,000 fans had applied to buy shares in the club. Just 8,500 'lucky' season ticket holders were given the chance to buy shares, for a minimum investment of £500 each, although most spent well over £2,000 of their savings on the club. So the average loss for each fan with shares would be about £400 each.

Douglas Hall pocketed £10 million as he sold 6.3 per cent of his stake to media and telecommunications company NTL. But more importantly, he also gave them an option to snap up the remaining 50.8

per cent of his shares. NTL, one of the top three cable companies in the UK and the creators of Eurosport, had until early June to accept.

Hall had made his mind up to eventually sell his entire stake, but his decision to sell 6.3 per cent left him with a controlling interest for the moment. The NTL move was expected to boost the share price, leaving the club ripe for sale, and Hall might pick up a massive 160p per share for the remainder of his stake. Such a deal would net him a further £81 million.

Fletcher, who was appointed as acting chairman of the plc following the return of Hall and Shepherd to the board, suggested the NTL deal had all happened very quickly. 'When the major shareholders returned to the board, we learned that there had been some preliminary conversation which may or may not have led to something, but there was nothing which meant us having to make a Stock Exchange announcement. But on Tuesday after an unfounded story in the press, we had to make a holding statement, and then we pulled out all the stops to get to where we are.'

If NTL did decide to take up the option to acquire the remaining stake, it would then be required to make an offer to all shareholders. Fletcher admitted that huge financial backing from companies such as NTL, itself worth $3 billion, was necessary to succeed in today's football world. He said: 'This is good news for Newcastle United, its fans and its shareholders. I think this is the way football is going to develop on a more internationalised basis. If the best clubs are to compete with Manchester United in Britain, and the Milans and Barcelona, they need the strength of a company like NTL behind them.'

Fletcher also paid tribute to the company which, through Sir John Hall and son Douglas, had been behind much of Newcastle's success. 'Cameron Hall Developments has been the controlling major shareholder for the last six and a half or seven years, and if you look at the progress of the company during that period, then it has been a period of success. I remember those dark days when I came to the club and we were almost in the Third Division. Although we still want to be playing better on the park, at least we are in the Premier League. I think it should be put on record what happened during their stewardship.'

NTL was seeking a foothold in the bargaining process for the right to screen live sport. Its president and chief executive officer Barclay Knapp said: 'We wanted a top club. Next to Manchester United, Newcastle has the best and strongest fan base nationwide. We're getting in at the start of a new era for TV and soccer.

NTL had until twelve weeks after the Monopolies and Mergers Commission's report on BSkyB's planned takeover of Manchester United to take up the option. The telecommunications company does 99 per cent of its business in Britain, where it employs a workforce of 12,000. Over the last year it had bought the Teesside cable TV franchise from Comcast UK as well as the two other cable companies, ComTel and Diamond Cable. Its cable network reaches 5.2 million homes.

Ba flew into Newcastle on Friday, December 18, but Gullit declined to confirm that the deal was done. He smiled: 'You don't sell the fur until you've shot the bear. And my cannon is loaded.' If Ruud did sign Ba, it would definitely be sexy football – Ba was voted sexiest foreign footballer in Serie A in a poll of 1,000 women. His reaction: 'It must be a joke. I don't believe it. What do they find sexy? Perhaps it is since I've changed my hair dye from yellow to blond.'

Meanwhile, Ruud's first signing was suffering from flu – Ferguson was out of the side. So there was an outside chance that Shearer would make a surprise early comeback. The England captain would be on the bench against Leicester.

Meanwhile Ruud urged the FA to close the game down for two weeks for the Millennium. 'I think it will be a time for players to be with their families. It will be a very special time. But then I would also like to see the game in England close down for two weeks *every* Christmas. They do it in Italy for two weeks and in Holland and Germany for a month. Maybe England just like to be different!'

For the Leicester game, Ruud invited a group of kids from a hospice he had visited in the week before Christmas as his guests of honour at St James's Park. He asked his team to arrive at the ground early to meet the kids, and sat the youngsters just behind him during the game.

Alongside him on the bench was indeed Shearer. Gullit said: 'Shearer had managed only three days training and that's not enough. I didn't want to risk him and wanted to play him when the opposition was tiring. He should be ready for the Christmas programme.'

Glass sealed the points with his third goal of the season midway through the second half, against a disappointing Leicester side which never managed a solitary shot on target. Both sides struggled to take a grip. Lee and Speed took a stranglehold in the centre of the park, but their work was wasted by the ineffective Andersson and Ketsbaia. Glass showed excellent skills when in one moment he lifted a Lee crossfield pass over the head of Frank Sinclair, wrong-footed Taggart and drove against Elliott, with the referee refusing all claims for a penalty. In a bid to add some spark to his lacklustre attack, Gullit sent on Shearer soon after the break for Ketsbaia.

Shearer's arrival produced the necessary lift. Leicester responded by sending on Pontus Kaamark to do a man-marking job, but the deadlock was eventually broken midway through the second half when, for once, Andersson's poor control worked in Newcastle's favour. As he tried to hold up a Barton cross from the left, the ball bounced off the Swede to Glass on the edge of the area and he finished with style.

Barton had signed a new three-year deal – even though, according to his manager, he had no left foot! The left-back attracted such backing from the crowd that they looked as though they were on the brink of elevating him to cult status.

In contrast, supporters hurled an amazing amount of abuse at Andersson, anxious to consign the Swede to the list of failed Newcastle centre-forwards.

Understandably, he looked as though he feared his every touch was going to go against him. Invariably it did. Gullit left himself open to derision when, ten minutes into the second half, he threw on Shearer for Ketsbaia and not the woefully weak Swedish international. But he said: 'I thought Ketsbaia and Andersson did what they had to do, and did it quite well. We know we can still do better and that we need more class in certain areas. But let's go one step at a time. We had two strikers out in Shearer and Ferguson, and I was quite pleased with things.'

One huge plus for Newcastle was the continued good form of Howey. In his fourth game back, he looked as polished a defender as you would find anywhere in the Premiership, taking care of the dangerous Emile Heskey throughout. Gullit backed him to resume an international career that earned him four caps before a catalogue of disasters befell him just before the start of Euro 96.

Gullit poked his head round the dressing room door and said he would see the players again on Boxing Day. He didn't leave for Holland immediately and was seen on Tyneside as newspapers linked him to a second AC Milan star, Zvonimir Boban, available for a nominal fee after putting in eight years' service. Newcastle initially discussed a loan deal for the experienced schemer who had captained Croatia, but that broke down.

It was the start of a controversial week for him.

7

Gullit accused . . . 'a semi-detached manager'

Ruud Gullit was caught in the crossfire five days before Christmas as Douglas Hall and Freddy Shepherd attended the club's annual meeting to be confronted by 350 United shareholders.

Angry fan Dan Leeson described Gullit's commitment as 'semi-detached'. He said: 'I read that he spends as much time in Amsterdam as he does in Newcastle. I know there were a lot of problems with that at his last club, Chelsea. This morning, is he in Newcastle or Amsterdam?'

Freddie Fletcher responded: 'I completely reject those remarks. It's a one-hour-ten-minute flight from Amsterdam. And if he wants to go back there from time to time, he can do. The board has every confidence in Mr Gullit. Their remit was to bring entertaining and attacking football to the club. We believe that's what the club wants, and it was very successful a few years ago. Mr Gullit works very hard and, as we speak, he is in Newcastle. It's no secret that he wants to sign players and he is fully committed to making Newcastle a successful team. The board are fully behind him.'

Shareholders at the fiery meeting voted 9-1 against Hall's election as well as 2-1 against Shepherd in the show of hands. Chants of 'It's a stitch-up' echoed around Newcastle Civic Centre. It was the first annual meeting since the two men were exposed by a tabloid newspaper criticising Newcastle's fans and the women of the city, and the supporters took the opportunity to attack. 'I find it sad that the present management has created such ill will from the city and supporters,' Alan Clark told the meeting. Even though Hall and Shepherd had previously apologised in writing to shareholders and season ticket holders, supporter Hilary Brown insisted: 'An apology from the pitch, especially to the women, would have been much more successful.'

Neither spoke from their positions on the platform as irate fans continued to fire questions. On a couple of occasions, stewards were asked to restrain over-excited fans. One Mr Leeson, said: 'I've never known Newcastle United be such a laughing stock.' Another, Brian Putnam, added: 'I feel very let down by the goings-on at this great club. Why don't they put the shares on the open market fairly and squarely?'

Fletcher stated that such a move could depress the share price even further. Mr Putnam said he was in danger of losing £58,000 after spending £250,000 on shares when the price was at its peak.

It was confirmed that Gullit would be given the go-ahead to tie up an £8 million Christmas double swoop for Domi and Ba.

It was also reported that Newcastle forked out £200,000 a year on hotel bills for Gullit. The story angered and hurt Ruud, and would later prompt a powerful defence of his position. Steve Clarke brushed aside criticism that the manager spent too much time travelling back and forth to Holland. 'I don't have any problem at all. It was partly my idea. I think it's important that he gets away and spends time with his family. The run-up to Christmas is always quiet. I can't see too many players being transferred in Christmas week. We were hopeful, but at the moment, there's nothing to report.'

It was business as usual for the rest of the squad preparing for the Boxing Day visit of Leeds, followed two days later by a trip to Liverpool. Clarke joined Gullit in advocating a mid-season break. 'It's come to a time now when football should shut down for the Christmas and New Year period. More and more, people want to spend that time with their family. It's not really very nice when you get out of bed on Christmas morning and sit with the children when they're opening their presents and then having to say, that's it, I'm off now.'

It was the Gullit-bashing season; one of his old boys, Gustavo Poyet, the Uruguayan international brought to Stamford Bridge from Real Zaragoza by Gullit two summers before, insisted he preferred the Chelsea style under Gianluca Vialli to the flamboyant tactics favoured by the Dutchman. 'Ruud Gullit and Gianluca Vialli are very different types of manager,' said Poyet. 'Gullit set great store by playing attractive football, whereas under Vialli we play more in the Italian manner. I have got on well with both ways. But now I am playing as an attacking midfielder, which is where I feel most at home. Gullit talks about playing sexy football – but I would much prefer to win the championship. I want to win the League with Chelsea, even if we don't do it playing in a spectacular style.'

Newcastle would go into the game at Leeds on Boxing Day looking to extend their unbeaten Premiership run to five games. The win over Leicester had helped them climb five places to tenth in the league table, the first time they had been in the top half since the end of October.

The day after the meeting, Clarke confirmed that his boss had taken a short break with his twenty-year-old girlfriend Estelle and one year-old daughter Joelle. Ruud insisted he was busy bringing in fresh blood from Europe, not taking a week's holiday back home. He felt compelled to issue a statement.

'I feel that after a difficult initial period, the team is beginning to take shape and it won't be long before I can finally call it my own. I believe I have chosen excellent backroom staff, which enables me to spend a reasonable amount of time searching for new talent to bring in. In fact, in the last seventy-two hours in particular, I have been in further meetings in Europe with players who we are currently targeting as potential new signings to bolster the squad and mount a serious challenge for honours in the not too distant future.

'I want to assure all Newcastle supporters that my commitment to the club, its players, and of course the fans, remains 100 per cent at all times. I am totally dedicated to the success of Newcastle. I was very sorry to read the stories in the press this morning concerning my visit to Amsterdam on Sunday. It is true that up until now my family has remained in Amsterdam and, as a father, I felt it only natural for me to spend a few days at this important time of year with my girlfriend Estelle and my baby daughter.'

Ruud was back at the training ground by 9am on Thursday for a press conference scheduled to unveil Ba. Instead, Gullit had to explain that Ba failed his medical earlier in the week because of a long term knee injury.

The good news was that the £23 million duo of Shearer and Ferguson were ready to be unleashed for the first time. There had been a five-week wait while Shearer returned to full fitness, then Ferguson went down with flu. 'We only seem to have trained together for five minutes,' said Shearer, 'but if there has been a positive thing to come out of my injury, it's that I have been able to sit in the stand and watch Duncan for the last few matches.'

With the hype over the most expensive strikeforce in English soccer history came great expectation. Shearer had waited for a new partner since Les Ferdinand's £6 million switch to Spurs eighteen months earlier. 'Even I am excited at the prospect of it,' he said. 'I feel great and it would be nice to start the New Year in a high position with something there to build on. I think we have a great chance to put a run together. If we beat Leeds, we will move up another two or three places and then Europe becomes a realistic target. I was delighted to get on against Leicester. Confidence is high after that win and it's important that we carry it on against Leeds.'

Leeds centre-half David Wetherall relished the challenge awaiting him. He said: 'Shearer and Ferguson are both strong and physical but that is fine by me. It suits me, in fact. I have always maintained that I'd rather face an aerial battering from a big striker than try to cope with a nippy little player who runs at you. Ferguson's threat is his sheer physical presence and, from that point of view, he is the best around. But it's not as though he can take me by surprise. I've faced him often enough and there is no way you could look at those battles and say he's had it all his own way. I've been fairly pleased with the way things have gone and I'll be up for it. He is difficult to handle and he can be intimidating. There have been times when he has won the battle against some teams before he's even gone on the pitch, such is his reputation. Players have sometimes hesitated about going up with him and challenging for a header, waiting for the ball to drop instead. I can assure you we won't be doing that if I'm playing.'

Incidentally, Wetherall reckoned the Scot was a pussycat compared to 'Fash the Bash' when it came to verbals, and Ian Wright who has been hosting his own on-the-pitch chat shows for the last fifteen years.

Ruud reacted quickly to the breakdown of Ba's move by launching a bid for Barcelona midfielder Luis Figo. Having let Gillespie leave, he had to find a supply route for Shearer and Ferguson. Gullit hoped a bid of around £6 million would tempt the Spanish champions to sell.

He was also interested in Figo's team-mates Boudewijn Zenden, the Dutch World Cup winger, and defender Winston Bogarde. Ruud was waiting for Paris St Germain to accept a £2.5 million offer for Domi, and had also expressed an interest again in Ronald de Boer. But Barcelona remained favourites for de Boer as long as their Dutch coach Louis van Gaal remained in charge. World class players thinking of coming to England are attracted mainly to the capital, which put Gullit at a huge disadvantage.

Ruud took charge of training on Christmas Day, as dressing-room gifts caused a stir. The players clubbed together to buy Shearer a special seasonal present – a Mary Poppins doll! For Pistone, it was reputedly a heart because they reckoned he didn't have one, and Hamann received a copy of Adolf Hitler's *Mein Kampf* at the Christmas party, more a joke than a statement that he wasn't liked. But the form of Speed, and his encouraging partnership with Lee since Batty's move, put Hamann's place in question in the media.

Ruud was high on optimism as he spread the Christmas goodwill. There was a special message for Batty, who would not be fit for the Boxing Day reunion. 'I thank David not only for his contribution to Newcastle United's cause during almost three years here, but also for the straightforward manner in which he told me that he wished to leave us to go "home". Family – and he is very much a family man – played a huge part in his decision to go back to the club he supported as a boy and played for as a teenager. Because of the honest way he explained things to me, it was easy to reciprocate and grant his wish to leave us for Leeds, and they are the only club he would have left us for, by the way. He has our respect and our best wishes for the future and I know that he will say the same thing about us.'

Ruud was full of praise for Barton and Shearer. 'The team is always the most important consideration for a manager, but a word here for Warren Barton, who has stepped into the left-back spot recently and done very, very well. He is not naturally left-sided, but he has such a good attitude that he has been very effective. Warren's a good professional and a good character to have in your dressing room. He is willing and eager, no matter what task you set him, and I was pleased to see and hear the backing he got from our supporters against Leicester.

'Alan Shearer was back for the last thirty-five minutes of the Leicester game. He had had only three days of training after his hamstring injury and hopefully, with a full week's training behind him, he will be ready to take on Leeds United from the first whistle. If we also have Duncan Ferguson recovered from the flu bug, our fans might even see the two of them on the same pitch!

'I hope you've all enjoyed a lovely Christmas. My New Year message is that I feel sure we will get better as a team and stronger as a club in 1999. I know how much a successful Newcastle United means to so many in the North East and beyond, and I very much want to be part of that success.'

The long-awaited unveiling finally took place against Leeds – but after just two sessions on the training ground it was perhaps unrealistic to expect too much. Shearer and Ferguson clearly needed time to establish an understanding. And service. Gullit wanted to remedy that with a transfer splash after admitting: 'A big cannon needs ammunition.'

Leeds' Harry Kewell snatched top billing on what was meant to be the Al and Dunc show. The injured Batty wasn't missed and Gullit admitted it wasn't Newcastle's day after Nigel Martyn made three brilliant saves from Ferguson, Glass and Dabizas. Shearer also had a header cleared off the line.

Questions now focused on Gullit's commitment after this 3-0 home defeat. There were few more vitriolic and withering attacks than that of Johnny Giles in his *Express* column, who delivered an undiluted condemnation of Gullit's management style. The fans wanted to hear about his rebuilding plans but they also wanted him to prove his dedication to the club; a New Year resolution, perhaps, to put down some roots on the Tyne. Gullit suggested that news of a major signing in the next few days would explain his absence in Christmas week, but also hinted at some sort of conspiracy after being stung by the questions raised at the club's AGM. Newcastle fans, of course, would not give a monkey's whether Gullit spent his week in Tenerife if their side were perched on top of the Premiership table.

Gullit refused to blame his personal troubles as the reason behind recent results. 'It's got nothing to do with it, I don't know why people are trying to make a fuss. Kevin Keegan lives here in the North East and works in London, Bryan Robson lives in Manchester and works in Middlesbrough. Nobody mentions this. I ask myself: why have a go at me? I ask myself: why is there a difference? Brian Kidd always prepared the team at Manchester United. Alex Ferguson never took training, as far as I know. I do the training here, and I prepare the team. I have given you very clear examples of other coaches. I don't know the shareholder who asked the question. I have not seen him at the training ground.

'Things are happening that are very good for the club but I can't always reveal what they are, and that's why criticism is unfair. I wanted to unveil Ibrahim Ba as my answer to those who have questioned my commitment, but unfortunately the deal fell through. Now I hope to have a new transfer breakthrough. In the next couple of days people might understand better. In the meantime I will take the stick.

'I am away doing all I can for the club and then this happens and I think, what the hell is going on? My conscience is clear. Management-wise, we do very well for this club and that's why it is out of order to say the things that were said last week. The chairman knows what I'm doing and only those who know what's going on can understand how I feel. I can't laugh about it. I can't win, but I have broad shoulders.

'The biggest disappointment is that we were in a good spell, playing good football and getting results. It's a major setback. We had too many players off form. You can get away with one or two having an off day but not three or four. We could have played for another hour and not scored. I hope we have learned something from this game. It's not just about the two strikers, the overall team performance wasn't good.'

The next day Estelle delivered a powerful defence for Ruud that any family man would understand. She said: 'Ruud is so often in training at Newcastle. He is always on duty for the club either watching players or talking to people. When I know he is busy, it's better for me that I spend time with Joelle and my mum.'

She insisted his frequent trips to Holland would continue and discounted a move to Newcastle, arguing it was all a matter of size. Of houses that is. 'The fact that we don't have a home in Newcastle has a practical reason. The majority of the nice homes in Newcastle are enormous. They are simply too big for us. I'd feel very small and insignificant there. I like a cosy place. I don't need swimming pools, luxuries or big houses. I like to be plain. Nothing flash.'

In their early days together, when Gullit was at Chelsea, Ruud and Estelle had shared a home in Knightsbridge. As Estelle explained to Dutch magazine *Beau Monde*: 'I enjoyed living in London with Ruud but I'd only just left school.'

With the flak flying, Gullit concentrated on the next trip to Anfield – where Newcastle had lost their last four Premiership matches. Another defeat over the festive period would put a European place even further out of reach. And he would be forced into further team changes by the news that Barton was out, after limping off early in the second half of the defeat by Leeds.

Ruud stormed out of Anfield after the Liverpool match bitterly upset at the sending off of Dietmar Hamann. Even in his *Match of the Day* interview he looked decidedly fed up. Who wouldn't after this 4-2 reverse?

Hamann got his marching orders from referee Stephen Lodge as Newcastle blew a two-goal lead. Booked ten minutes earlier for a foul on McManaman, he got a further yellow followed by red after what was nothing more than a clumsy challenge on Berger. Gullit came rushing from the bench to rage at the nearest linesman. Shearer, who tried to point out to the Barnsley official that Jamie Redknapp's challenge on Gary Speed a minute earlier was also a bookable offence, was cautioned for his verbal blast. Then Gullit restrained Steve Clarke as he, too, made a pitchside dash to the trouble spot.

Livid Liverpool fans then got involved in a shouting match with Gullit, who turned round to have his say as police moved in to restore order.

Gullit said: 'A club like Liverpool doesn't need any favours. It was a big disappointment for me today. Just to protect myself I don't want to say any more. I wish you all a good Christmas and a happy New Year.

'Unfortunately certain things spoiled it for us today. Good luck everyone. Liverpool took full advantage of that and did well.'

With that, Gullit departed the press room to head back north, reflecting bitterly on that decision and the way his team were finally overpowered after taking a two-goal lead through Solano and substitute Andersson.

A furious Hamann branded Berger a 'diver'. Although Gullit gagged his players and refused to comment on the flashpoint, Hamann could not contain his frustration and broke the club's vow of silence. He said: 'It was a joke. I didn't even touch the Liverpool player. He was diving. I have no complaints about my first yellow card even though it came a bit late. I have been sent off in Germany but never in circumstances like this. If we had finished the game with eleven players then I think it would have been three points for us. It has to be one of the worst experiences of my career.'

Overlooked in all the controversy was an injury to Ferguson, who said: 'I had felt a niggle for a couple of weeks but I didn't know what it was. Then I felt it in the first half but I wanted to try and keep going in the second half. However, with sitting in the dressing-room at the interval, I came out out cold and the pain was just too much. Wee Glassie knocked a ball down the left and normally I'd have been away. I'd just couldn't move for it and I knew something was seriously wrong. I had to come off.'

John Barnes was meanwhile heading for a showdown with Gullit. He had yet to make a first-team appearance under him and was upset at not being given a slice of the action in the defeat at Anfield, after being named as one of the substitutes. Georgiadis, Dabizas and Andersson were all sent on as second half subs, leaving Barnes frustrated and wondering why Gullit had once more overlooked him. His contract ran out in the summer but there would be a decision before then. At thirty-five, Barnes needed to quickly sort out his future.

The club issued another staunch defence of Gullit the next day. Incensed at the reports that they had been landed with an annual bill of £200,000 for his hotel accommodation, Shepherd responded. 'As chairman of Newcastle United, I would not be doing my job for the supporters if I did not comment on the rubbish that has been reported about Ruud's so-called time off and the cost of his hotel. Ruud has had no more time off than Kenny or Kevin had, and I see nothing wrong in having a couple of days off before Christmas to see his family. In fact, he never stopped working during that time. He makes a point of letting me know who he sees and what is happening at all times.

'Secondly, the so-called £200,000 hotel costs are once again a fabrication so I say to the mischief makers: stop making up these stories and report the true facts to the supporters of Newcastle. They don't deserve this rubbish.'

Gullit even promised to take legal action where appropriate. 'I like to do my job well and as long as you tell the truth, I have no worries whatever. But if you tell lies about me and also try to harass my family in Amsterdam, then it stops.'

The same day Didier Domi was unveiled as Gullit's second acquisition for a fee of £4 million and became the twenty-third French player to join the Premiership. A French youth international not yet twenty-one, he cost £3.25 million immediately plus a further £750,000 when he made a number of appearances.

Domi had made just over fifty appearances for PSG since making his debut in the 1994–95. He was in the team beaten by Barcelona in the final of the European Cup Winners' Cup in 1997, but had been out of the side since coach Artur Jorge took over earlier in the season.

Gullit observed: 'He's a very good positional player. That is something we are not used to in England as people want players who can tackle and run. But if you are in the right position, you do not have to tackle, which is a great bonus. A good example for me of that is Ronald Koeman. He was not very fast but was a very, very good positional player. He didn't need to be tackling all the time, because he understood the game. Those are some of the qualities that Didier has, but he's also very quick and has a good technique.

'I see him as a future French international, of course I do. He wants to play for me and that made it easier for us to sign him. I don't know whether other clubs were in for him or not, but players do tend to want to play for me. That's why Newcastle wanted me. Also I think France offers good value for players. Look at Arsenal and the players Arsene Wenger has bought. I took Frank Leboeuf to Chelsea as well and he did not cost too much.'

Gullit defended spending so much on a twenty-year-old. He said: 'Nowadays, the youth players are also getting more expensive, especially when it is an international and someone who has already played for several seasons for Paris St Germain. It's not as if it's someone who hasn't had any experience. You know what you're going to get.'

With Pearce out of favour and Barton acting as a makeshift left-back before injury let Pearce back in, Domi would find himself involved sooner rather than later. He took over Batty's number four shirt and was earmarked for his debut when Gullit's former club Chelsea visited Tyneside in January. 'I will not be overawed by the likes of Leboeuf and Desailly,' he said.

Supporters' leader Kevin Miles backed Gullit to turn the struggling club around in the New Year. After a bleak Christmas with defeats against Leeds and Liverpool, conceding seven goals, Miles reckoned that once Gullit removed the 'dead wood' and brought in the players he believed would take the club back to the pinnacle of the Premiership, then the change in fortunes would be swift.

Miles said: 'As soon as Kenny Dalglish was sacked, I think all Newcastle fans realised this would be another season of transition. Ruud Gullit inherited a squad he claims was not his own and one he knew would need a lot of rebuilding. He made it clear he wasn't satisfied with the quality of the squad. I think a lot of people will be reconciled by the fact that he had a lot of work to do and if you look at his track record with regard to signing people when he was at Chelsea, there were never many duff signings. He has a reputation for bringing in people relatively cheaply and they have turned out to be worth their weight in gold. Somebody like Gustavo Poyet, who nobody had heard of, yet has played extremely well. He seems to have this knack of identifying quality players, so it all bodes well for the future. People have got to be patient. He has a team who are capable of beating anybody on their day, and if he does bring in more quality new signings, then I don't see any reason why we can't be optimistic for the New Year.'

Miles hoped for a repeat trip to Wembley for the FA Cup final to put a smile back on the face of Tyneside football, despite a tricky third round tie at home to Crystal Palace. 'There's nobody harbouring any illusions we're going to win the Premiership this season. But the Cup has yet to start. Newcastle fans, in between Christmas and New Year, are always confident we are going to win the Cup, and Gullit has a good Cup record. The partnership up front between Alan Shearer and Ferguson is also in its infancy. Duncan was a good signing anyway, so we have high hopes for them.'

8

St James's Park curse . . . farewell to Fergie already . . . the FA Cup run begins with Crystal Palace

---

As the New Year began, Newcastle braced themselves for the inevitable news that Duncan Ferguson would be sidelined until March with hernia trouble. Ferguson was not in the squad for the FA Cup game with Crystal Palace, to alert everyone that he was in a bad way. He suffered Gilmore's Groin, requiring surgery. It was a massive blow to Gullit, who had been able to field his £23 million strike force of Ferguson and Shearer on only two occasions since the Scot arrived from Everton at the end of November.

Gullit had been plagued by misfortune with Shearer missing a month with a hamstring injury and Ferguson struck down by flu, while several other key players were also unable to put together consistent runs.

The squad gathered at Ramside Hall Golf Club, near Durham, and Ruud arrived early with his golf clubs. He admitted he still hadn't quite understood the pomp and ceremony and age-old tradition of the FA Cup, even though he won it the year before last with Chelsea. However, he knew its significance as something special, as well as being the provider of an instant passport into Europe. And it offered Gullit his only remaining chance of any success this season.

Hence the pressure built up on Tyneside in anticipation of the visit of Terry Venables' side. Newcastle, out of Europe and out of the Worthington Cup, knew just how much importance their fans attached to a second successive run to Wembley. The disappointment of the previous season's 2-0 defeat in the final by Arsenal lingered, and there was hope that perhaps a Gullit-inspired team could reach Wembley once again. Ruud pointed out: 'One problem is that I would rather be playing another Premiership team in the Cup. When you play someone from the other divisions, it seems to me that suddenly the rules tend to change. The other clubs are favoured more by referees and I don't know why. Also, Palace have nothing to lose when they come to Newcastle. We, on the other hand, have everything to lose.'

Venables, who won the FA Cup with Spurs in 1991, relished the prospect of an afternoon back in the spotlight, convinced Palace had a realistic chance of an extended FA Cup run.

Tel rejected the notion that Shearer – without a goal since early November – was no longer the player he was during Venables' time as his national team coach. He said: 'Shearer's had a tough time with injuries and for a while there I was worried he might not be the player he was, but I think he's back to his best. I wouldn't say that I brought the best out of him, he did it himself. There's no doubt in my mind that he and Duncan Ferguson will be a powerhouse between them, it's just a matter of time.'

Another player looking forward to a reunion with Venables was Steve Howey, who had won his four England caps under El Tel. But despite Gullit's positive comments about him before Christmas, Howey's future at Newcastle was yet to be resolved: 'They haven't come to me. I have had no talks, no indication and do not know what the situation is. Nor why things have not been sorted,' he said. 'Nothing has been done about it yet, so I am able to talk to other clubs.'

Palace's Matt Jansen was once among the Newcastle fans in the Milburn Paddock cheering on Peter Beardsley and co. Now the twenty-one-year-old Carlisle-born striker aimed to put them out of the Cup. Almost a year before he had scored the shock winner in front of the Leazes End in a league game. He said: 'I think some of the Newcastle fans knew me as an ex-Carlisle player and a lot knew I supported Newcastle. I wanted to sign for them at one stage, so a goal against them didn't do me any harm!'

Shearer's motto is 'First is first and second is nowhere.' So he was pretty sick about hitting the post in the FA Cup final just before Arsenal scored a second to clinch the Double. Shearer was eager to return as he said: 'It's for the fans that we want another exciting cup run, for them that we want to go back to Wembley and this time get our hands on the trophy. We are expected to beat Crystal Palace and I believe that we will, but we must beware. They came here in the Premier League in March when nobody gave them a chance of winning and they turned us over. This is a good FA Cup tie for Palace and a potential banana skin for us. The only trick in cup football is to be in the hat for the next round.'

Robert Lee also warned of the danger of being hot favourites but stressed: 'We are looking more and more solid defensively these days and the return of Steve Howey has been a massive boost for us. He has looked in fine form and has been like a new signing – but I quickly told him not to get too used to the idea of wearing that captain's armband of mine, because I wasn't going to miss too many matches. This has been a curious season for me in terms of missing games. I've been out of so many, yet I've had a virus, I've had a suspension, I've had a bruised hip, but nothing you could call a proper injury. My hip injury in December was even just a training accident and although I can't reveal the culprit, let's just say he was tall and Greek! Now we're at the halfway point of the season, we can look back over the first five months and assess things clearly. After the unsettling period around the end of August the players have settled down well. The lads are getting used to the way the manager wants to play and wants to train, and are getting used to Steve Clarke, too, who is doing such a good job alongside Ruud. When things change behind the scenes it all takes time, but things are settling down nicely and we're all now firmly aiming for a successful 1999. A convincing victory over Crystal Palace in the Cup would be just the right launching pad for a very happy new year.'

Dalglish used twenty-four players and accumulated fourteen goals with 271,635 fans watching on the road to Wembley – and finished up empty-handed. Now Gullit was out to go one very important stage further. 'I would love to take Newcastle back to Wembley and win the Cup again,' he wrote in his programme notes. 'I saw at first hand how disappointed the Middlesbrough fans were as Chelsea's danced in celebration. Getting there is a great achievement, but winning is divine. This is, hopefully, our first step this season along the way to Wembley Way.

'My New Year wish for Newcastle United fans everywhere is to give you more winning days in 1999 than you had in 1998, and if one of those winning days is in London on 22 May I'll be more than delighted.'

Palace stayed two nights at the Gosforth Park Hotel. Freddy

Shepherd made a point of buying one of the players and the manager a few drinks on New Year's Eve, and he was spotted chatting with Tel long into the night – no doubt the subject of Matt Jansen arose!

The game itself, on the first Saturday of 1999, turned out to be a typical Cup scrap, full of incident. But despite the 2-1 win, there was little sign that Newcastle's luck was going to improve in the New Year.

'There must be some sort of curse on this club,' said a bemused Gullit. 'Everything is slipping out of my hands. Red cards, injuries, illness, suspensions. It's all making it very difficult for me. But we will beat it because we have a lot of faith. We will not need the Wizard of Oz.'

Gullit believed the fifteenth-minute dismissal of Given was harsh after the keeper was found guilty of handball outside his area. 'The referee was only ten yards away and didn't see it,' he said. 'His assistant was twenty-five yards away and did see it. That was the difference.'

Enter substitute keeper Steve Harper; first touch picking the ball out of the back of the net as Bradbury headed home Morrison's delightful right-wing cross within seconds of Given's dismissal.

Speed pounced with the equaliser with a rare right foot drive following a Barton free-kick. But it was Shearer's unwavering tenacity that kept Newcastle going. His sixty-eighth minute winner arrived just as Newcastle were beginning to pin Palace to the floor.

Shearer seemed to take an eternity after chesting down a left-wing delivery from the excellent Barton. He had found himself in the exact situation countless times before.

'I was screaming at him to hit it first time,' said Gary Speed later. I thought the chance had gone, but he knows best and that's why he is the striker he is.'

One crucial strike from Shearer had kept the Geordies' season alive. But it was his all round display that grabbed the attention. Captain in the absence of Lee, he had led ten-man Newcastle through a minefield.

Gullit's relief over this hard fought battle was tempered by Ferguson's absence – more reason to believe he was jinxed. 'It seems to be the same all the time,' he explained. 'Someone comes in to play alongside Alan and then they are either ill or injured. I have never known anything like it. But I have spoken to Terry Venables about my frustration, and he understands. If there's a curse, then we must try to do something about it. We can't be in this situation all the time with strange incidents occurring. We have to turn it around.'

Next up would be Bradford at St James's Park, as Newcastle were number nineteen out of the bag in the fourth round draw at Lancaster Gate. Chelsea were drawn away to debt-ridden Oxford United and Vialli's men were immediately made 11-2 favourites by bookies William Hill, who fancied Manchester United to beat Liverpool after installing them as 7-1 third favourites behind 13-2 Aston Villa, 8-1 Arsenal, 10-1 Liverpool and Leeds, 11-1 Newcastle and 12-1 Spurs.

Transfer speculation was still rumbling and the word was that Sunderland boss Peter Reid wanted Howey. Reid was planning for the future as the Wearsiders prepared to return to the Premiership. Arsenal and Spurs were also alerted. The Geordies were keen for Howey to stay, but with Tony Adams' future in doubt, the Gunners needed a new central defender.

Philippe Albert was wanted by First Division Bradford. City could afford the £1 million fee, but the small matter of paying his wages was an obstacle.'

Middlesbrough and Tottenham challenged Newcastle over £4 million Romanian target Constantin Galca. Spurs were especially keen on the twenty-six-year-old Espanyol midfielder, yet another name on Gullit's list after a recommendation from Chelsea's Dan Petrescu. Gullit considered a new bid for Ipswich's Kieron Dyer after a £5 million bid was rejected, while he remained unconvinced about a move for Steve Stone. Forest boss Dave Bassett had wanted to interest Gullit in Stone to generate cash for new players himself.

Ruud's former player Eddie Newton considered rejecting a new contract at Chelsea to talk with Newcastle. Newton, twenty-seven, who scored one of the goals in Chelsea's 1997 FA Cup Final victory over Middlesbrough, was a free agent at the end of the season.

Alessandro Pistone was furious after being told to train with the reserves, and was so disillusioned with life on Tyneside that he contacted the PFA for advice – blowing any minute chance he had of battling his way back even as a squad member. Gullit earlier insisted he needed another left back, someone who was 'regularly available and not injured all the time'. That player turned out to be Didier Domi.

Ruud watched the exciting rugby final on a wet and windy Tuesday night at Kingston Park as Newcastle Falcons beat Bedford 'to spread my horizons'. So estatic was he at the victory that he headed straight to the dressing room at the end to offer his congratulations to Rob Andrew and his players. Not exactly au fait with the rules, he was impressed by their fightback and with the 'very physical' aspect of the sport.

News came the following day that Kenny Dalglish was to return to St James's Park – as a player to honour one of the club's most celebrated former players, Peter Beardsley. He and Kevin Keegan were ready to pull on their boots once again for Beardsley's big night, as was Gullit. 'Ruud has been asked to play, and depending on his fitness he expects to play some part in the game,' said a club spokesman.

Keegan would play in the game, against Celtic, provided that a neck injury healed sufficiently, while Manchester United striker Andy Cole was one of the first to accept.

Meanwhile Ruud was desperate to give some of his players a sunshine rest. Peter Schmeichel had been pictured in Barbados sunbathing with permission of Alex Ferguson. 'I'd love to be able to do that with my players,' said Ruud. 'Everybody knows that I am in favour of a winter break. The players need a rest. I have only just been talking to Johan Cruyff about the Champions League, and we agree that the most difficult bit for Manchester United is going to be the last part of the season. That's why we believe they are going to win the Champions League. The problem for them is they have so many games to play and Alex Ferguson knows this. The reason for a break is not because it is winter but to give the players a rest. A break would benefit the League and ultimately you would be doing your English football a favour.'

The last time Ken Bates shook hands with Gullit it was to hand him his P45. The venue was the plush Conrad Hotel foyer in Chelsea Harbour on the day of his amazing exit from the Bridge. When they met up again at St James's Park on January 9, the hand that sacked Gullit after he won the FA Cup for Chelsea would be extended again. Surely it was bound to be the most acrimonious reunion of all time? The circumstances of the Gullit departure would have done justice to a John le Carré plot. In fact, there were so many twists of the knife even le Carré would have rejected it as far fetched.

Yet Bates insisted there would be no animosity when they met up again. 'It is not in my nature,' retorted the Chelsea chairman. He had not spoken to Gullit since the day he was sacked, 'but then again, why should I have done? We move in vastly different circles and our paths haven't crossed. We left on good terms personally. We shook hands. I said that we should stay friends because we live in the same world of football and you never know, one day our paths might cross again. Now our paths will cross again, and I will shake hands with him again if I see him. I will be in the directors' box and if he comes into the directors' lounge I will be more than happy to speak with him and shake his hand.'

Bates anticipated a classic football encounter rather than worrying about dented egos and events of the past. He went on: 'In view of Ruud Gullit's reputation for wanting to play good football and given Chelsea's reputation for exciting football, it should be a magnificent game of football. I cannot understand why this match is not live on Sky so millions can enjoy it rather than just those lucky 40,000 Geordies at St James's Park.'

Everyone expected Bates not to hold back about the reunion with the dreadlocked genius he kicked out. Bates knew everyone expected it and opted to do exactly the opposite. He was diplomacy itself when he said: 'The only reason he left us is that we couldn't afford him.'

Gullit's version was vastly different. He said: 'Everybody knows it wasn't about money. It's pretty transparent that that was the big stick with which they hoped to beat me, and it failed. Because it didn't work they had to come up with another reason, they were plentiful.'

One of those 'reasons' emerged when Bates accused Gullit of being a 'playboy boss' more interested in 'pizza adverts' and selling Ruud Wear, his personalised fashion line. The accusation that he was not dedicated and committed to his work on the training ground ensured that first Aston Villa and then Spurs ignored him. Little wonder that when Gullit resurfaced at Newcastle he was bitterly upset when he was attacked as a 'semi-detached' boss at the AGM. One can imagine a smirk of satisfaction from Bates when that story hit the headlines. Naturally enough, that was an issue Bates chose not to comment upon.

From my own conversations with Gullit, I know how much he craved to be successful a second time in the Premiership, and that he had deliberately taken on a big challenge rather than accept a managerial job at a club where success was guaranteed.

In essence the Chelsea game was still Gullit's old team versus Gullit's new one, with a touch of Italian refinement from Vialli. Less sexy, more efficient. From Hoddle to Gullit to Vialli, Chelsea had become title contenders – with the Gullit hallmark.

Gullit focused entirely on his quest to beat his old club. Deep inside remained a deep affection for his 'lovely boys' at the Bridge. Equally there was a residue of anger and hurt. Those negative thoughts were not directed at the players, not even at Vialli who took his place. It was Gullit who had brought Vialli to the Bridge on a free transfer from Juventus recognising his gifts as a player and an influential figure in the dressing-room. It was only injury and illness that cost Vialli his place in Gullit's starting line-up. Vialli was benched for no other reason, certainly nothing personal, despite ugly insinuations that it was a question of egos and jealousy.

But Gullit felt betrayed by some of his backroom staff. He told me he would not make the same mistake twice. If he ever got another job he would appoint his own right-hand man. That is why his first move was to recruit Steve Clarke. But it would fill Gullit with pride, not envy, if Chelsea were crowned champions.

Barton warned his team-mates to beware of Wise. The pair were both ex-Wimbledon men and Barton, who had recently signed a new contract after producing a string of excellent displays was showing the kind of commitment Gullit wanted. But he accepted it had become increasingly difficult to stay in the side following the arrival of Domi and he was prepared to play anywhere. 'All I want to do is play and I'll do that in any position that is required. My preferred position is right-back but I am prepared to play anywhere to stay in the team.'

But unhappy Hamann was contemplating a move. 'I was a first-choice player at Bayern Munich and there is no reason why I should not be in an average English premier league club.' Hamann kicked his manager right where it hurts in an interview in German soccer magazine *Kicker*.

'If I am not a standard part of the team, it makes no sense to stay,' he added. This from the man who earlier in the season had said: 'All my expectations have been fulfilled, there are favourable working conditions, the service is excellent and there is a welcoming atmosphere which makes it easy for foreigners.'

Behind Durham's Chester-le-Street cricket ground, there was a larger than usual lunchtime media contingent the day before the game as Ruud held court, with comments guaranteed to hit the headlines of every tabloid, and even the broadsheets.

'I'm very calm at this moment, but I'm very excited also because I will be seeing my players again . . .'

Yes, 'my' players.

There was no longer any doubt: Gullit thought of Chelsea as 'his' team, the vast majority of their side being his players. He suggested: 'I think Gianluca has to go for the title this season – there's no hiding from it anymore. But it's easy for him. He has the players there, the right system and the rotation system as well. Everyone learned from what I did there, so I did my job very well. My methods are still in practice, and this season Chelsea must go for the title. I was going for it last season and I had the team in second place when I was sacked. I didn't talk about going for the championship, but that was my plan. Now it's a possibility that Vialli can do it. The players who are there were successful for me, and they have gone on to achieve more since I left. They are my players. I put the team together and that makes me very proud.'

Gullit was also prepared to shake hands with the man who axed him. 'He has said that he will shake my hand when he sees me and, yes, I will do it. You can't keep thinking about the past, and I've forgotten about it now. The most important thing is that you get on with life. A lot of bad things have happened to me in the past, but you have to forget about them and just get on with things.'

Accepting he had a good way to go before Newcastle could look anywhere near as slick as Chelsea, he held no grudge against his successor. Gullit said of Vialli: 'I think he is doing exactly what I was trying to do. In the beginning he tried to change to a 4-3-3 formation but he lost all his games. Then I saw him admitting that my rotation system was good. No one can play in the team all the time. That's a reality, I didn't invent it. You need to rotate players.'

Meanwhile, Gullit launched a £4 million bid for Crystal Palace striker Matt Jansen. 'We have had some contact with Palace,' he said, but added: 'The first figure they mentioned was £6 million. That is not even close to our valuation. The player hasn't done anything yet in his career but we want to improve the team and we know he comes from up here. If they are reasonable, it is possible. If not, it's off. It's purely about money. I've found out that they're in some trouble so they're trying to get some money. It's not the way to deal with Newcastle. He's over-valued.' A further complication was that Jansen's former club Carlisle had a written agreement by which they received a percentage of any future sale. Jansen's agent, Simon Fuller, formerly manager of the Spice Girls, called on his mobile, advising no comment on escalating speculation.

Gullit did sign Louis Saha, a French under-21 international striker, on loan with the option of a permanent deal at the end of the season, and he was linked with Pietro Parente from Torino in Italy's Serie B.

In Genoa, the Luca-Ruud confrontation was the subject of much debate at their old club Sampdoria. David Platt played with both and remained a close friend of Luca's. The new Sampdoria boss said:

'Luca's grateful for what Ruud left him. He accepts that he wouldn't be anywhere near where he is if it hadn't been for Ruud. Sure, Luca has gone in there and changed one or two things around, but things were already moving at Chelsea under Ruud. Luca took that view and felt there was no point in tampering with too much. But he's added to it, not just with the players, but with his personality. Ruud detached himself and created a bit of friction. He's a different personality to Luca.'

Platt also knows Shearer well, and offered this advice to Gullit. 'It's probably hard for Alan at the moment. Shearer's a match-winner but can only make the difference in a team that's playing well. He's never been the sort who gets the ball, beats three players and scores a goal from nothing. He needs the right service to give you thirty-odd goals a season.'

Last word to Ken Bates ahead of the match with Gullit's new club: 'I didn't sack him, I didn't renew his contract. Perhaps you've been reading the *Sun*, otherwise you'd understand the subtle difference.'

The story all the papers would be telling after the match was that Gullit's old boys had beaten his new boys. Wild scenes of jubilation greeted Chelsea's first League win at St James's Park in twenty games, dating back thirteen years. It took them back to the top of the table. The Chelsea fans unfurled a banner saying, 'Ruudi and Clarke, thanks for the memories, we still love you,' but by the end they mockingly chanted, 'Sexy football.'

Despite encouraging signs and a blistering start that might have produced a goal or two, Newcastle went down to their third successive league defeat by a single goal. Gullit conceded: 'It was an emotional day for me, I was very quiet, very relaxed about it. It was good to see each other again, talk with the players, it was good to see them again "live" and good to see that what I left is in such good shape. If you look at a game like this, the difference is that one team has the quality throughout to decide a situation that is tight. Chelsea have that.'

Gullit's attacking 3-4-3 formation, with Shearer the spearhead in a diamond formation up front, worked in an impressive start which encouraged the crowd, but once Petrescu scored, Chelsea took command. Gullit observed: 'We were very adventurous, and did very well. We are struggling a little bit with pace, so I had to find something else to enable us to play in their half. We created so many chances in the first half, but got nothing.'

Gullit was delighted with Domi making his début at left-back, and pleased with Hamann's first half display but it was difficult for anyone to shine once Chelsea took a grip after the interval. Eventually, to loud cheers, Andersson, on the right side of the attacking diamond, was replaced by Louis Saha. Gullit was quizzed as to the disappearance of young Dalglish, and explained: 'The most vital thing is to keep the ball, and to lay it off. He was struggling in that aspect and he has to work on that. Rather than the ball bouncing away from your feet, you have to play others in possession and that's what he has to learn to do.'

Whatever happened on the field, there was never any doubt there would be more hostilities off it. Vialli accused Gullit of trying to be 'smart' by mischievously putting extra pressure on him to deliver the title, but Gullit said: 'I am saying that they have the potential so they must win it. Surely I am paying them the biggest compliment!' It was interpreted as a provocative comment. So there was still no love lost. There was no handshake. When asked if he had seen Vialli Gullit said: 'Yes, I've seen him for ninety minutes! Why would I have seen him when he's busy focusing on the game?'

And had he seen Ken Bates?

'I haven't seen him, also. I don't know, very strange questions.'

Vialli got his own little dig in. 'This was not Ruud Gullit's Chelsea or Gianluca Vialli's Chelsea. This was just Chelsea versus Newcastle. Ruud has done a great job at the club and then he left. I tried to continue where he left off by doing things my way. He did very well and everybody knows that. If he wins the title at Newcastle he'd have done very well here. But things do not happen at a club just because of one man and if he did very well here then it will be on the back of Kevin Keegan and Kenny Dalglish!'

Graham Rix offered a handshake on the final whistle, duly accepted by Gullit; Vialli was in the middle of his players celebrating in one corner of the ground with the travelling Chelsea fans. As for either Gullit seeking out Bates, or the chairman looking out for Gullit to shake his hand, that was never going to happen. Neither was there any real intent on the part of Vialli or Gullit to pass any pleasantries to each other.

The day after the match Dietmar Hamann criticised Gullit's style of management. He talked of rifts in the dressing room between the foreign and British players and expressed surprise at Gullit's absence from training before Christmas.

Hamann said: 'I've had a lot of bad luck and obviously the fact that the manager who signed me was sacked after two games has not helped. But it is obvious now that Ruud Gullit does not want me here. I was not in the team against Leicester just before Christmas, so the following week I really wanted to prove my worth to the manager in training. How can I do that when he isn't even at training? Gullit had not spoken to me at all – but then he doesn't speak to anyone much – so I decided I had to go to him. He just said: "We'll have to wait and see and talk again in five weeks' time". But as far as I'm concerned, I have made a decision and it looks as if I will leave in the summer.

'Newcastle paid £5.25 million for me and I'm playing for Germany, so you might expect the manager to phone when you are injured or to tell you what position he wants you to play in. I was good enough for Bayern Munich, so I should be good enough to play here. I can't negotiate with clubs because Newcastle have not officially told me they will let me go, but I have had offers from Spain, Italy and another English club.

'We have English players in one corner of the dressing room and the foreign players in the other. Our position in the League is unsatisfactory but I get the feeling the English players don't realise it. When we go on the team bus they are laughing and joking before the game. There is a fine line between having confidence and the wrong attitude.

'We are selling and buying players week in, week out. It creates a negative atmosphere. We have fifteen internationals at this club. They should give us time to become a team.'

Ruud was more concerned about signing Matt Jansen, who effectively went on strike by pulling out of Crystal Palace's 3-0 defeat at Bolton. But he made a point of telling his moaning players to put a sock in it. It was aimed at imports Hamann and Pistone. Pistone did not speak out in the press, but of course Hamann did.

Gullit insisted: 'Supporters don't like players to moan. They earn a lot of money, and fans want to see them battle and play well. They only want players who can do the job and who will work hard. If you moan all the time, then you get the crowd against you.'

Both players had demanded regular first team football. But Gullit pointed out: 'Nobody here is guaranteed a place. It just doesn't happen in football these days. Hamann has had some problems in adapting his game to the English style of play. It is much quicker here than it is in Germany, and he has to adapt.'

While Gullit urged both men to prove their worth on the training ground, Shepherd went a step further in a bid to end the controversy, warning that if it continued, players would be fined the maximum two weeks' wages.

In contrast, Laurent Charvet had played in every Premiership game under Gullit. Everyone else had been either injured, ill, suspended or 'rotated', but the twenty-five-year-old from Cannes emerged as a steady influence on an often shaky defence.

The Frenchman displayed his admiration for Gullit when he revealed: 'I was playing for Chelsea when they sacked Ruud and I was astonished. We were second in the league, in the semi-finals of the Coca-Cola Cup and in the quarter-finals of the Cup Winners' Cup. After he went, I had to wait two more games before winning back my place. I had plenty of time to think about him leaving. It had staggered me.'

Charvet went on to play nine more games under Vialli's leadership. At first, Chelsea said they did not want to keep him. But then, just as he was about to return to Cannes, to whom he was still under contract, Vialli changed his mind and asked the versatile defender to stay.

'By then it was too late,' Charvet explained. 'But when Newcastle came in for me during the summer, I was very happy to return to the English game. Then Kenny went and I found myself working with Ruud again. Nothing had changed so far as he was concerned. He was still very relaxed, very full of life and someone who you enjoy working with. That's just how he was at Chelsea. And yes, I do think he can transform Newcastle in a similar way to the job he did at Chelsea. Certainly he has the basis here. It's a big club with great support and it can be a very good team. But it will take time, and he needs the support of people. Support from the press and the fans.'

Equally comfortable at either right back or centre back, Charvet had been voted Newcastle's Player of the Month. 'I am very happy here, and you can see also that Ruud is building for the future. He has just signed Didier Domi from Paris St Germain. He is a tremendous prospect at only twenty, and has every chance of becoming a full international. We do have a lot of foreigners here at Newcastle, but that was something I got used to at Chelsea. It's the players who make an atmosphere at a club. It depends on personalities.'

Gullit was still trying to make significant changes to his squad and he urged new Nottingham Forest manager Ron Atkinson to consider Stuart Pearce in his future plans. 'People like Pearce and John Barnes should not be lost to the game. These players need to stay in football. I hope it's possible for Stuart to be given the chance to go into coaching,' he said.

Paul Dalglish wasn't perturbed about his future despite being linked with Birmingham. Geordie fans were mystified that Dalglish was not given a chance ahead of the unpopular Andersson. But Gullit explained: 'Paul still has to work on a lot of things. It is vital for him to keep the ball and not let it bounce off him. Also, he has to be able to play it wide. He is struggling with that and so we are working very hard with him. He is still young and came into the game very late. He did well for me when he came into the side, but he is nowhere near the finished article.'

United were still keen to sign Matt Jansen but they faced stiff competition for the player from Blackburn, Everton, Arsenal and Villa. His affinity for Newcastle was thought to tip the balance in their favour, but they just had to wait. 'We have made a bid and done everything by the book,' confirmed Shepherd. 'But now it rests with Palace.'

Gullit was in no mood to be held to ransom. Palace rated their striker at £6 million, but he insisted: 'If they are not going to be reasonable, then it will be off. We have made what we consider to be a fair offer for the player.'

Jansen, who turned down a £1 million move from Carlisle to Newcastle a year earlier, said: 'I came close to joining Newcastle, but they offered me a lot less than other interested clubs.' Now the youngster, who once said he was 'willing to crawl along the A69 from Carlisle to sign for Newcastle', had another big decision to make.

Talks began over Howey's future with Shepherd stressing the club's determination to keep him. Shepherd added: 'Ruud will only bring in top-class players, as we have shown with Duncan Ferguson and Didier Domi. We have to be big enough to admit we have had major setbacks, but from now on the only way is forward. Once Ruud gets the team as he wants it, I am confident exciting times will return. He is the man do do it.'

Team-building was their big chance to win over disillusioned fans worried about the club's future ownership. Shepherd said: 'We, the board, are determined to hand the club's future success back to the players. We want them to have high profiles, we want them to hit back at the snipers. The only way to prove we're worthy of the fans is to bring them real success, and I believe Ruud and players like Alan Shearer will do this. Even if we have to accept this cannot happen overnight, I am confident the manager will bring back the glory. We are a huge club, a unique club in that few others have such a massive profile. If something happens at Newcastle it is almost guaranteed to hit the back pages. We must make certain that from now, and certainly next season, it is for the right reasons. Ask Alan Shearer what he wants and he will say, to make Newcastle United a truly successful club for the fans. I believe we will achieve this together.'

Gullit had been criticised for his tactics by some, but Gary Speed reckoned they were spot on. He relished his new central role: 'Now that I'm in the middle, I'm far more settled. You are always involved in the action. We've had Stephen Glass playing well out wide and he's a lot more effective than me. Ruud's called it right.'

And Ruud vowed not to walk away from the biggest challenge of his career. He was determined to turn Newcastle's fortunes around after ten points from a possible thirty-six in the past three months.

'I have a two-year contract, with an option on a third, and it's my intention to see it out,' he said. 'You never know how things are going to turn out in football. I learnt that when I was sacked at Chelsea. But I am learning about myself and giving more all the time. I am totally committed to Newcastle and if things go according to plan, I will be happy to stay. The situation is difficult at the moment and it will take time. The hardest part is getting rid of some players who don't want to be here and others who are not willing to go. I was brought here to clean up, and that's a bad job. We won four games in a row, but I knew the sh** would come. It's the biggest challenge I have ever faced – and the most different. But I expected it.'

Gullit said he was joking when he recently claimed that there was a 'curse' on the club, but there was no doubt he had been hit hard by injuries, illness and suspensions. Given and Hamann were both suspended, while Saha was the latest to suffer the striker jinx. 'When I want to do something in training the first person I have to see is the doctor!' said Gullit. 'You need characters in this situation and we have the players here who can turn it around.'

Ruud wanted to see the ugly face of Newcastle and lay to rest the 'sexy football' tag: 'We are ready to play ugly football now if it gets us points!' The football purist was prepared to make sacrifices. 'It's the first time I have had to adopt this sort of attitude but we've had to open our eyes and be realistic. I'm not going to lie about our situation because that would be a nonsense. We've lost three games in a row and it's points that we need.' Knowing Newcastle had almost slipped through the relegation trap door the previous season, he made early plans to ensure the same dismal end to a campaign did not happen again. Newcastle prepared to go to Charlton with Ruud admitting: 'I think it's a game that we simply have to win.'

Domi's first live televised appearance in English football at the Valley held no terrors for him. He had cut his teeth in a European final at eighteen when he played for Paris St Germain against Barcelona in the 1997 Cup-Winners' Cup final in Rotterdam, and he said: 'To play as a teenager in a big final against one of the best teams in Europe was a great experience. Now I would love to do what Patrick Vieira and Nicolas Anelka have done at Arsenal. We grew up together and we are good friends. Their success in England was part of the reason I chose to come to this country.'

Shortly before the match there was mixed transfer news as Gullit pulled out of the chase for Matt Jansen after increasing an initial offer of £4 million. On the other hand Pistone was wanted by PSV Eindhoven boss Bobby Robson. Benfica had been set to take him on loan but he was injured in a reserve game.

But television viewers were not to witness the Newcastle victory that Ruud had claimed was so vital. Gullit stormed out of the Valley in a huff, convinced Newcastle had been robbed of their first away win in four months. He looked thoroughly fed up as Newcastle tossed away a two-goal lead and were pegged back by lowly Charlton four minutes into stoppage time. Cursed again, as Dabizas was sent off for two bookable offences and Shearer incurred another suspension after collecting his fifth yellow card.

Ruud's assertions that Newcastle deserved to win the game, and that Shearer was harshly treated by referee Peter Jones, were scoffed at by Charlton. And with just two wins in thirteen games, Gullit was beginning to stretch the patience of his Geordie public. But he said: 'You do all your technical work on the training pitch, but when people get red and yellow cards they don't deserve, that is out of my hands. I don't know what Shearer did wrong. It's a big disappointment because he doesn't deserve it. How much bad luck can you have? It was the same story at Liverpool last month – the course of the game was changed by things that were out of my hands. It's been a crazy day and a crazy week.'

Gullit's complaints cut no ice with Charlton boss Alan Curbishley, who said scornfully: 'I've just listened to Ruud on TV and I don't think I've seen the same game. Ruud was very disappointed after the game as if everything had gone against him, but it's been like that here for eight weeks. And I heard Ruud talking about his injuries but we've got about ten players out at the moment and we haven't got anything like the squad at his disposal.'

Shearer was booked for a first half challenge on Pringle, who expressed 'amazement' that anybody could dispute referee Jones' verdict. Pringle said: 'If Newcastle are complaining, they should see the state of my boot. Shearer's tackle caused a split several inches long

and I had to change boots at half time – that's how fair the tackle was.'
For Shearer, whose only recent goal had come in the FA Cup win over
Crystal Palace two weeks earlier, there was a fourth different strike
partner in as many games in Ketsbaia but the pair combined well in
the build-up to both Newcastle goals, Shearer playing provider for
Ketsbaia's piercing runs.

However, Pringle's late strike saved Charlton from an unwanted
Premiership record ninth successive defeat, and Shearer had now gone
900 minutes without a goal. Gullit defended him. 'He helped set up
both our goals very well, and that side of his contribution is also
important.'

Gullit seemed still to be disgruntled on Monday as he pointed the
finger at his predecessors Dalglish and Keegan.

'A lot of good players were sold – but they didn't get the same
quality back and I am stuck with that. I have to change that again. The
Board were very cautious with me at the beginning because the
previous managers had spent £90 million. They had backed them all
the way.'

Keegan and Dalglish actually spent £97 million, leaving Newcastle
£50 million down. Keegan's spending spree of £61 million was
cushioned by selling players for a total of £21 million, while Dalglish
fared slightly better, forking out £36 milion and recouping £26
million.

Gullit was so far in the black; £12 million on two players, Ferguson
and Domi, while disposing of Guivarc'h, Batty, Watson and Gillespie
for a total of £14 million. But he was far from happy with some of the
players he inherited; it was not easy to ship them out. 'It's hard,
because you have to hurt people. We do need more quality in certain
areas.'

His next move was for the dreadlocked twenty-four-year-old
Nigerian defender Taribo West. West hinted he was only interested in
a loan deal because he wanted to win his battle at Inter with coach
Mircea Lucesu. 'God made me a star, the coach has put me in the
shade, but I will be back,' said West. Gullit wanted West's presence to
boost Newcastle's chances of a cup run.

Meanwhile the club were facing another hike in the overall salary bill
if they agreed a new deal with Howey, currently earning £6,000 a
week. Armed with the knowledge that a number of other Premiership
sides wanted to sign him and that Gullit wanted to keep him, Howey
hoped for a big increase. Initial discussions indicated he expected to
double his earning power.

Gullit watched the reserves on Tuesday afternoon while Shepherd held transfer talks with Inter. He planned to fly to Milan to try to finalise West's personal terms – it was believed the player would demand around £1.5 million a year. And any deal with the Nigerian international would allow Howey's advisers to point out the vast difference between the salary of their client and that on offer to newcomers. More talks were planned with Howey's negotiators, who were seeking no less than £18,000 a week, topped up with a signing-on fee.

In the evening, Ruud was in the VIP box at Bradford watching his next Cup opponents against Crystal Palace on a bog of a pitch. He hoped his team would not have to cope with that in a replay. Gullit had gone on a personal spying mission at Wimbledon before Chelsea's 1997 FA Cup semi-final at Highbury, when he felt he spotted the way to beat a team that had proved difficult to overcome in the league. Normally, Gullit concentrated on his own team's preparations rather than worry about the opposition, but here again he chose to closely scrutinise Bradford, paying them a huge compliment as tricky cup foes.

Meanwhile, Keegan was given the all-clear to make a farewell appearance at Newcastle. The Fulham boss had recently had a neck operation, but was fit enough to play in Beardsley's testimonial at St James's Park. 'It's great news,' said Beardsley. 'Kevin was special and did a great job of turning the club around. It's been hard for the men who came after him, but it was always going to be hard to follow Kevin.'

On the following evening a lavish dinner was held at the Marriott Hotel for the panel of judges to announce the latest Hall of Famers. As a member of the voting committee I voted for Ruud as my number one choice. Present at the dinner were Ruud's agent Jon Smith, Les Ferdinand, fellow panellist Gabby Yorath and Howard Wilkinson, plus chairman of the FA Premier League Hall of Fame, Sir Geoff Hurst. The public announcement was to be made on ITV on the morning of Newcastle's match with Villa ten days later. Ruud was honoured alongside Tony Adams, Ian Wright, Mark Hughes, Ian Rush, and David Seaman.

Meanwhile, Peter Beardsley backed Shearer to end his Premiership goal drought. Beardsley, who teamed up with him when Shearer arrived at St James's Park from Blackburn in July 1996, said all strikers go through lean spells and pointed to the lack of a regular partner as a partial explanation. Despite former Arsenal striker Alan Smith suggesting Shearer ought to become a little more selfish in a bid to open the floodgates once again, his former team-mate urged him to carry on what he was doing.

'Alan Shearer doesn't need any advice from me,' said Beardsley. I haven't seen that much of him this season but he's still the top striker in the country for me. He's seen and done it all before. People say he's going through a barren spell but I'm sure Alan won't be too worried by it, and why should he?' Shearer was still leading scorer for the season with nine in twenty-two starts, six of them in seventeen league games.

The League Managers' Association voiced concern that Kenny Dalglish's case against Newcastle would not be heard until May. Dalglish was seeking compensation from the club via an arbitration tribunal – the first time a case from the Premier League had been heard by the tribunal. LMA chief executive John Barnwell was concerned that the case was going to take so long to reach a decision. 'It is a ground-breaking situation because it is the first arbitration tribunal since the inception of the Premiership. It has been delayed too long. The arbitration tribunal was put in place to act speedily. We look forward to progressing as soon as possible.'

With Gullit's own honeymoon period well and truly over, everyone at the club was desperate to improve relations with the supporters, which had been deteriorating ever since Dalglish's unhappy departure. The charm offensive began over diet Cola and canapés in a restaurant adjacent to Durham County Cricket Club. Ruud and members of the media were brought together to lay out the ground rules for a more harmonious relationship, to lower the barriers built up between Newcastle United and its supporters.

In an informal, off-the-record engagement, Gullit said it was imperative that the club should look forward, that the agenda should not be set by a few malcontents. He was happy, the future looked good, and everybody smiled, shook hands and said what a worthwhile exercise the evening had been.

The detente was not to last very long! Less than forty-eight hours in fact.

It was not the supporters, though, who were first off the mark with their criticisms. The same day, David Batty labelled Dalglish's team as 'bottlers' because of the Wembley defeat by Arsenal. 'The whole day just fell flat. We'd had a poor season in the league, so the Cup was keeping interest alive. But there was maybe a feeling beforehand that we expected to be beaten. People said to me that the week leading up to Wembley was the best in a player's career. But for me it just didn't turn out that way, for whatever reason. It was a big disappointment, and the final itself wasn't the most enjoyable game I've played in. We just weren't up for it and that was reflected in our performance.' Matt Jansen also lined up to have a pop at Newcastle after he signed for Blackburn for £4.1 million. He turned down a move to St James's Park because he claimed Brian Kidd's club had more ambition. Jansen suggested he pulled the plug on the move rather than Gullit, who felt the fee was going up all the time. As it turned out he went to Blackburn for just a fraction more than Newcastle offered. Jansen had demanded £1 million a year, which would have made him one of the highest paid players at the club. The Geordies were quoted £6 million by Palace and denied getting as far as offering him a contract.

Gullitt switched his sights to the First Division's top scorer, Bradford striker Lee Mills, soon to display his talents at St James's Park in the FA Cup.

9

Training ground row: Gullit *vs*. Shearer

Gullit encourages his players to be outspoken – the Dutch have an open philosophy – but he stressed: 'What you don't need is to have headlines in the papers saying this has happened or that has taken place. What's said between me and the players should stay between me and the players, just as conversations at other places of work stay between those concerned. I don't discuss what I talk about with Alan Shearer or any other player, but the facts are that I have the utmost respect for a great player and a great leader. Alan knows what I want from him for Newcastle United and I know that he can deliver what I want. He is certainly delivering it, despite the people who said he would not be the same player after his injury. He has tremendous self-belief and mental toughness. He knows what he wants – he wants to be successful, he wants Newcastle United to be successful, he wants England to be successful. He thinks about things carefully before making his responses. I have the greatest possible admiration for him. He has achieved many things in his life and he will achieve many more because he wants them so badly.'

The papers broke the story of a training room bust-up on the morning before the important FA Cup tie against Bradford. The *Daily Mail* reported: 'Alan Shearer has had a blazing row with Newcastle boss Ruud Gullit which will increase the chances of the England skipper leaving Tyneside. The uneasy alliance between manager and star striker exploded into a verbal set-to witnessed by a number of other players . . . Shearer has never been at ease with Gullit's often aloof style. He is also believed to be unhappy with the treatment of

136

some of his team-mates by the Newcastle boss. Everything came to a head in a bitter bust-up which has so far not been healed.'

Shearer responded: 'I have never talked about dressing room secrets and I never will.' However, it was suggested that he was hurt but didn't hold a grudge after Ruud called him a 'selfish' footballer who only wanted to score. Shearer was moving into a new home in Newcastle, and remained committed to helping bring some success to his home town club, it was said.

A sniff of a rift opened the floodgates for a series of anti-Gullit stories. Paul Dalglish was reportedly caught up in the crossfire over his father's legal actions, summoned to the manager's office and asked by Gullit to resolve the differences with his father.

Ruud received a comforting call from Jon Smith, who told him he was on the back foot and needed a more positive press. 'Back foot?' enquired Ruud. 'I had to explain the term to him,' said Jon, who was about to engage in countering the political spindoctoring used to damage Ruud's cause.

If there was a deepening rift between Gullit and Shearer, the most powerful figure in the United dressing room, it was masked over for the benefit of the FA Cup drive, even though the rumours that there was dissatisfaction increased after Rob Lee was axed for the Charlton game and then left out of the forthcoming Cup tie against Bradford, with the club saying he was injured.

Shearer, whose only two goals in four months had come in Cup games, admitted: 'This is a huge game for us and one that we can't afford to lose. Everyone here is aware of that and it's important that we get the right result.' Last season Shearer had returned from a serious knee injury to hit the goal that took Newcastle to Wembley. Now Shearer's form had dipped and there was even talk about whether he was good enough to keep his England place.

Bradford striker Lee Mills, enjoying the best run of his career, would have little sympathy if his twentieth goal of the season dumped Gullit out of the Cup. 'I suppose it's been hard for him, taking over a big squad – half of which he doesn't want. But he knew what he was taking on. So there is no point moaning.'

Dietmar Hamann spoke to Gullit following the reports that he had been critical of the club and its training methods. He said: 'All I want to do is let my football do the talking.'

Ruud desperately wanted to repeat the Chelsea cup experience. 'Nothing would give me greater pleasure than to be manager of Newcastle United at Wembley in May. We'll need to be on top form to dent Bradford's confidence, but I certainly believe that we have the talent and the determination at this club to go all the way in this most glamorous and compelling of competitions. The players need to believe in themselves and our supporters need to believe in the players. There will be a special buzz about St James's Park. I have come to appreciate just how much the FA Cup means to the fans here, and at other clubs in England, of course. It's a big, big competition, one that really fires the imagination of supporters, much more so than domestic cup competitions in Holland and other countries throughout Europe. It's a big day for Bradford City, who are in such good form that they will line up with their confidence high and a belief running through their players and fans that this can be their glory, glory day, when they take a Premiership scalp, just as they did at Everton two years ago.'

On the day of the match, Gullit's rift with his star striker showed no sign of healing. Just before kick-off the two men passed within a few inches of each other on the touchline without exchanging words or glances.

But the acting Newcastle skipper set up the first for Hamann, scored the second himself and was involved in the build-up for Ketsbaia's third. Shearer's goal came just as the fans were beginning to show their frustration at another lacklustre performance – the First Division side's superiority in the first half was embarrassing. When Hamann put Newcastle ahead after thirty-three minutes it was totally against the run of play.

Gullit skipped the post-match press conference, suffering from flu. Stand-in Steve Clarke admitted: 'The scoreline flattered us a little bit. We had our fair share of luck. Bradford had quite a few chances when the scores were level. If they had taken one of them it might have been a different story. Alan Shearer got one chance in the match and went through and stuck it in the net. That's the difference between the two divisions.'

And as the Bradford players admitted, you don't realise just how hard the England skipper really works until you find yourself on the receiving end. Explained Shearer's marker, Darren Moore: 'What is amazing about Shearer is the way he keeps working. His work rate never faltered against us. He really puts it in. He is one of the most physical strikers I have ever played against, but I mean that in a good sense. His willingness to work really impressed me.' Keeper Gary Walsh chipped in: 'I don't think the way Newcastle played suited Shearer's style, and you can't blame him for being frustrated by that. Newcastle did not impress me. But you have to admire the way

Shearer keeps going. Other players with such a high profile might have stopped.'

A few days earlier I had notified Ruud's agent Jon Smith of rumours that Mohamed Al Fayed would try to buy Newcastle and install Kevin Keegan as manager. It was laughed off by Shepherd and Fletcher when they visited Jon at his Wembley offices.

But the speculation had clearly been widespread as Louise Taylor wrote in the *Sunday Times*: 'With Kevin Keegan due back in Toon on Wednesday, when he will play in Peter Beardsley's testimonial, this was a tie Ruud Gullit dared not lose. Happily for Newcastle United's manager, the recent rumours that Keegan, who despite managing Fulham still lives locally, would be replacing him have now receded.'

The Cup draw was to Ruud's liking: Blackburn at home. He said: 'They knocked us out of the Worthington Cup after a penalty shoot-out at St James's Park in November and we drew 0-0 at Ewood Park in the League last month, so maybe it's our turn for a victory.'

Manchester United were the 11-4 Cup favourites, then came 4-1 Arsenal, 5-1 Chelsea, 8-1 Leeds and 12-1 Newcastle and Spurs.

Keegan's influence certainly still exerted itself over some players. Philippe Albert wanted to sign permanently for Fulham because Gullit would never pick him for Newcastle. He had joined Keegan's FA Cup heroes – they knocked out Villa – on loan until the end of the season, but hoped to stay at Craven Cottage for good.

Keegan was delighted to have the former Belgian international in west London. 'He's not only a great player, he's great to have around the place. He absolutely jumped at the chance to come here. He'd been playing in the reserves at Newcastle and training with the kids – and he deserves far better than that.'

The reception for Rob Lee at Peter Beardsley's midweek benefit match suggested the fans were far from keen on the idea of him being allowed to leave. On top of that, Keegan's appearance on the field only served to remind everyone of the fans' craving for his brand of free-flowing, entertaining football.

KK made a dramatic seventy-sixth-minute entrance. Chants of 'Keegan' echoed around a packed St James's Park. The fact that Celtic ran out 3-1 winners with Beardsley grabbing a last-minute penalty mattered not. Dalglish senior and junior made their appearances in the sixty-eighth minute to a warm reception from both sets of fans.

Just before the game, Ruud was informed that his £4.2 million move for Taribo West had collapsed despite an offer of around £27,000 a week, after painstaking negotiations. West said: 'I know that Ruud was

upset and I am sorry about that because I love him and would love to
play for him, but I decided I did not want to live in Newcastle. I have
had the best out of my time in Serie A and for me the time is right to
go to England, but I am afraid Newcastle would not suit me. I didn't
fancy playing for them, but I would like to play in England next season.
I am aware there is interest from Chelsea, Spurs, Liverpool and maybe
even Manchester United.'

Bruno N'Gotty was Ruud's alternative but it would take time to
prise him from AC Milan, even though he only moved there from Paris
St Germain in the summer and wasn't holding down a regular first
team place.

Altogether it was not proving a good week for Gullit. There were
revelations from his former wife in the papers to go along with the
persistent rumours of dressing-room rows.

So Jon Smith organised a number of one-to-one interviews for
Gullit to set the record straight. Ruud put it all down to a combination
of jealousy, spite and the fact that he is Ruud Gullit!

He insisted he and Shearer were not at loggerheads. 'I do not find
him cold and get on well with him. He has an inner strength. He is not
outspoken immediately. He reflects and lets things rest in his mind.
Next he wants to know what is going on. He then says what he thinks
and he needs to be like that. There was no row between us, but that is
what people want. Let's get at Ruud Gullit and Alan Shearer. Again I
ask, why? The trouble is that when you are successful, like Shearer,
everyone wants to make an image of you. He has to distance himself
from that, otherwise people will eat him alive. It is simply not true that
we do not get on or that he is for sale. He is the pinnacle of what I am
trying to build here and people just do not understand what is going
on. They do not listen. But I do not mind what people think anymore.
There is not an issue between Shearer and me and it is cheap to say so.
It seems everything I do has to be justified. Let's do Gullit and Shearer
again.'

Gullit also dismissed suggestions that some of his players did not like
him and that he packed his dressing room with foreign stars. 'I have
signed just two players since I became Newcastle manager – one a Scot,
the other a Frenchman. As a manager I have to make important, tough
decisions that will make people unhappy. As a person I do not like it at
all. Some people do accept the decisions better than others. I often go
home and say to myself, "It was a rough day today. I do not like it, but
I have to do it. We know we need better results."

'The people of Newcastle must not look back to Kevin Keegan.

Cherish the memories, but do not compare. We have to go on. There are players who are very happy, but their views never come to the surface. I want players to have a reaction when they are unhappy. I want suggestions, things out in the open if there are problems. Not from the same players, from everyone. Yet there is not going to be a happy dressing-room all the time. What I ask is for people on the outside to be fair. It has been one thing after the other – Ruud does not get on with his players, he is cold, he signs too many foreign players, he lives in Amsterdam. Ah yes, Amsterdam. I do not live there. I visit there, where Estelle and my child are. Sometimes I do not go home for two weeks. On other occasions I go home for one day, maybe two. And I will continue to visit my family. No one will stop me.

'My message to the good, passionate people of Newcastle is this: I was brought in to bring success and that is what I aim to do. I am going to do everything I can to give you what you want. The feedback I get from supporters is supportive and Newcastle is like a football village. Everyone is a fan – and they are not stupid. Along the way there will be difficult decisions and they will be bad for certain people. I am still at the beginning here and I am taking it step by step. There are hurdles to jump and sometimes you hit those hurdles. I believe the future is good for Newcastle. I am sure we are going to succeed. I have been hurt, but it has not dented my enthusiasm.

'I love this country, yet the treatment I get is not fair. English coaches do not have the same treatment. Take diving. We're told diving is here because of the foreign players' influence. Why? What is this thing against foreign players? When Nicky Butt dived, it was quickly forgotten. We do not get such treatment. Also, can you imagine the reaction had a foreign player been to jail, or had a drink problem? He would be slaughtered every day. We have a saying in Holland, that big trees catch a lot of wind. When you are successful, there are always people who want to take that from you. Jealousy is part of life and I have to deal with it.'

There was better news from the treatment room as Duncan Ferguson prepared to take the first steps on his return to training, starting gently with a bit of weight work to maintain general fitness. Nothing more strenuous. But at least he was back at the training ground. Shearer would face Villa on Saturday despite a troublesome back complaint. Their boss John Gregory had tried hard to sign Shearer but explained: 'Newcastle said there was no way he would be leaving and told me to go away, so I did.'

A lunchtime press conference on Friday at Chester-le-Street, but

Ruud was fed up with questioning from the media interrogators. He told one, 'You have to do your homework,' when accused of concentrating too much on the older players. And when the question over his relationship with Shearer was raised for the umpteenth time, he turned on the questioner. 'You come like a parrot,' he said. 'Come with something original. Every time the same question, there's something odd. I'm not irritated but every week the same question, to fill the headlines with the same question. This is old, old.'

Ruud was then asked if he would be interested in the England job after the dismissal of Glenn Hoddle. 'I don't want to talk about that, I don't want to be involved . . . that pleases me, at least something new!' When pressed for his views on who he would recommend for the England post, he said: 'I don't know if somebody wants it.' Should there be an overseas manager? 'I don't know, not my problem. Not many people keen to do it, must be a reason for that.'

As for Shearer, Gullit said: 'Alan is still the best striker in the Premiership and I wouldn't swap him for anyone. Despite the stick he has taken recently, you will be surprised by what he is going to show you. We, the staff, have a lot of faith in him, and the players have a lot of faith in him. There's nobody better. You only have to see him working on the training ground to know that he is a very good leader.'

In a clear reference to incidents on the training ground, Gullit insisted: 'The whole context of things seems to get out of proportion at this club. Somebody sees me in discussions with a player, then it is described as a row and then someone else says there's been a fight. There is always a lot of chit-chat around this club, that's the problem at Newcastle. But I will always have discussions with my players because that is what I want. I want to know what is in their minds and what they want. I don't have fights, I have very good discussions about things. Some players express themselves better than others. Some express themselves in group situations, but with others you have to do it in private. Everybody wants to know what is going on at this club, it's a problem of the area.'

At the end of a week when true Geordie spirit was at the fore with the Beardsley benefit, one of their most popular local heroes, Steve Watson, was now to return with Villa.

Gullit's new foreign target was Silvio Maric, the Croatia Zagreb star who shone against the Geordies during a recent European campaign. Sources in Croatia claimed the deal was almost done. Gullit was coy. He refused to tempt fate following the breakdown of big money moves for Dublin, Ba, Jansen and West. The arrival of Maric would put added pressure on Rob Lee, who was now a target for West Ham and Southampton.

Gullit was the only overseas player in the second group of six players inducted into the Hall of Fame as the announcement was made. In a live link up at St James's Park he was asked where this would rank alongside his multitude of accolades and achievements. 'This is one of the best honours you can get, it means you are not forgotten after a while, and that you have done something appreciated by a lot of people.' Barry Venison asked whether he had miscalculated just how tough a job it was at St James's. Gullit replied: 'I knew it was a big job. That it was that big, I can't imagine. There is a different environment than anywhere else in the world. Everyone in the area has the attention of the club, every day they have to fill the newspapers, everybody wants to be informed.'

The match against Aston Villa, following Gullit's Hall of Fame award, was a good way to end a bad week. After having all his domestic dirty washing hung out in public by his former wife, plus all the headlines over his handling of his players, Gullit was delighted to have watched 'the best performance since I came here. We were hungry for it. We wanted it. Our people were battling for each other,' he enthused after beating them 2-1.

This was also Shearer at his best and Gullit said: 'I was pleased with his performance. There has been a lot of press on his back, but he has put that aside now. It is one weight less on his shoulders. He played well but also showed he is a good captain because he battled hard for the team for ninety minutes and that was good to see. He is the sort of player that every team must keep an eye on, even when they are chasing the game like Villa, and that has to be to our advantage.

'Alan is eager and a very proud man. However, he has been under very difficult surgery, and I know all about that. You always remember how well you were playing before your injury, it's one of the problems. But you can't expect to come out of an operation better than you were before. They take something out of your body, and so you can no longer be the same. You have to learn to adapt, and Alan has done that. You can't always do the things you could. But he can be as great a player as he was before. He has been playing well recently without scoring. But against Villa, he did both. I still think he's the best striker there is. But he doesn't have to show anything to me, because I know that.

The three points was the important thing, but we've had a few false dawns here before. And so it's no use beating Villa and then going to

Leeds next week and getting stuffed. It will be a waste of time if we can't go on and build from here.'

The Sunday papers, though, were less confident that either Gullit or Shearer would be part of the process. 'We Want You Back, Keegan', screamed the back page headline in the *Mail on Sunday*, suggesting moves through third parties had been engineered by the club's prospective new owners NTL. Equally informative was the *Sunday Mirror* headline that Shearer would be on his way to Chelsea in a summer move, possibly with Flo going in part-exchange.

10

Shearer offered new five-year contract. But Saints defender says: 'He's on the way down'

Ruud felt by the beginning of February that he was emerging gradually from a dark tunnel, finding answers.

'I have discovered a whole lot of answers and that makes my job interesting. But I would rather have got those answers in a different way. The way we have found the answers during the past couple of weeks has not been pleasant for me or for the club. A lot has happened and it has not helped me.

'I would rather it had been different. But it's when things are not going well that you find out about people. You find out who is willing to fight or not, who is giving up, who has trouble with pressure, who is going to moan and who is going to take responsibility.'

Gullit told his players that anyone who was not 100 per cent behind him and not willing to fight for the cause could leave. He had the backing of the board despite the rumours to the contrary. Keegan would not be making a sentimental return.

Shearer, back to his best against Villa meanwhile, took a complete break from football for a week. He was suspended for United's trip to Leeds.

It began to seem, too, that the future of several members of the squad was beginning to take shape. Charlton had decided they wanted John Barnes to help them beat relegation. Barnes trained at the Valley and Alan Curbishley planned to snap him up on a free. Barnes had made only one appearance as substitute for Newcastle this season but believed he had something to offer in the Premiership.

Rumours that David Platt had been told he could have Shearer for Sampdoria at the end of the season didn't look too clever after the former England captain was on the next plane back to London after being kicked out of his new coaching job! It was suggested that Platt and Shearer had spent some time at Lake Como two weeks ago, discussing the possibility of the deal.

Rob Lee was told he could talk to interested clubs or he could stay and fight for his place. Gullit said: 'We want to extend Rob's career, sometimes playing him, sometimes sparing him. It's almost impossible for a man of thirty-two to play every game. This is a very good solution for his age, but only if he wants it.'

Lee had missed the last six games through injury, and was no longer guaranteed a first team place. He hinted that he would be on his way. 'Of course I want to stay at Newcastle but sometimes you don't always get what you want. You can never tell whether you're in a manager's plans or not. We have had disagreements but we'll just wait and see.' Gullit indicated he would be handing the captain's armband to Shearer but Lee had heard nothing officially about his role as club captain.

Gullit hoped to tie up his swoop for Maric, who was expected on Tyneside. Lee Clark was also being tracked. The twenty-six-year-old midfielder, Sunderland's record buy at £2.3 million, had made the short move from St James's Park eighteen months earlier. But he was unhappy at being the target of abuse from a minority of Sunderland fans.

Pistone launched a broadside at English football as he joined Serie A strugglers Venezia on loan until the end of the season. He blasted Gullit for axing him, and for having the temerity to speak to him in English! He accused English people of being prejudiced against him and his Italian compatriots.

Gullit took his total spending above the £15 million mark on February 4 when he completed the £3.3 million signing of Silvio Maric. Maric signed a five-year deal, pending his work permit being granted, although his switch to the Premiership left Croatia Zagreb far from pleased. Gullit finally saw a glimmer of light as his successful move for the highly rated Maric put a smile back on his face. He sounded optimistic as he said. 'My five months here have been my most testing time in management. It's all been an excellent test for me. My job is to rebuild Newcastle and I am delighted with the three signings I have made so far.'

With Shearer suspended, Gullit would start with Louis Saha up front against Leeds, partnering Ketsbaia. Saha was from the same footballing background as Nicolas Anelka and might move permanently to Tyneside. 'I like the look of him in training,' said Gullit. 'But I will need to see him in a few games before I decide. But he has good technique, a good left foot and is very brave. He has played in the same under-21 team as Anelka and we shall have to see how he does. Certainly I would have no fears about playing him against Leeds.'

So much for the rumoured divisions in the cosmopolitan Newcastle dressing room. Solano's sixty-third-minute winner took them to within five points of Leeds and the manner in which it was achieved was the perfect response to accusations of disharmony and disunity.

Steve Howey did as much as anyone to render David O'Leary's potent side completely ineffectual, and his partnership with Laurent Charvet was a perfect indication of the strength of the bond Gullit had forged in his developing side. Charvet's injury time block to deny Haaland an equaliser Leeds scarcely deserved typified an eleven-man contribution to a victory celebrated as if it was FA Cup final day at Wembley.

Gullit said: 'We showed that the rumours about our spirit was not true. The players said all this disunity talk has been thrown out the window. It upset them more than anyone. The players made me happy. They worked very hard for it and the joy they had pleased me most. I can see signs we are getting there. It's taking time. We may not have the formula, but we are working towards it.'

It was a win achieved without Shearer and Dabizas, as well as Domi, who was preparing for the under-21 international with England. Newcastle's luck had changed for the better – one defeat in six games and still the chance of reaching the FA Cup quarter finals.

On Monday Gullit paid tribute to John Barnes after allowing a 'very complete' player to leave. The manager said: 'He deserves what his desires are. He's been very successful. He has a good vision of the game and although he was not always the quickest, he understands the game. That's why he is able to anticipate situations, and he also has very good technique. That made him a very complete player.'

It had been apparent for some time that Barnes did not figure in Gullit's long-term plans, and the Dutchman hinted on several occasions that he believed coaching could be the way forward for him.

Charlton completed the signing until the end of the season. and Barnes wanted to become a Premiership manager by the beginning of the next season. He had seen several of his former international team-mates, such as Glenn Hoddle and Bryan Robson, step straight into top club jobs, while Chelsea had employed two player/coaches in succession in Gullit and Vialli. Barnes said: 'I would like to start my managerial career as high as I can. I want to be thrown in at the deep end like Ruud Gullit, Glenn Hoddle and Gianluca Vialli. At the end of the season there could be a high turnaround of managers and I hope I can get something.'

Silvio Maric, meanwhile, was laughing off two-year-old comments he had made about English women and food. He insisted his outburst, reported in a magazine in his country during the Champions' League qualifier between Newcastle and Zagreb, was intended as a joke. 'It was all a bit of a joke and should never have been in the paper. I wouldn't be moving to England if I really meant it, would I? When I talked to the Newcastle directors last week, they told me I was the first foreign player to say how much I liked your weather. People said it always rained, but it was beautiful.' Maric passed a medical on Tyneside on Friday before flying back to Croatia for the international against Denmark, and would return to the North East as soon as his work permit was issued.

'This cannot be a coincidence,' Ruud said enigmatically when he took his place at the back row of the Royal Box for the England-France international. There I was, sitting right behind him. He seemed glad to see me.'

When Anelka struck the underside of the bar and it looked as if the ball might have crossed the line, he said: 'I thought at Wembley they gave those!' Later that night he dined with his old pal Frank Leboeuf at San Lorenzo's. With the Frenchman demanding double his salary, and Ken Bates not liking it one bit, could it be that Ruud would make him an offer he couldn't refuse one day?

Shearer, who captained England at Wembley, was also the man Gullit had chosen to lead the Tynesiders into a new era. His decision to appoint Shearer as his new skipper was the clearest indication yet that manager and player were determined to work together for the cause. Explained Gullit: 'Alan is captain of his country, and that is very logical because he has a presence among players. He is charismatic and that is a plus for you. But I see him as the long term captain of this club also. I think that will suit him. He is the right type of player to do it. It is not a major issue at the moment, but there will come a time soon when it will be. Then we will make an official decision on the captaincy.'

Shearer, taking over from Rob Lee, said: 'It was a proud moment for me. As a kid growing up in Newcastle I had always wanted to play for Newcastle United, but I never thought about being their captain. I was a centre-forward and I thought captains were defenders or midfield players. Before I said yes to Ruud Gullit, I discussed it with Rob, who is someone I respect and admire enormously, both as a man and a player. We have been good friends for a long time and he's been a terrific Newcastle United captain since he took over from Peter Beardsley. Rob told me that there was nobody he would rather hand the armband to than me, so now here I am, a Geordie boy captain of both his club and his country. It's well-nigh impossible for me to put into words just how proud I feel.'

Ruud posed for Sky publicity pictures with boxing pin up Joe Calzaghe before his defence of the WBO title against Robin Reid in Newcastle. Ahead of Sunday's Cup tie, Keith Gillespie declared himself fit to play against his former club. He had scored the goal which beat Sunderland in the previous round. And Chris Sutton relished the prospect of trying to outgun his old striking partner Shearer. 'Alan has had a hard time with injuries just like me this season. He's had a hamstring problem and it's taken him a few games to get back into his stride. But he is always going to be a threat if he gets the right service. We were successful together.'

Gullit enjoyed the rare luxury of choosing from virtually a full squad. Domi returned from injury; only Dabizas was suspended. Shearer returned in place of Saha and was desperate to put the misery of England's midweek 2-0 defeat by France behind him by taking it out on his former club Blackburn.

The successive wins against Villa and Leeds had lifted morale. There was a new spring in the step of Shearer: 'Everybody is playing well and confidence is sky high. We are all looking forward to the Blackburn game.'

The deposed captain wrote in the matchday programme about the 'marvellous' team spirit at the club – despite the 'disagreements' with his manager! But Gullit had got the players in the right frame of mind. Shearer had badly missed being involved for the Leeds game and was in the mood for the Cup tie. He explained: 'I was delighted the lads won at Leeds in my absence, but I was dragged around the shops in London all day and I kept looking at my watch thinking what I would be doing if I was at Elland Road. From all accounts we did extremely well.

'It was only the second ban of my career, but it could happen a lot more now more yellow cards are going around. If you play the physical way then you are going to pick up yellow cards. But I hope I don't have to go shopping again for a long, long time.'

Shearer was also getting tired of the constant questions of whether he was back to his best. He had shown his irritation to that one while with England at Bisham Abbey. 'I don't know how many times I have to say this, but I have felt fully fit for some time. I feel good, strong and very fit. Maybe it is only because the team is doing so well, winning the last few games, that I have been given that extra recognition. As long as you're honest with yourself and know you've given your all, nobody can ask more of you.'

There was just one player with some reason to be unhappy. Rob Lee, declared fit by Gullit on the eve of the clash, was not even among the substitutes. Gullit had arranged to take his players to Portugal as a thank you for recent good performances. Instead it would be a replay at Ewood Park as Blackburn's Aussie keeper Filan prevented Newcastle scoring for the first time in five matches.

United's best chance came when Hamann, performing solidly alongside the impressive Gary Speed, switched play with a delightful ball to Shearer wide on the left, and he held up play intelligently before knocking a perfect pass into the path of his strike partner Ketsbaia. He did not need to be asked twice before trying his luck, but his right foot curler beat both Filan and the far post.

Star man Speed was stretchered off fourteen minutes from time with his left leg strapped in a splint having fallen awkwardly after a challenge on Sutton. Tests later revealed just a minor knock on his leg and not the break he had feared.

Newcastle had produced some of their best football for months but would have to do it all over again if they were to get through to a home tie against Everton. Duncan Ferguson was hoping for victory in the Cup replay to confront his old club. He said: 'Part of my heart will always be at Everton. I had great times there, but I also had a special relationship with the fans. However, it was their decision to sell me. And, once I knew that Newcastle had come in for me, I didn't want to talk to anyone else. This has been a great move for me.'

Shearer was now ready to commit himself to Newcastle for the next five years, giving the clearest indication yet that his future was on Tyneside. Talking on stage at Newcastle's City Hall, he said: 'I can't see any reason why I wouldn't sign a new contract. I still believe this club can win things. I have got two years left on my current contract, and it could take that long before we win some silverware. But I expect to see out my contract. And I am sure that someone at the club will open talks on a new deal soon.'

Shearer was appearing with Rob Lee as part of Durham county cricketer John Morris' benefit year. During a question and answer session, Shearer was asked if he wanted to leave Newcastle. He said: 'I have turned down Inter Milan, Barcelona, Juventus and Manchester United, so that should show how much it means to me to play for Newcastle. I am expecting someone to open talks within the next few weeks because, in the current climate, you can't allow contracts to run into the last eighteen months, especially with the way the Bosman ruling is now.'

Shepherd saw Shearer eventually as Newcastle manager, first as player-coach. Would the manager's job interest him? 'I would not rule out management. I was offered the player-manager's job at Blackburn at twenty-five and it didn't appeal then. It doesn't at the moment. I still intend to play for a few years, but management and coaching do interest me.'

Shearer's sense of timing was impeccable. With Keegan, his former manager, installed at Lancaster Gate with a four-match contract, the England centre forward scored twice as Gullit notched up three consecutive league victories with a 4-1 win over Coventry at St James's Park.

Keegan might not have needed the prod, but Gullit was grateful. Shearer's first was a thunderbolt, his second a tap-in after Hamann's free kick was fumbled by Hedman. Decisive proof that a happy player is an effective one. Negotiations to keep Shearer on Tyneside were imminent.

Shearer would be returning to Southampton and Blackburn within five days, hoping to get a first win at both his former clubs. He had been back to the two grounds eight times. He visited Southampton on six occasions (four while with Blackburn) and returned to Ewood Park twice – all without a victory. He said: 'I was not aware I had never won at either ground since I left. It's a strange one and I'll be hoping to put it right.

'This has been a big week for us. If we get something at Southampton, it will set us up for the Cup replay. I am enjoying my football and the team is playing well. We are creating chances and defending well – and not just the back four.'

Solano, charged with the responsibility of supplying Shearer, was convinced his jinx would end. Solano said: 'Alan is back to his best now. I know now why some people say he is one of the best strikers in the world. I have seen it for myself.'

Ruud's biggest decision was who would partner Shearer? Ketsbaia had been dropped for the Coventry game, despite his three goals as Shearer's partner in their last four games together, and his replacement Saha had capped his home debut with a goal against the Sky Blues. Saha got a thumbs-up from the master.

This was the week when Kevin Keegan was confirmed as part time England coach. Shearer was enthusiastic about Keegan's appointment, as one might expect. He said: 'If ever there was a man for this occasion it is Kevin Keegan. Kevin is just what we need to give everyone a lift.

'He'll come in like a whirlwind and everyone will be swept along by his energy and enthusiasm because he's such an infectious character. I watched his press conference on television on Thursday and just listening to him talk about the job made me feel I couldn't wait to get the England shirt on and play for him. I am sure he will have had the same effect on players up and down the country.

'Not that I am taking anything for granted – that's something you can never do with Kevin. He might have said I'm going to be his captain, but I know I will have to show I'm worthy of a place in his team before he picks me, because he doesn't have time for favouritism.'

Steve Howey believed England were in for a treat, with former Newcastle assistants Derek Fazackerley and Arthur Cox joining Keegan. Howey said: 'Faz is the best coach I've worked with – and I've seen a few at Newcastle, including Kevin, Kenny Dalglish and Ruud Gullit.'

Newspaper gossip again had Keegan lined up to return to Newcastle at the instigation of NTL when his England contract expired, with Gullit's contract paid off. Ruud and the club were not impressed.

There was also speculation that Guivarc'h was in trouble at Rangers. Coach Dick Advocaat was said to be ready to unload him unless his contribution improved.

The weaknesses was again revealed in the 2-1 defeat at Southampton, but as usual Shearer was the focus of attention. 'There is a lot of frustration in his game because he is not the player he used to be. I think it's time for young players like Owen to take over. Shearer is on the way down.' Saints defender Claus Lundekvam delivered the stinging assertion that England's premier striker was no longer the player he was.

Lundekvam appeared to get Shearer's elbow in the face after just eleven minutes of a game that saw all the recent good work evaporate.

England's skipper was booked, although TV replays showed that Lundekvam may have been struck by the ball.

Gullit delegated press conference duties to Steve Clarke, who struggled to explain why Solano, who hit the bar with a free-kick and had been Newcastle's most creative influence, was substituted at half-time. 'It sometimes happens that a player's doing well and he's taken off for tactical reasons.'

A puzzling Newcastle performance did not bode well for their replay at Blackburn. Shearer was out of sorts in front of goal, reacting too slowly to Solano's excellent through pass and enabling the keeper to block. Then Howey was panicked into a botched back-pass and Beattie danced round Given to score. Worse was to follow as Domi impeded Egil Ostenstad's jump and Dodd drove in the penalty.

Howey then grabbed a fistful of Beattie's shirt as he threatened to charge clear again and a red card seemed certain but referee Graham Poll, possibly judging that Dabizas was coming across to cover, surprisingly opted for yellow. That prompted Gullit to desert his director's box seat and join Clarke in the dugout.

Despite being clearly the more accomplished side, Newcastle never recovered their poise after such a sloppy start and Hamann's far-post header was too little, too late.

Shearer, who had stuck two goals past Lundekvam and Southampton earlier in the season, refused to be drawn into slanging matches in the press. But on the 'elbowing' incident, he was adamant: 'I never touched him. The ball hit him in the face. It was frustrating to be booked so early because you have to be careful after that, and it stopped me from enjoying the game.' He now had his mind on the Cup replay: 'What happened on Saturday has made us all the more determined to get the right result.'

Howey agreed to sign an improved four-year deal that could also see him treble his weekly wage and take in a testimonial.

Speed was given a one-match suspension after picking up his fifth booking of the season against Southampton. If Newcastle overcame Blackburn in the replay, he would miss the quarter-final tie against Everton. However, Maric would be available for that match, provided his work permit came through as expected.

Shearer missed training on Tuesday with flu and did not travel on the team bus in case he spread the bug on the journey from Newcastle. Gullit would ring him in the morning just in case he was better but

Saha and Ketsbaia were on standby. Glass was definitely out with a knee injury and Ferguson was not ready.

Without Shearer, Newcastle's FA Cup talisman who had struck eight goals in twelve FA Cup games, seven in the last nine matches, Newcastle's chances of beating Blackburn looked slim. But the fans found a new hero as they sang, 'Que Saha Saha, we're going to Wembley.' Louis Saha's cracking goal had put them into the quarter-finals, and the manager wanted to sign him: 'He's a young player and he's very strong for the size that he is. He works very hard and he has a good vision of the game. You can see that his technique is also very good, and he can only become better. He's here to try and impress everybody and he's doing that.' Gullit was enthralled by Saha's goal, made by the impressive Hamann.

The hard-fought victory was revenge for Blackburn's penalty triumph in the Worthington Cup. Even without Shearer and Ferguson, Newcastle were organised and worth the win. Hamann was particularly impressive under the admiring gaze of his old German national team boss Berti Vogts (Vogts was at the game with Manchester United boss Alex Ferguson, who was giving him a VIP tour of English football). And Saha looked totally at home in a starting line-up packed with nine foreign legionnaires from all parts of the soccer globe.

Before the Saha winner, Hamann hit a free kick from thirty yards out. The ferocity of the drive stunned everyone except the diving Filan, who plucked the ball away from the top corner. Then Saha took a clever ball into his feet and fed back for Ketsbaia to unleash a low shot tipped away by Filan at his near post. Ketsbaia posed a constant threat with his link play with Saha. They almost inspired a second goal in the seventy-fifth minute. Saha popped up at the heart of his defence to head a clearance to Ketsbaia's feet and the Georgian was away. He fed Garry Brady, whose shot was brilliantly saved by Filan, only for Charvet to smack the angle as he pounced on the loose ball.

Gullit said: 'We thoroughly deserved the victory and the bonus, of course, is that we have been drawn to play Everton at St James's Park. The system we play suits this team now, everybody knows what they have to do. We were patient and our patience paid off. So I was delighted for everybody connected with this football club.'

Maric flew into Newcastle, his work permit sorted out, as his new team-mates were playing in the FA Cup 150 miles away. 'I got straight into Russell Cushing's car and the game was on the radio. Fifty minutes had gone and he told me we were winning 1-0, which was very good.'

He wanted to be the first Croatian to play in the Cup final. Maric trained with his new team-mates and hoped to be handed his debut on Sunday against Arsenal. Maric would have been a Manchester United player if Croatia Zagreb had not blocked his move to Old Trafford six months earlier, and was widely regarded as one of the most sought after midfield players in Europe. He admitted: 'A lot of clubs spoke with me and I spoke to Alex Ferguson at Manchester. But Zagreb said that they wanted me to stay and sign a new contract. They would not let me go. But then Newcastle came in for me and I said, please, can I go this time? Fortunately for me, they said that I could and I am delighted to be here.'

Gullit wanted Maric to operate just behind Shearer and Ferguson. It would take time for him to settle in England, although nothing could compare to surviving in wartorn Zagreb.

Said Gullit: 'He will have to adapt to this country and it will take some time. He trained with his new team-mates today and he was very emotional. You have to understand that he has made his move at a stage of the season when teams are performing at top level. The tempo is very fast here now and the training is quick.'

Meanwhile, Saha declared his intention to be the Toon Army's answer to Anelka. 'Nicolas and I go back a long way,' he explained. 'We played together as boys in France and he has achieved a great deal since he joined Arsenal. I would like to do the same with Newcastle. I have always looked up to Nicolas. He's always had this determination to succeed, from his days in the French youth set-up. I share those ambitions and have dreamed that one day I could follow in his footsteps. I watched him score at Wembley in the FA Cup final. Now maybe I will get the chance of playing at Wembley. That is every footballer's ambition – even those from abroad.' The French duo would face each other at St James's Park.

The Geordies were much fancied to overcome Everton and march into the Cup semi-finals for the second year running. But, under Gullit, last year's beaten finalists had more guile about them and supporters were beginning to sense that Wembley was in the air again. 'We cannot afford to think about that yet,' warned Gullit. 'We still have our goals to aim for in the Premiership.' Ruud's mind was concentrating on Arsenal.

Shearer and Anelka were going head to head. Both had thirteen Cup and league goals from virtually the same amount of games, but Anelka had already outshone Shearer, scoring twice in France's humiliation of England at Wembley, and Wenger said: 'He is the best player in the world, better than Ronaldo and younger than Shearer. If you ask me who he plays like most, then I would say Ronaldo. There are so many similarities. Both have power, grace, good touch and vision. The only thing Nicolas needs is the patience and attitude of Alan Shearer.'

Shearer had emerged from his sickbed but had yet to train with the first team, and would need a late fitness test. Nevertheless Newcastle went into the game brimming with confidence. Gullit insisted: 'I no longer see games like this as a test for us. We have had enough tests, but now we feel confident and on an equal footing to teams like Arsenal.'

In the event Shearer did come back and Ketsbaia made way as he linked up with Saha. It was only the second time the pair had started a game together.

But it was Didi Hamann, whose career on Tyneside could have been short-lived following barbed comments about a dressing room split, who popped up thirteen minutes from time to cancel out Anelka's first half strike. It was a goal straight out of the top drawer and proof that Gullit's revolution remained on course. Newcastle had hit rock bottom when they lost at Highbury and flopped against Arsenal in the FA Cup final. But this was a new-look outfit under Gullit.

Arsene Wenger's disappointment was tempered by his appreciation of a much improved Newcastle performance. 'They have improved greatly since we played them last. Ruud has created a better spirit and they appear to be a far more dangerous team than they were.'

Behind the delighted Hamann's smile was the worry that he faced a one-match ban after picking up his fifth booking and with Lee back in contention and Maric champing at the bit, he would have had to sit by anxiously before fighting for his place once again. But he was now playing the sort of football that prompted Dalglish to pay Bayern Munich £4.5 million for his services.

Gullit mused that his team's gradual improvement was 'not the egg of Colombus'. But at least Ruud was no longer walking on eggshells.

11

Ruud is Tyneside hero after quarter-final triumph . . . Shearer suceeds pal Lee as captain

Enormous strides were being made toward profound changes at St James's Park.

A list circulated in the dressing-room for those requiring the services of an English language teacher. Many of the French contingent indicated their interest while the jokers among the English pack put each other's names down. After earlier suggestions of splits within the camp and foreign cliques, that kind of dressing room banter hinted at greater harmony.

Gullit added: 'What I see ahead is a Newcastle United getting stronger and stronger. Nobody is hungrier than I am to put a trophy in the cabinet at St James's Park. I felt this was the right job for me, I still feel that way.

'I expected the job to be difficult, that's the first thing. Jobs at this level don't become available if everything is running smoothly. The pride and the passion of the people who follow Newcastle United appealed to me – that's a positive thing and I'm happy about it. I understand, of course, the interest of the supporters. The football club means so much to them, also. As I say, I love their passion. It's one of the things that attracted me to take this job.

'People ask me if I can achieve here what I achieved at Chelsea, who had also gone many years without winning a trophy, and my answer is that for a manager it's about starting points. The starting point I had here after Kenny Dalglish left was obviously a lot different to the one I had at Stamford Bridge, where I had also been a player, of course. I started here after Newcastle had played just two Premier League games this season and – a crucial point – I had missed the pre-season preparation work. So I inherited not only somebody else's players who had not done so well the previous season, but also somebody else's preparation for the new season.

'What you hope, of course, is that you can make things better quickly at your new club. But to do that you have to have not only the right players but also the right environment and atmosphere. You have to work hard and create the atmosphere you want and then it can take time to assemble the players you know you must have before you can start to think about winning trophies. Chelsea was a different experience to the ones I had in Italy with AC Milan and Sampdoria, and Italy was different to Holland where I began my career. But you learn from all your experiences and I believe, of course, that what I have learned has equipped me to make a success of managing Newcastle United.

'Make no mistake, becoming manager of this club was a huge challenge. But if you don't see it as a challenge then you can't get the best out of yourself. I was more than happy to take it on and I'm enjoying the challenge. But it does take time to get a squad of players to think the way you want them to think, you can't achieve it immediately. That's true in most professions, but I guess especially so in football. What you try to do is create the right atmosphere and environment in which to work.'

Gullit was happy with this three main purchases, and insisted it was no reflection on some of the players he had to sell. 'As a manager, your life revolves around making decisions every day. Sometimes it's hard for fans to understand why their favourite player has been sold; and I won't discuss individuals who have left here, but it's no bad reflection on players like Watto and Batts that they are no longer at Newcastle United. When you get an offer for a player, you simply consider if it's in the best interests of the club to accept it. Your circumstances and your own requirements at the time help you to make the decision. Managers live or die by the decisions they take – the trick is to make more right ones than wrong ones. Whatever the size of the squad, the most important thing is quality not quantity. You need at least twenty quality players, thirty can be too much, but I would say that twenty is a minimum number. What you must never do is buy just for the sake of introducing a new face into the dressing room. It took us quite some time before I signed my first player for Newcastle, who happened to be Duncan Ferguson. But I was happy enough because I knew I had got the player I wanted. It's the same with Domi and Maric, you know they are going to be good players not only for the present but also for the future of the club. Good players with the right attitude, that's what you need.'

A chairman judges a manager on results, but also on how wisely he spends the company's money. Shepherd said: 'I think he's spent the money brilliantly. His first buy was Duncan Ferguson, and you can only get excited when you think about what we might see from a partnership between big Dunc and Alan Shearer. Duncan has been so unlucky with the groin injury that kept him out for so long. Ruud's second buy was Didier Domi and if there's a better left back in the Premier League I'd like to see him. The lad is only twenty, yet he's come here from Paris St Germain and just been absolutely top class, so quick and so positive. Be honest, how many football fans over here had heard of Domi before Ruud signed him? Not many, that's for sure. His third buy was Silvio Maric, a midfield player with a reputation for scoring goals and we all know how difficult they are to find. He'll be a big name over here unless I'm very much mistaken, so the message is that we're very, very happy with the calibre of player Ruud has brought to St James's Park.'

But Ruud was shocked by reports in Holland of an affair with the interpreter involved in the signing of Maric. Estelle was naturally distraught. Ruud acted to halt the lies that originated in Holland and spread to a newspaper in this country. Jon Smith acted swiftly to ensure the paper had Ruud's version of events.

Of paramount importance to Ruud was to protect his young girlfriend and baby daughter. In his quest to transform the team, he had suffered months of pain and anguish. 'When I have been trying to make Newcastle the best, I have had a lot of personal things to deal with which make the job more difficult. I am putting smiles on the faces of the players because they are enjoying their work. You can see it in their eyes – and the eyes don't lie. But almost every month there has been a piece in the papers by my ex-wife and I have always had to deal with that sort of thing.

'It is the same with the Alan Shearer thing and the gibes about me being a part-time manager. That hurt, believe me. In fact, one of the nicest things that has ever happened to me was the chairman giving me a private jet and telling me to go back home for Christmas Day because he thought the part-time stuff was just rubbish and I needed to be with my family. Also, people thought me and Alan had a fight and that we couldn't get along. OK, I can't prove it so I just have to shut up, wait and then when things go in the right direction, let people admit: "There is no bad atmosphere in the dressing room, things are OK with him and Shearer." '

Jon and Ruud contacted me for my views regarding adverse media coverage. I suggested Ruud ought to take legal advice to silence the lies in his home country, the stories which were bound to make their way over here to discredit him.

Ruud hated the image people had of him of being 'arrogant'. The truth is vastly different. 'When I am at home, I forget my football. I prefer the child in myself. I like the simplest things. I like to laugh and joke. I like to make the players laugh and joke. When things got us down here some time ago, we went on a paintball trip. We won. I have a sort of defence mechanism, a shield that comes up when people want something from me. You have to understand that a lot of people always want something of you. They want your attention. They want to be seen with you. All kinds of things. It is always negative. People come up to you and say: "You going to lose again Sunday?" And then they laugh. If you're playing cards, they laugh and say: 'You're going to lose again.' In the age we live in, people find it very difficult to be positive about their fellow man. Why is it never what a nice shirt you have, what a nice car you have? People in our society always approach each other in a cynical way. Everywhere, not only with me. I don't like that approach. It is easy to fall into that trap. You have to make an effort not to do it. If you do it, it is like closing a door on someone immediately. Everybody has jealous people talking about them, but my jealous people always get in the newspapers.'

As Gullit turned his attention back to the team in the run-up to the FA Cup quarter-final, there were two significant disappointments. Ferguson was out until Easter. He wanted to return for the quarter-final but he was still some way off the pace.

And the plan to give a first outing to Maric was scuppered by First Division Sheffield United. The Blades were due on Tyneside for a reserve team fixture but after boss Steve Bruce told officials that his injury-ridden club could not raise a side, the game was called off. Now the only way Maric could be given a run-out before the quarter-final was to play in Thursday's Northumberland Senior Cup tie at the home of local non-league outfit Bedlington Terriers. Gullit did not see that as an option, and arranged a behind closed doors friendly, as Maric was earmarked to make his debut against Everton in the Cup, with

Speed suspended.

Perez answered an SOS to go back to Lyon after the tragic death of the club's goalkeeper Luc Borelli in a road accident. Serrant was on the move to Huddersfield. He had not been near the first team since giving away the penalty at Everton.

Fiorentina and Real Betis were linked with Hamann, as interested clubs hoped the patched up row with Gullit might not last. But Hamann seemed finally fit, happy and a fixture in Gullit's central midfield.

Bruce Rioch failed in a move to sign Paul Dalglish, while Gullit denied receiving a £2.5 million offer for Greek internationals Dabizas and Georgiadis from Olympiakos of Athens. Ruud himself was on the trail of Holland's Ruud Van Nistelrooij. The twenty-two-year-old striker with Bobby Robson's PSV Eindhoven, rated in the £4.5 million class, was the leading scorer in the Dutch league and would be perfect cover for Shearer and Ferguson.

United's improved form made them favourites to book a place in the last four, but recent games between the sides had been close. Ian Rush's forty-third FA Cup goal had set the Magpies on the road to Wembley in last January's third round tie at Goodison Park, but a 0-0 draw on Merseyside the following month and a 1-0 defeat courtesy of Michael Ball's penalty in November had followed since.

Peter Beardsley was backing Newcastle to put out his former club Everton and go all the way. 'I've said from the third round that this is United's year to win the FA Cup and with a fourth successive home draw, I'm not about to change my mind. It's just a pity they've got to beat another of my old clubs along the way.

'I was there last May when they were beaten by Arsenal and despite the result it was an absolutely incredible day. I took my son Drew with me on an early morning train from Newcastle which was packed with United supporters and we came back with them twelve hours later. They were cheerful and optimistic all the way to Wembley and just as cheerful on the way back. They are truly amazing and it's for them I want to see United back at Wembley a couple of months from now. If they are in the final I'm confident they will bring the trophy back to Tyneside.

'For my money, Ruud Gullit is doing a terrific job. He's so shrewd tactically. I know from talking to players how hard he works on the training ground, and the players he has signed so far have been top class. Now Ruud's signed Silvio Maric from Croatia Zagreb and this lad is a great talent, he can link with other players and he can score goals. I'm sure the Geordie fans are going to love him and I'm just as sure that Ruud Gullit will get it absolutely right at Newcastle. I have been very impressed by Didi Hamann, his goal against Arsenal was an absolute beauty, all quick feet and a superb right-foot finish.'

Duncan Ferguson would definitely not be fit to face his former club. The big man was still two weeks away from a return. But Maric would make his FA Cup bow in the number ten shirt that used to belong to Barnes. Gullit had a space to fill because Speed was suspended, and Lee and Maric were in contention. Ruud said: 'I have options but I have been impressed with Maric this week. He was tired and drained by the long wait for the move to go through and he's had a lot of attention directed at him. He needs to be more fit but he looks better every day. He just needs to train and play.'

Shearer would play, although he was still troubled by flu. Interviewed for *On The Ball*, he described his relationship with Gullit. 'The dressing room is good and will improve as time goes on. There is no problem between me and Ruud Gullit. There have been plenty of newspaper stories that would upset the apple cart, but nothing has happened. The majority of the foreign players speak English, we go out together once in a while to unwind and get to know each other. That has happened despite what you might read.'

Shearer was inspired by the graphic memories of last season's semi-final when his goal beat Sheffield United. 'I am the same as any other Geordie and I can't deny that we now have a tremendous chance of getting into the semi-finals again. The memories of all the smiling faces at last year's semi-final will live with me for a long time. I'd like to think we could take the fans back to Wembley again this year and hopefully go one further and win the Cup.'

Rob Lee was set to return, and would be the only player who featured in last year's third round win over the Merseysiders.

The outcome, however, was just the same. Newcastle were beginning to look like a real team at last. The Geordie fans rose to Ruud after the 4-1 win over Everton and the misery of his early struggle on Tyneside was forgotten. The body language from the touchline told its own story; punching the air, beaming, this was one of his most satisfying moments.

The Toon Army chanted Gullit's name for the first time since he arrived and he admitted: 'It was a great feeling, really great, to hear the crowd do that. I would not say this was my most satisfying moment. There have been one or two others this season. But this is the FA Cup and something so special, and this is a one-off moment that I will cherish.'

The enigmatic Ketsbaia scored two, made a third for Shearer and generally ran Everton ragged on a rain-soaked afternoon. Georgiadis also joined in the fun by emerging from the bench to score his first goal for the club.

Shearer was now Gullit's skipper on a full-time basis, as Lee returned to first team duty only to find that his good friend had retained the armband. 'I would have preferred it to have been in different circumstances,' said the England skipper. 'But you had better ask the manager and Rob about the situation.'

It had been made clear that if Shearer turned it down, it would go to someone else, not Lee. Shearer said: 'I had worn it before, of course, when Rob wasn't playing, but I always knew I was keeping it warm for someone I admire and respect enormously, both as a man and a player. Believe me, though, it's a fantastic feeling to lead the team.'

The possibility of a repeat of the 1998 FA Cup final was kept alive as holders Arsenal and Newcastle were kept apart when Peter Beardsley made draw. Arsenal would do battle with the winners of the Chelsea-Manchester United replay following their goalless draw at Old Trafford, while Newcastle took on the winners of the Barnsley-Tottenham quarter-final, postponed because of heavy snow. But Gullit said: 'The draw does not matter, I wouldn't say it was a good draw for us – it did not matter to me which team we have to play. Anything is possible now.'

The door was thus left ajar for the possibility of Gullit facing his former club in the final. Before that, there was also the prospect of David Ginola in action against his former club in the semi-finals. Shearer was delighted: 'If we're going to win the competition then we are going to have to beat the best somewhere along the line.'

Newcastle would travel to Old Trafford, the scene of last year's triumph over Sheffield United in the last four, for their semi-final. Wembley would host a semi-final between Arsenal and Chelsea if Vialli's side overcame Manchester United in the replay, while Villa Park would be the venue if Manchester United won.

Meanwhile, Gullit might have had a wry smile as Shearer went on record as saying that footballers had far too much power for their own good. As one of the highest paid players in the country, he said he thought the money now being paid to top stars had put the players in a position of power that could be detrimental to the game.

In the BBC documentary *The Football Millionaires* with Alan Hansen, previewed at Planet Hollywood, he said: 'I started off at Southampton as a trainee on £22.50 a week on the YTS scheme. But the money involved in football nowadays has escalated so much that it is unbelievable. There will never, ever be a better time to be a footballer than now. Players can demand things and, more often than not, rightly or wrongly, they get what they want.'

Gary Speed's availability after suspension gave Gullit several options in midfield for the midweek game at Forest, as he was desperate to claw his way up the Premiership table. 'I think we deserve to be higher than twelfth, and between now and our semi-final, I want to see us start to climb the table. Speed is available again, and he has been a big plus for me.'

There were Shades of the Chelsea rotation system as Gullit left out four players, two-goal hero Ketsbaia, Lee, Dabizas and Solano. In came Speed, Georgiadis, Charvet and Saha. Newcastle won 2-1.

Another Shearer milestone – his fiftieth goal for the club put him on target to score his 150th league goal at the weekend, when Manchester United came to St James's Park. 'It would be nice, very nice to score my 150th against United, although it would have been better if the game had been at Old Trafford,' Shearer said. That remark referred to the fact that every time he plays there, a packed house never fails to bombard him with ninety minutes of abuse.

Shearer put Newcastle ahead from the penalty spot after Richard Gough, making his Forest debut, tugged at his shirt. Newcastle replaced Speed with Lee at the break, and Forest lost Gough with a pulled muscle three minutes into the second half. Their manager Ron Atkinson was forced into more shuffling after fifty minutes when Louis-Jean was sent off for bringing down Domi. Forest fans, already none too impressed with Shearer's part in the penalty incident, were now further angered by Domi's theatrics. Howey picked up a calf injury, while there was also a doubt about Speed for Saturday.

Gullit didn't need to motivate his players for a high-profile clash with Man United. In fact, he indulged in some inverse psychology by insisting the really big game of the week had been at Nottingham Forest! 'This is not our most important game, and that's not pie in the sky. Anybody will tell you that the really tough games are the ones against teams scrapping for survival.'

Gullit nevertheless expected Alex Ferguson to field his strongest side, irrespective of their Champions' League return at Inter Milan the following week. Ruud was still unable to field his own best team as Howey and Glass joined Ferguson on the sidelines, but at least Speed had recovered from flu. And Maric was itching to show Manchester

United what they had missed.

Gullit took Alex Ferguson aside just for a few minutes before kick-off at St James's and told him what to expect in the San Siro, once his domain as an AC Milan superstar. He warned: 'It will be very hostile. It will be like a boiling pot. The least little thing could explode. They are going to be provoked a lot. It all depends how they cope with that. There was one moment when it happened at Old Trafford and immediately some players got involved. Keane was involved and there was a yellow card.

'You must, must focus on the game all the time. There will be intimidation, theatre, backchat. It will be very clever. They will be trying everything to get you out of your concentration. There is no way in this country that you can experience that because it is cheating. But it is the Latino mentality.'

Unfortunately Gullit's side were off the boil at St James's Park and were a letdown in a 2-1 home defeat. Stam's mistimed lunge on Hamann gave Solano the chance to beat Schmeichel with a twenty-five-yard free kick. But just as Geordie hearts were lifted, Andy Cole collected the equaliser and then, five minutes after the break, the winner.

As for the Shearer v Cole debate with Keegan now in charge of England, two-goal Cole was applauded off the pitch by the fans who used to idolise him. Cole revelled in his return to Tyneside. Just like the previous season when he scored the only goal of the game, his cutting edge was the main difference between the two sides. 'I'm enjoying playing with Dwight Yorke,' he smiled after taking his season's haul to twenty-one. 'He's just the sort of partner I have been searching for since I played here alongside Peter Beardsley.'

Rob Lee had appeared only as a second-half substitute against Manchester United and he pleaded for a fair price if the club intended to sell him. Newcastle wanted around £2 million but Lee hoped that would not inhibit interested clubs. 'Players don't have a say in how much they are worth, but if the club is looking to sell me, I would hope they would set a fair price,' he said.

He had joined Newcastle from his only other club, Charlton, for what proved to be a bargain £700,000 in September 1992, first playing wide on the right before heading into the centre to establish his partnership with Batty. His industry and commitment made him a crowd favourite, and his reception when introduced as a substitute in four of the last six games was more than warm. He had not been afraid of fighting for his place and had been honoured to be handed the captain's armband by Dalglish when Peter Beardsley's days came to an end, but Gullit's decision to pass that on to Shearer brought matters to a head.

There was happier news the following week as Duncan Ferguson returned to full time training. Gullit was sticking to his frequently expressed rule that he would not rush any player back before he was fully fit. But that still allowed Ferguson to target an FA Cup comeback, an almost identical situation to four years ago.

He said: 'I had a groin operation within months of moving to Everton and I came back in time to play in the 1995 FA Cup Final. The similarities are strange.' Everton beat Manchester United at Wembley that year and Ferguson, who came on as substitute, added: 'I hope it's an omen. Certainly the semi-final is a realistic target if I can get match fit and put in a couple of reserve games. I'm itching to play for Newcastle.'

The Newcastle management went the same day to see the Barnsley v Spurs quarter-final. When Ruud tried to get into Oakwell a doorman refused to let him in until he produced a ticket. Steve Clarke was sent to another stand for the necessary passes. Gullit ended the day a few seats behind George Graham, Alan Sugar and David Pleat as he watched Spurs win with a wonder goal from David Ginola.

Graham said: 'It was typical Ginola. He can be quiet for forty-five minutes and then he can come alight for twenty minutes. But I'd like to see him score with a few more tap-ins, getting into the box more. But he is a match-winner and although he's got some deficiencies, we've got to put up with them!'

Steve Howey also earmarked the semi-final for a return, and a date with David Ginola. He admitted: 'David is in the form of his life. He's magnificent when he's on song, but we have to be ready to meet the challenge.'

Stuart Pearce was at the time collecting his MBE from the Queen. 'It was a different sort of nervousness to going on to the pitch before a match, he said. 'The Queen seemed to be very knowledgeable about football.'

Although he was clearly now getting to grips with the enormous task he had taken on, Gullit declined to commit himself beyond his two-year deal. 'I can't say I'm going to stay for three or five years,' he said. 'You can't, too many things can happen within the space of a week or two.' But his contract remained unsigned. 'It is signed in spirit and it is not a problem,' Guillit said.

He unveiled a blueprint that could one day result in Clarke taking over or indeed even Shearer managing his hometown club. Gullit wanted an old Liverpool-style infrastructure implemented, with all future coaches emerging from within. 'It is important that we plan for the future at Newcastle and maintain a certain philosophy all the way down the line. The fans want and expect open, exciting, attacking football, and that means all our coaches should be working towards the same thing. The same system. People should come from within. It's not about bringing in big names from outside, because managers come in and buy and sell their own players and the style of football changes. This exciting style is also what Newcastle represents to the rest of football.

'For example, I don't know if Alan Shearer wants to be a coach in the future. I don't know what his ambitions are. But maybe he could start as the second or third coach and work his way up. I don't know if he wants to. He hasn't given me any indication that he does. But if he wants to coach here, then he could step in and learn from the ones who will already be in place.'

Gullit needed to concentrate on more immediate tasks, such as Saturday's match against West Ham. Newcastle travelled to Upton Park without the suspended Hamann. Gullit selected Maric, who would then fly on to one of the most volatile locations in European football, playing for Croatia in their first meeting with Yugoslavia in Belgrade since the troubles ended there.

Spurs were also represented at the game as George Graham dispatched his assistant Stewart Houston to Upton Park where Gullit's team lost 2-0. His report on Tottenham's semi-final opponents made encouraging news.

Gullit would only stand a chance of upsetting the odds against Spurs with all his players available. He admitted: 'We played some good stuff but did not have the firepower, which made it difficult.' Maric made no impression either for himself or in support of Shearer. Saha showed glimpses of individualism, but the most telling was to lose possession to send the Hammers on their way to Kitson's goal (against his old club) when Newcastle were on the attack. Little wonder that when Gullit was first asked about Shearer, he smiled and said: 'I am not going to talk about individuals.'

Gullit was the first to concede that his game plan to provide width and service for Shearer had failed, but was not amused when asked why he only had one striker. 'I had three strikers,' he said, 'did you not see the same game?' He explained his strategy: 'I had Maric and Saha up front, Domi and Griffin to get forward and they have to cross the ball. On some occasions it went well, for the most part it didn't.'

Neil Ruddock signalled to the depth of his trouser pocket to illustrate the position in which he held Shearer all afternoon. With a beer gut in decline – it didn't stop the Toon Army from singing 'You Fat Bastard' – he was still able to stop Shearer. He had his close pal just where he wanted him.

Ruddock said: 'Alan Shearer is still solid and very hard to mark. The couple of times I did lose him the distribution to him was absolute crap. Newcastle didn't get behind us to feed him, they had no penetration, they played in front of us and we were more than happy. But Alan couldn't get away. Newcastle even had two wingers but still couldn't get the ball to Alan. His head went down a bit because of the poor service. Newcastle played some very good one-touch football in the second half but I can't remember one aerial challenge with Alan, usually we're knocking each other around. Service like that is just not good enough for him or Newcastle.'

Ruud had a taxi waiting to dash away from Upton Park at 5.15. Robert Lee would have liked to have stayed in east London – permanently. He said: 'You have got to be playing, and if you're not playing, you look elsewhere. My mum and dad still have a house near here and I have a home in Hornchurch. Unfortunately, I have got to go back up north tonight.'

The chairman responded to suggestions over the next few days that the club were examining a back door entry to the UEFA Cup via the Inter-Toto Cup. Shepherd said: 'Never mind the back door, we want to get in through the front door, and that means either winning the FA Cup or qualifying through our league position with a strong late run.'

Just before the transfer deadline, Paul Dalglish signed on loan until the end of the season for Norwich. It would not be long before the move was made permanent for £300,000. Transfer deadline day itself passed without any activity; but there would be huge changes in the summer. Gullit planned to move on virtually an entire surplus team: Pistone, Andersson, Lee, Dabizas, Dalglish, Albert, Pearce, Georgiadis, Serrant, Hamilton, Keidel and Perez. Ten of those were signed by Kenny Dalglish.

Said Gullit: 'The squad was too large when I came here. I believe that the correct number to work with is twenty-two, and that's what I am working towards.'

Newcastle's problems in attracting top flight players to the North East underlined the importance to the club of an effective youth policy. And they needed to start young. Gullit planned to nab the best kids by advertising for them to attend a 'Talent Identification Day'.

Successful seven to eleven-year-olds would win a place at the club's youth academy and grow into the stars of the future.

Recruitment officer Peter Kirkley, who brought Paul Gascoigne to St James's Park, said: 'The manager knows how successful this idea was at Ajax. The interest is phenomenal and I've no doubt we will find a lot of talent out there.' No homegrown players had come through the ranks for years. NTL pledged a £5 million outlay on youth development if they gained control of the club.

Ferguson meanwhile was still battling to make the semi-final but was forced to pull out of a reserve team comeback. Gullit admitted: 'I honestly don't know if he will be ready for the semi-final. I can't put a date on it.' Glass was certainly out of the semi-final and faced a second scan.

But looking to the more immediate future, optimism was running high before the Easter programme of games.

Shearer said: 'First things first, our absolute concentration has to be on beating Tottenham, we can't afford to let our thoughts drift beyond that.'

12

Qualification for Europe as semi-finalists! Newcastle go back to Wembley . . .

Ruud thanked UEFA for granting a bizarre passage into Europe. United were guaranteed a place in next season's UEFA Cup, even if they lost to Spurs in the FA Cup semi-final! A smiling Gullit insisted: 'It's a nice idea. Thank you, UEFA!

'I thought this might have arisen if we had reached the final. But whatever the outcome, it will have no bearing on our determination to go all the way. Winning matches is a lovely feeling and this doesn't take away our intentions to win it. We just want to go forward.

United gained the coveted European place as all three other semi-finalists had almost certainly guaranteed their places in Europe – Manchester United and Arsenal in the Champions' League, Spurs as Worthington Cup Winners in the UEFA Cup.

It seemed almost to be an April Fool joke. However, the joke was on clubs like Leeds, West Ham and Aston Villa, as they would have wanted the spare UEFA place to go to the club finishing fifth in the Premiership. It would be the second year in a row that Newcastle had got into Europe through the back door as they had qualified as the FA Cup runners up when Arsenal won the Double. The previous year they became the first to benefit from the second placed team qualifying for the Champions' League. Ironically, in 1969 when they won the Fairs Cup, their last major honour, they qualified in ninth place because there could be only one entrant per city – so third-placed Everton, Chelsea in fifth, Spurs sixth and West Ham eighth were overlooked!

Gullit kept a room full of journalists waiting for two hours after training the day before the match at Derby. 'He's been delayed . . . he's gone for a run . . . he's having a shower.' One reporter said: 'He'll turn up without apologising, sit down and talk utter bloody shite for ten minutes, then he'll dash off.'

After all the adverse publicity, Gullit was not always receptive. He wouldn't give any real clues to his team selection. 'I'm not gonna show you my cards – why should I?' But he insisted his players must not ease up, despite their unexpected UEFA bonus.

Shearer was out again – this time with an ankle injury picked up in training. With eight days to the big tie, Gullit didn't seem too alarmed. 'Alan's injury is not a worry to me and I would expect him to play in the semi-final. I think he will be okay, but it is too early to say. He's walking but it doesn't mean he's fit to play.' Gullit also had Ferguson on the verge of a comeback. 'Duncan trained today and did well. We shall have to see how he recovers from that session. I can't say for definite that he will be involved tomorrow, on Monday, or against Spurs in the semi-final. We have to work day-to-day with him.'

Successive defeats by Manchester United and West Ham had seen the team slip back into the bottom half of the table, and Gullit admitted that the two-week lay-off since the game at Upton Park was far from ideal. Barton was suspended. Hamann, hurt during his country's 2-0 win over Finland in midweek, would play no part at Pride Park and was doubtful for the Premiership visit of Spurs on the Monday.

It was also announced that sales of club merchandise, largely made up of replica shirts, had dropped by over £2 million from £5.5 million to £3.3 million over a six month period. Figures in the club's half-yearly review highlighted the fall during the six months leading up to January, with United's turnover also down from £31 million to £25.2 million, while the operating profit tumbled from 10.3 million to 5.7 million. Shepherd refused to blame past indiscretions for the fall in profits from black and white shirts. He said: The situation was over a year ago and we have drawn a line over that. We are looking to the future now and there's a buzz around St James's Park these days.'

A few more games like this one and the buzz would be well and truly back. Ruud gazed up at the lower half of the Premiership table displayed on a TV screen in the Pride Park press lounge. 'It's alright, Ruud,' came a helpful voice, 'you're in the top half now.'

It could have been ten goals. This was back to the Keegan days – only then, the team *lost* 4-3! And there was the first hint from the travelling fans of acceptance of Gullit, as they chanted his name near the end.

Gullit said: 'I am a very happy coach today. Perhaps neither Jim Smith nor I would be happy with some of the defensive football, but I thought we were very good in attack. I sensed that my players were up for it. After two successive defeats it was important we won.'

This was a line-up minus Hamann, Howey, Ferguson and Glass as well as Shearer. But even without their top scorer Newcastle were well capable of ramming all the Euro moans down a few throats, particularly after Villa and West Ham drew 0-0 on Friday night. Smith's team were run ragged, leaving the Bald Eagle so bemused he had five strikers on the pitch during the closing stages.

Competition at last! 'I'd be perfectly satisfied to play Tottenham in next Sunday's FA Cup semi-final with this team,' insisted Gullit. 'I always look at what is best for the team and not the individual. Who plays depends on form. People select themselves and, for sure, there are places up for grabs.'

Gullit turned his attention to a week when his personal battle of wits with George Graham would shape the entire season. First, the dress rehearsal in the League on Monday. Gullit grinned: 'Maybe George and myself will be playing tactical games on Monday, maybe not. Who knows? I will send out my best available team, because we owe it to our supporters to give everything for three points in the League game. At the moment, I have no special plans to handle David Ginola. He is a good player, you don't need to tell me. But maybe he won't be quite so good if Tottenham cannot give him the ball. We will see. That is my main concern.'

Ruud felt he had won over the fans. 'They like me. At least, I feel they do. Sometimes they hear bad things about me, hurtful things like I spend too much time away from the place. But I think they ignore them. They know it's just spite, just talk. The thing is, they have great expectations. They want this club to achieve things. It's a burden, sure. But the heaviest expectations are the ones I have of myself.'

The *Mail on Sunday* led their back page with speculation that Fulham owner Mohamed Al Fayed would want Gullit to replace Keegan if he took up the England job full-time. However, Gullit told me he would stay at St James's Park however many millions he was offered by Al Fayed.

In a practice match Gullit experimented with Garry Brady in a wide position, a possible strategy to cover the Ginola threat as well as provide crosses for Shearer. He congratulated Spurs on their Worthington Cup triumph. 'I have been asked if that makes them less dangerous in terms of Sunday's semi-final on the grounds that they have already qualified for next season's UEFA Cup. I'd say that it makes them more dangerous. Winning is a lovely habit to get into and having won one trophy, George Graham and his players will be nice and relaxed and very keen to win another.'

In the end, both sides forgot the winning habit for Monday's game. But Gullit felt he had learned enough in a 1-1 draw to mastermind Spurs' downfall. He smiled to Clarke at the end and was already planning towards the semi. He explained: 'The good thing is we knew why the game went like it did. We had players who were very tired. We had no possibility to replace those players because the others were injured. But still, we controlled the last twenty minutes of the game and we should have won it. So that gives me and my team a psychological advantage for the next game.'

Graham felt *he* had gained the upper hand. Spurs were the better side and Anderton's forty-ninth-minute penalty would have won it for them had Ketsbaia not cracked in a terrific twenty-five-yard strike thirteen minutes from time.

The biggest shock was Gullit's inclusion of nineteen-year-old rookie midfielder Jamie McClen, a local lad. McClen was so far adrift of the first team that he did not even feature in the match programme that displayed the latest squad photograph. Twenty-five players were ahead of him in that respect, but Gullit had never been afraid to follow his instincts. McClen replaced Lee. Gullit explained: 'Robert Lee was injured and couldn't play and I had to improvise.' There was no sign of Shearer, nor the half-expected appearance on the bench of Ferguson. For the 36,000 who turned up to steal a preview of Sunday's tie, it was a waste of time and money.

Shearer had recovered from his ankle knock but Charvet was a new doubt for the semi-final after injuring a knee. Howey, on the way back from a calf injury, would be the obvious replacement.

A chauffeur-driven car took Gullit from Newcastle to Manchester on Wednesday to appear on ITV alongside Kevin Keegan as the star analysts for Manchester United's Champions' League semi-final first leg with Juventus . . . so time for Ruud to catch up on some sleep!

Duncan Ferguson successfully made his comeback in a private friendly at St James's Park, scoring in a 6-0 win over local part-timers West Allotment. Howey also proved his fitness with a ninety-minute work out.

Newcastle's top earners would pick up bonuses of up to £100,000 a man for reaching the final. The squad were on a bonus system that netted each player five per cent of his annual salary should they beat Spurs. So the club's top earner, Ferguson, would collect £100,000, Shearer in the region of £90,000.

Training in the morning, golf in the afternoon on Thursday, and then one of Ruud's many routine management meetings with Fletcher. Then he did the rounds at a couple of social clubs to meet the fans accompanied by Fletcher and director of marketing Alec King. Gullit was given rapturous applause. He answered a variety of questions ranging from transfer targets to who did his dreadlocks!

Ruud dispatched Clarke to Stamford Bridge for the first time since his departure to check on some Real Mallorca players. Dani didn't disappoint with a precious away goal, but nor did he fail to catch the eye of Arsene Wenger, who was ahead of the queue to buy him.

Ruud had agreed to be interviewed by me on the eve of the semi-final – and again before the final if he got there! It was a promise he had made when I told him after the third round during a meeting at the Copthorne Hotel, that he was heading back to Wembley. He said he would be only too willing to oblige if my prediction came true.

Inevitably, Ginola, the one-time darling of St James's Park, was the main topic of conversation. While the Frenchman was a candidate for player of the year, he still managed to upset many opponents. But there were no complaints from Gullit.

As a player who was similarly in the spotlight, Gullit knows it is a back-handed compliment to be jeered and abused by the opposing fans – it means fear. He didn't expect such abuse to be aimed at Ginola, or indeed the other former Geordie hero Ferdinand. 'These two guys have done very well for this club and they will always be remembered by the fans for what they have done. On this day they will be our enemies, of course, but after the game they will be given our full respect.' Ginola was not to be the sole focus of Gullit's attention.

On Shearer, Gullit said: 'I don't know what psychological impact Alan will have on Spurs, that is for them to say. But he is looking good and I am happy about that. It's the semi-final, remember. They all want to play, they all want to go to Wembley.'

At the training ground, it was the traditional, FA-organised 'open day' for media access. The players were, supposedly, all freely available for interview but, spotting a growing gathering of journalists, some sneaked out into the car park via a fire door. Not Shearer. Inevitably asked about Ferdinand and Ginola, he said: 'There are very few people of David's ability around and on his day, he's very, very difficult to stop. Let's hope he has an off-day. Les is going through a bit of a barren spell at the moment as all forwards do at some stage throughout their career. I hope he starts scoring goals on Monday morning rather than Sunday.'

Shearer, the only Englishman to score for Newcastle all season, would be the first Geordie to lead out an FA Cup final team for seventy-five years if Newcastle got through. He said: 'It's got to be the wildest dream of any Geordie, leading Newcastle out for an FA Cup final, and it would top it off for a Geordie to lift the FA Cup at Wembley. But to skipper Newcastle at Wembley would be a great, great feeling, one you would never forget. It would give us the chance to make up for last season's defeat. I know everyone says we didn't play particularly well but if we had had a little luck, I still believe we could have won it.'

Freddy Shepherd said how great it was to have a Geordie captain in Shearer, and Robert Lee was hurt. 'Well, obviously my problem is that I'm not a Geordie,' snapped the Londoner, who had spent seven years wearing black and white stripes and whose two sons spoke with North East accents. 'Alan and I are still very good friends, we wouldn't let something like this drive a wedge between us, but I don't think it was the best choice of words by the chairman. I was very proud to be captain of Newcastle. It meant a lot to me, it was a great honour.'

Disagreements with his manager? 'It's a private matter.'

Do they talk?

'Oh yes, of course.'

More positively, Gullit felt Lee's career could be extended by his squad rotation, but Lee responded: 'I don't think my age is a problem. I don't feel any different to the way I did four or five years ago, I was a late developer and I think my career has got a long way to go yet.'

BSkyB's £623 million bid for Manchester United had meanwhile been ruled out by the Government after the Monopolies and Mergers Commission's report on the offer. It meant the NTL take-over of Newcastle, which was dependent on the outcome of BSkyB's bid for Manchester United, was also in doubt.

Once again, though, affairs off the field were driven from supporters' minds by a thrilling performance on the pitch as the Magpies won their semi-final 2-0. Estatic fans chanted, 'Ruudi! Ruudi!' There was even a hug and a handshake for Shearer from Gullit at the end!

Gullit had clutched his 'lucky' crucifix as Shearer stepped up to take the vital penalty in extra time. He explained: 'I'm a very good Christian, and I was stroking it for luck. It's something I do before games, and at certain important times through the match. Every one has little things to help them relieve the tension. It's a dream for me that we are in the final – I'm very, very grateful and happy that God has given me this opportunity to go back to Wembley. It's incredible that I am going back there again after coaching for just two and a half years. It is very emotional for me, to think of that walk out of the tunnel.'

Shearer capped an aggressive, driving display with an explosive twenty-yard shot which finally killed off Tottenham's hopes. Gullit was delighted. 'Shearer is Shearer, he can score goals whenever he wants.'

The key moment was the unpunished handball in the box by Dabizas after fifty-eight minutes. Barton felt aggrieved when he was pulled up for a foul on Armstrong but when Sinton placed the free kick in the air Dabizas threw up his hand and clearly made contact complaining he had been shoved by Campbell. Conversely, in the 108th minute when Campbell blatantly handled, referee Paul Durkin could not miss it. Gullit had already brought on Ferguson and later Maric and it was Ferguson whose flick was handled by the Spurs captain. Shearer scored at the same end of Old Trafford where his winner had taken Newcastle to Wembley a year earlier. Once Newcastle were ahead it was just a question of holding on but with a minute to go Shearer took a Maric pass in his stride on the edge of the area and cracked it into the top corner.

Shearer said: 'I think our fans got us through it in the end. They were magnificent and the atmosphere was incredible, especially when we needed it in extra time.' He appeared to be the calmest man in the stadium as he converted the vital spot kick. 'It may have looked as if I took it with a lot of authority, but my backside was going, I can assure you. It was always going to be a close game, and when we went into extra time I knew tired legs would come into it, which made it even more difficult. The second goal was good because my legs had gone and I was knackered, so it meant I could walk around for the last minute. It was pleasing because I don't score from long range anymore – or so I'm told.'

Gullit's amazing affinity with the FA Cup continued. The one down side was an injury to Howey after thirty-five minutes, challenged by one of his own defenders at a routine throw in. He was stretchered off with a calf injury which was threatening to rule him out for the rest of the season.

Gullit looked forward to a pulsating final, but he wouldn't react to the fans having chanted 'Attack, attack, attack,' unheeded by Dalglish, during the last sterile Wembley performance. He said: 'I am getting asked if I can pledge to put on a show to pacify the fans. But first and foremost we've got to put out a team that can beat whoever the opposition might be at Wembley.' The other semi-final had finished 0-0, so a rematch with Arsenal was still possible. But Gullit stressed: 'You don't think about having to put on a show. It's all about winning and what we have to do to win the final. Once we know who we are facing we will study them and see where their weaknesses are.

'We will be a better team in a month's time with Duncan Ferguson being that much fitter because he is not only important in the air but also a very good footballer as well. He gives Alan Shearer someone to play off, and that helps him. Alan scored a lot of goals when he had Les Ferdinand here doing that job, and Duncan does the same for him. You could see the big difference it made when Duncan Ferguson came on, and with it the relieving of Alan Shearer as the target man. Every time Duncan had a flick, Alan was near by and he could control the game. I think it made a big difference to him. He has been missing that sort of thing for a long time.'

Newcastle shares rose 6p to 81p after that result, while Spurs' stock sank 5p to 67.5p. But no one's stock rose more than Ruud Gullit's on Tyneside.

'Incredible is the right word for the Newcastle fans. The reason I say that is that it's easy to support a club which is doing well and keeps winning trophies, but at Newcastle we have thousands upon thousands of fans who have given the team magnificent support despite the fact that it's thirty years since the club won a major trophy. I have been here only a few months but I quickly realised how special these fans were. They have never lost their belief in the team and that has helped the team to believe in itself.'

Shearer concurred: 'There can be only one better feeling than winning a semi-final and that's to be Cup final winners, and that's the feeling I want for our magnificent supporters at Wembley. I have had the pleasure and privilege of playing in some great atmospheres but Old Trafford surpassed anything in my experience. Many, many players before me have sung the praises of Newcastle United fans, but I do want each and every one of them to know that the players at this club felt proud to represent them and to give them the victory over Tottenham their fantastic support deserved.'

Shearer backed Duncan Ferguson to help bring the Cup to Tyneside. His introduction had freed Shearer of the role of target man and ensured Sol Campbell had his hands full. 'It enables me to pick up the pieces,' said Shearer. 'Otherwise, I'm fighting and scrapping for everything against the big man in defence. I'm willing to do it, it doesn't bother me. I do it for the team and I do it for the football club because I love the football club. I'm prepared to sweat blood up there on my own for them. But when Dunc comes on, it takes a bit of the pressure off me and enables me to have a little bit more space because the big man has to pick him up. He was tremendous when he came on. He won everything in the air and I was able to benefit from that.'

The one unhappy man after the patch was Steve Howey, whose injury jinx continued – he was out for eight months with a ruptured Achilles tendon. As a result Gullit and Shepherd made the short journey to Paris to agree a fee of around £4 million with Paris St Germain for twenty-six-year-old Alain Goma for next season. Gullit had been on the trail of the player for some time, but made his move after the verdict on Howey. Goma would take Gullit's spending to close on £20 million.

The London *Evening Standard*'s TV guide on Wednesday showed what it thought of Newcastle's Cup chances: 'Highlights of tonight's FA Cup semi-final replay. To save the foregone conclusion of the final against Newcastle, it would be quicker and simpler to present the winners of this game with the Cup.' A wonder solo goal from Ryan Giggs won it for Man United in extra time, after Bergkamp's penalty was superbly saved by Schmeichel in the last seconds of normal time.

So the final would be a repeat of the 1996 Charity Shield, but that is where Newcastle hoped the similarity would end. Alex Ferguson's side won 4-0 that day in what was Shearer's first competitive game for the club. Shearer observed: 'I'm sure it will be a lot different this time. It wasn't a very good introduction to football with my new club, but this will be something completely different. Having said that, Manchester United are the best, and I have always said that if we are going to win the FA Cup, then we will have to beat the best.'

Ruud knew no one in the country outside of Tyneside, and probably even the majority of Newcastle fans, gave his side a prayer against Manchester United. But he insisted: 'We have shown in our two Premier League games against Manchester United this season – a draw at Old Trafford and a narrow defeat at St James's Park – that we can play well against them and I have every confidence that the players will do a good job for this club against a team I rate very, very highly. People ask me if we can win and the answer is that of course we can win. Favourites are there to be beaten.'

Newcastle expected to bank more than £1 million in sales of new replica shirts in the week leading up to Wembley. They were due to announce details of their kit before their last League game of the season against Blackburn. But with their Wembley date booked, they wanted to sell as many as they could in the week leading up to the final. The new strip featured white socks, as requested by Gulllit. 'I think teams play better and look better in white socks,' he said.

Gullit was still concerned that Ferguson was not yet ready to play a full game as Newcastle prepared to face struggling Everton in the League the weekend after the semi-final. Howey, Charvet and Domi were also out, with Dabizas suspended. But Gullit had few qualms about fielding what would be one of the youngest defences Newcastle had ever put out in a top-flight game. 'Beharall is a little bit quicker than Caldwell but he is technically a good player. They're very young and inexperienced, but of course you can only get experience when you let them play.'

In the end, Big Dunc did not make an appearance of any sort as his former club edged nearer safety with a gritty performance in a 3-1 win at St James's Park. Gullit criticised his players' hunger. 'What's the point in having five or six gears if you are only going to use four? It's like having a Ferrari and not using it to its full potential. There was something missing from our game. But then you can't give 80 per cent instead of 100 and expect to win. Everton had more hunger than us. We didn't have sufficient desire, and I blame the experienced players for that. They have held their hands up.'

With Shearer shackled by a strongman trio of Watson, Short and Unsworth, United's two genuine chances were limited to penalty kicks. Shearer's first was saved by Myhre with Everton one up, but he succeeded at the second attempt to make it 2-1.

Shearer said: 'We were all on a high after beating Tottenham, so our mood was very buoyant for the game. We shot ourselves in the foot conceding a goal after forty-three seconds and then when I missed the chance to pull us level from the penalty spot it looked like it wasn't going to be our day. But we have no excuses and we don't seek any. We have nobody to blame but ourselves.'

Seeking to minimise the risk of any further slip-ups, Gullit banned the FA Cup from the training ground on Monday. Sponsors Axa intended to have the original 1911 trophy photographed with Rob Lee as he handed out sets of kit to six junior clubs. But the famous old trophy never made it past the gates as Gullit and Lee agreed that it was bad luck to touch the Cup before the final.

Nevertheless, fortune still seemed to be evading Gullit with the news that NTL had pulled out of their £160 million takeover, and inevitably it was reported in the media that Gullit's ambitious transfer plans would be curbed. Committed to £42 million to increase the St James's Park capacity, Newcastle would still operate with plenty of vigour in the transfer market, but NTL had promised to widen their horizons even further.

The club were surprised by the swiftness of NTL's decision. But having noted BSkyB's rejection, NTL became pessimistic about their own chances. Leading stockbroker and football analyst Vinay Bedi, of Wise Speke, said: 'Many people expected the NTL bid to be given the go-ahead, so it's a little surprising they haven't stuck it out. The big question is whether Ruud Gullit will be told the same as Alex Ferguson at Manchester United – that he can't have as much money in the summer as he originally thought.'

Gullit insisted the failed takeover would not hinder his rebuilding. 'My position has not changed, and I am not working with one hand behind my back. I will continue to scour England, Europe and the world for players. I still have my targets and I'm still planning to bring players to the club. I am comfortable with the situation. It is not a problem.

'Things may be different for the club in the long term, but for me it has not changed anything. I go to the directors and say that I need this and this, and we try to go for it.' It would encourage Gullit to offload players, which he intended to do in any case.

Gullit admitted the Cup Final was preying on his players' minds in midweek as Newcastle drew 1-1 at Sheffield Wednesday. 'I can understand all the hype around and the feelings of the players. If you have not won any silverware, all the time you are waiting for that moment, but if you have, then you are more relaxed. I remember my first trophy and it was the same experience. You get nervous, thinking about being part of it and not wanting to get injured.' His advice to the players: 'Just win the FA Cup and then you will know what I mean!'

The North East radio reporter summed up the draw with Wimbledon when his first words to the listeners back home at the final whistle were: 'No injuries sustained.' With Wembley ever closer, Gullit and Clarke instantly dissected the game, an animated Ruud throwing his hands out to illustrate a point as they left the field at the end. Nothing to play for in the Premiership? Not so. Newcastle tiptoed through meaningless fixtures like this, but for Gullit there were Cup final places up for grabs and thoughts turning to next season.

The only parallel to the final was that Peter Jones was in charge, the man who would referee at Wembley. Shearer provided the only moments of high involvement for the huge following of Geordie fans. He popped in his twentieth goal of the season, a lead held until Hartson finally managed his first goal since moving to the Dons from West Ham.

Gullit offered Beharall a second game in the centre of defence and he responded with a solid performance, but up front, in the absence of Ketsbaia, who had taken a knock on the head in training, Shearer got precious little help from Andersson.

Hartson turned up with a goal but where was Duncan Ferguson? The outcome of the final could hinge on the Scot, but the mystery was that he had not been seen since that brief but telling contribution in the semi-final. The North East was awash with rumours that Ferguson was crocked again, fuelled by an appointment with the specialist on Thursday. And on this evidence many felt Newcastle might as well not turn up at Wembley unless Ferguson took some part, even if it was only another cameo appearance from the bench.

A few days later Gullit thought he had agreed a £2 million deal for Dynamo Kiev right-back and captain Oleg Luzhny. But it was easy to understand why he wanted it kept secret. Once news leaked out, it alerted Arsenal and with the option of playing in the Champions' League, it looked as though Luzhny would go to Highbury and Gullit would miss out on a key signing having made the first move.

Middlesbrough were also interested and Bryan Robson flew to Germany to hold talks with Kiev before their European Cup semi-final defeat by Bayern Munich. But Gullit acted swiftly to pip Boro.

So, no sign of holding back in the transfer market. Gullit also made a £6 million bid for Real Mallorca's central defender Elena Marcelino, whose arm was the subject of a controversial bite by Dennis Wise during the first leg of their European semi-final against Chelsea. Reports indicated that Gullit had offered a £10 million package to land Dani – but did people have the wrong Mallorca star? President Guillermo Corbella insisted Newcastle sent a fax outlining a deal for the forward but a club source said: 'There has been no such fax. Dani is not on Ruud's shopping list.' In any event, Dani only wanted to sign for a club in the Champions' League, and held out for a move to Arsenal.

Gullit was also linked to Read Madrid's Dutch international midfielder Clarence Seedorf. It was even reported that Seedorf had turned down a big money move to Italy to join Gullit on a four-year deal. The twenty-three-year-old midfield star had the chance to move to Juventus or Lazio but said: 'I've sampled football in Italy and Spain and now I want the challenge of playing in England. Newcastle would suit me fine. I'm a Dutchman and I have the greatest respect and admiration for Ruud Gullit.' Nobody at Newcastle was prepared to comment on the deal before the Final but it seemed a significant step in a massive rebuilding job. Gullit was also still tracking Boban and Blackburn keeper Tim Flowers.

Keegan's decision to allow two players from Arsenal and Manchester United to be released from international duty in Hungary prompted a public rebuke from Gullit. He wanted Shearer rested as well, for a friendly many regarded as pointless.

Gullit said: 'If Alan was to be selected while players at Manchester United and Arsenal were not, then of course I would object. Shearer was involved in the World Cup, and he needs a rest as well. But if many of the top players are going to be left behind, then what would be the purpose of going? I know this is only a friendly game, but the timing of it is all wrong. The FA might as well call off the game. Either they all go or the game should be off.'

Shearer's enthusiasm to captain his country was undiminished by the lack of interest in the midweek friendly. While some remained at home, Shearer had no qualms about playing in Hungary. 'I'm here aren't I?' said Shearer in Budapest. 'That suggests an awful lot.' Shearer joked he felt like one of the few 'over-age' players in a bizarre looking squad.

Keegan laughed at the suggestion that it had been decided Shearer would play only one half. 'That's come from the Hungarian coach, that one,' laughed the England manager.

Players were naturally keen to ensure they were available for the final. Now Laurent Charvet battled to recover from injury. The knee ligament tear he had picked up caused Gullit concern, particularly after losing Howey. Beharall, just offered a new long term contract, was on Cup final stand by even though he had started only two games. Either he or another youngster Aaron Hughes would partner Dabizas.

Ferguson put in double training sessions and was in with a chance of facing Middlesbrough at the weekend..

Promising youngster Jamie McClen agreed a new long term contract along with Beharall, and Ketsbaia made his peace with Georgia after vowing never play for his country again following a bust-up with national coach Vladimir Gutsayev. He picked up his thirty-fourth cap in the friendly with Norway, four months after saying he was finished with international football.

Ferguson lasted sixty-three minutes in his first start of the year in the 1-1 May day draw with Middlesbrough at St James's Park, as he was carefully nursed toward the final.

Sorry! Don't mention the 'F' word. Ruud fined anyone at the club £10 each time they mentioned the final, himself included! He explained: 'It's a £10 fine every time we mention it. We will not talk about the F-word until F-week . . . I had better be careful, it has already cost me £30. I've told the whole squad they have to pay and it goes into the pot. After the final we will have a day out to spend it. I have had it going since the semi and I don't want to hear it. I had the same at Chelsea and we won the Cup. It's not a serious thing, just a bit of fun.'

Gullit's press conference then collapsed into a sort of Basil Fawlty 'Don't mention the war' scenario. Still, there was a relaxed approach to the impending final, which was more than could be said for the previous year when a totally jaded Newcastle side staggered onwards before eventually losing.

Gullit was happy with his team's spirit despite the 'semi-final syndrome' – no wins since it! At least the side had come back from a goal behind as Shearer salvaged a point from the penalty spot after Domi had been hacked down.

There were more indications on Monday that Newcastle's luck really might have changed when Andy Griffin walked away from a horror car smash. He escaped unharmed when his £60,000 Porsche ran into the side of a moving Metro train at a railway crossing. His car was a write-off, the bonnet almost ripped off and debris from the vehicle scattered along the track by the crossing at Callerton Park on the outskirts of Newcastle. An eyewitness said: 'We looked inside the car and the airbags were inflated. The firemen said, "Let's hope he's all right for the Cup final!" We didn't know what they meant. Then they said it was Andy Griffin and we couldn't believe it.'

Gullit was relieved, but a little bemused. 'He's okay, he's just having a rest. I don't know how you can drive into a train. I really don't know, but he's okay. We were more concerned about the Porsche!'

Gullit dismissed the reports that Seedorf was set to join. Speaking as he cast his eye over 1,000 young footballers at a special talent-spotting event, he said he was mystified by claims that he had clinched a deal for his compatriot. The Seedorf package would be too costly – £10 million over four years.

Gullit was frustrated too that his team would miss out on prestigious pre-season friendlies against Real Madrid, Feyenoord and AC Milan . . . to play at Stoke and Reading! Because of contractual obligations, Newcastle had to face the Endsleigh League teams as part of deals for Griffin and Hislop.

Ruud wanted to fix up games against the biggest clubs in Europe having arranged three matches in Holland in July. He snapped: 'We have obligations in this country and it really p****s me off. I don't have a problem, but if you have the chance to play Real Madrid, Feyenoord or Milan, it's better for you to play against high quality opponents. Then you can measure yourself, then you know where you stand. Stoke or Real Madrid – there's a difference. It's no disrespect to Stoke or Reading, but it would have been a good chance for a lot of the young players to play there in the Bernabeu.'

As Ruud looked ahead, there were further signs that the Dalglish era was soon to become a distant memory. Stuart Pearce planned a meeting with Gullit for the final verdict on his future. At least Pearce had lasted longer than fellow veterans Ian Rush and John Barnes, who were also brought in by Dalglish. But he made his final appearance in a Newcastle shirt when he played for the reserves against Blyth in the Northumberland Cup final. He had not started a Premiership game this year.

Ralf Kiedel and Perez also played their last games before being freed. And Guivarc'h feared he had played his last game for Rangers! In contrast, Ketsbaia was promised a job the following season by Gullit.

Shearer was given assurances about his personal safety at Leicester. He was public enemy number one at Filbert Street after kicking Lennon in the face last season. Police were on alert for his first return.

Shearer insisted: 'It's history. It happened a long time ago and as far as I'm concerned it's forgotten. The less said about it the better. I've been booed at other grounds before and I'm sure I'll get it again in the future. It won't bother me.' Gullit said: 'It's interesting that all this should come up again a day before the game. I'd have thought Leicester supporters would have forgotten about it by now.'

Glass was unexpectedly in contention for Wembley after knee surgery and a six-week lay-off. Charvet and Griffin were not in the party which headed south to Filbert Street.

With Gullit's players terrified of referee Uriah Rennie's red card and an automatic exit from the final, the game itself looked more like a quest for Fair Play points than a competitive performance as Newcastle lost 2-0 at Leicester. Ferguson lasted one anonymous half and the only other talking point was a comeback for Glass, less than five weeks after Gullit had written off his season. First half goals from Izzet and Cottee did not flatter Leicester.

Gullit wanted Blackburn to pull off a shock result against Manchester United midweek. Rovers had to win at Ewood Park to stand any chance of survival, their final game was on Tyneside the next Sunday and Gullit felt he would rather be involved in a match with something at stake. 'It's maybe not realistic, but I would rather Blackburn beat United so that our last game before the Cup Final doesn't turn into a non-event,' he said.

Saha had originally been ruled out for the rest of the season after fracturing his cheekbone, but made such a swift recovery that he was now able to link up with the French Under-21s. He was dreaming of Wembley again. 'I would love to score another FA Cup goal for Newcastle. The memory of my winner in the Blackburn game will stay with me forever.'

Charvet resumed light training. But not everything was going to plan. Blackburn were relegated after a goalless draw against Manchester United. Gullit's team had picked up only one win in nine, failing to win a game since the semi-final. It all added up to a worrying Wembley countdown. And next day Ferguson, back in full training, was sent home suffering from a heavy cold.

Meanwhile, Gullit was well advanced with his plans for next season. 'The FA Cup seems to get in the way sometimes. It is hard to get it right in one season, I am looking forward to the next one. It will make a big difference to have a pre-season to experiment with on tactical things. I have had to do that during this season and it is not the best solution.'

Gullit's emphatic declaration in his final programme notes: 'Whatever you might have read or heard, rest assured that I am more than happy to continue working for Newcastle United. Many, many thanks – and I'll see you here next season.'

He praised the players and went on: 'There are others I must thank, starting with Freddy Shepherd, Freddie Fletcher and the board, who have supported me in everything I have tried to do. Their ambition for this club is tremendously encouraging and it's a pleasure working with them. My staff have worked hard all season long and I thank them for their efforts.

'Below the level of the first team, the reserves finished champions of their Pontin's League Second Division as well as winning the Northumberland Senior Cup. The under-18s reached the semi-final of the FA Youth Cup, while the under-17s convincingly won their group in the Academy Youth League and also reached the semi-final of the National Championship play-offs. So there has been progress at every level of this football club and that's something many people can be proud of. Newcastle United has a bright future, in both the short and long terms.

'I firmly believe that we can come away from Wembley with the FA Cup next Saturday. We are playing a great team, one of the best in Europe, but I am confident that our players will rise to the occasion and produce a terrific performance. We have already qualified for a place in the UEFA Cup next season, of course, and that's something to look forward to, but we are determined to go into that European competition as the FA Cup winners and nothing would give me greater pleasure than to see thousands of smiling faces lining a Tyneside victory parade next Sunday. And that brings me to the fans, the super, super supporters of Newcastle United, who have been so patient and so loyal throughout a difficult season. As I've said many times, without their support we can do nothing. With it, everything is possible. What we all know for certain is that they will support us from first whistle to the last and millions throughout the world will undoubtedly marvel at their fantastic backing at Wembley. It's a pleasure and a privilege to work for a club which has such outstandingly loyal and understanding supporters.'

Despite another mundane offering, the players did their traditional lap of honour, and it was a typically enthusiastic send-off to Wembley. Shearer missed the 1-1 draw with Blackburn because of a slight ankle injury while Ferguson was not risked. Ketsbaia and Maric were paired in attack. Lee, restored as captain in the absence of Shearer, was also battling for a Wembley place.

Everyone was glad the League programme was now consigned to history. Six matches without a win since the semi-final was hardly the sort of form to take to Wembley. Despite one win in ten, Gullit said: 'I am not worried, I have still seen a lot of good things. I know what the team's true capabilities are, and I think we have a very good chance of winning.'

At last everyone was free to mention the F-word!

Kitted out in Giorgio Armani Cup final suits, the squad posed for a group picture the next day while Ruud inspected his sparkling light blue new club car, parked 'inconspicuously' right outside the door of reception for everyone to admire. Cruise Flannels sponsored the 'three-buttoned, single breasted jacket with flat-front trousers in mid grey wool crepe', according to Elaine Sullivan's press hand-out.

As we relaxed at the Chester-le-Street training headquarters, I was given half an hour in a one-to-one interview with Ruud, just as I did before his first Cup final appearance. His routine mirrored the build-up to the final two years earlier. This time it wasn't Middlesbrough, and his team were not favourites, but one of the biggest underdogs of all time. I suggested that outside of Tyneside, the whole nation didn't think it was worth Newcastle turning up. 'Good. Very good. Very, very good,' responded Gullit. 'I like that.' He laughed, and laughed.

Preliminary discussions had opened between Shepherd and Gullit's UK representative Jon Smith on extending his contract. With managers' salaries escalating as rapidly as star players', Gullit would have to be offered a three-year contract worth £5 million – on a par with Duncan Ferguson – particularly as he was being linked with a return to his old club Sampdoria, who had been relegated from Serie A. Gullit was concentrating on the preparations for Wembley, declining to consider his future until after the final. He had already pledged to stay next season. There was an option for a third year, but his decision would not be based on the season's final outcome but on family reasons, his first pre-season with his new team and the kind of progress made in the early stages of the Premiership. Gullit's ultimate aim was to qualify for the Champions' League to take on the domination of the Big Three – Manchester United, Arsenal and his old club Chelsea. Gullit observed: 'I am concentrated on the final, but there is no reason why I won't stay longer at Newcastle although football is so strange nowadays, you could be anywhere tomorrow. For those reasons, I do not make any suggestions about my future. I am more cautious.'

When Gullit won the Cup with Chelsea, his reward less than a year later was the sack. Now he was thriving on Tyneside, dispelling all the myths about being a playboy, part-time coach. Gullit no longer endured backstabbing about his hectic lifestyle. He lived out of a suitcase at a Quayside hotel and took the forty-minute flight to Amsterdam whenever he could.

He was focused on the final, but he also had plans for next season. 'I never thought we could reach a final at Newcastle, especially in the beginning with all the problems I had. It is a major achievement to win a European place for next season. Next year will be a difference, with a whole lot of things which are improving already. One of the main things I will concentrate on is not giving away sloppy goals.'

Ruud's Revolution would definitely include Shearer. 'He will be here next season, of course he will.' When I asked Gullit about his relationship with Shearer, he said: 'We have a relationship between a coach and a player – that's normal. I don't understand, all season I am asked about Alan Shearer. I am not asked about any other player in the same way. It is simple. I have the same relationship with Alan Shearer that I have with all the other players: I am the coach and he's a player.'

Gullit loves nothing better than a challenge, and this was the ultimate – the Gods versus the Mere Mortals. The FA Cup final was seen as little more than stage two of Manchester United's quest for an historic Treble. A stepping stone bordering on an inconvenience en route to the Nou Camp and the big one against Bayern Munich. Wembley, according to Alex Ferguson, would be such a nice day out that he wouldn't have to bother with his first-choice forward line, as he saved his key team for the Champions League final. Maybe not. Though Newcastle would certainly stand a better chance if their manager played himself!

There are always firm favourites, but this was viewed as a formality. The invincibles from Old Trafford against the no-hopers from St James's Park. It would rank among the greatest Cup upsets of all time if Gullit's side could shatter Manchester United's quest for the Treble in what was thought the simplest of all three stages.

The country still had trouble taking Manchester United to their hearts, still found it difficult to will Ferguson's side to beat even the Germans in the Barcelona final. But Gullit explained that Manchester United are extremely popular in his home country and throughout Europe, even if they are widely loathed in England. 'The whole of Europe would want Manchester United to win the Champions' League, they really do want it in Holland – and that's not because they are playing the Germans! There is so much sympathy in Holland and I am sure elsewhere for Manchester United because of the plane crash, because they try so hard to become European champions again, and because of the way they play their football is so much related to the Dutch mentality of the game. I suppose they are not popular in their own country because everyone hates them winning all the time. That is very small-minded. I can understand the people not wanting them to win everything, but they must respect what they have achieved. I admire Alex Ferguson and I respect his team's achievements.'

As well as myself, Ruud was interviewed by Sky TV and ITN, switching rooms at the nearby Durham County Cricket club. That evening he launched an auction at Eldon Garden in support of the people of Kosovo, organised by the chairman's wife. He intended to open the event, which kicked off at 8pm, auction the first item and go to dinner with myself, Jon Smith and his assistant Nicky, who travelled on the morning Heathrow flight and met up with their North East rep Roy Aitken. It was close to 11pm when we all arrived at Trattoria Uno in the Quayside. Ruud tucked into a double helping of chicken wings and showed off his new toy – the James Bond mobile phone with fax and computer organiser. He was the first to leave. 'I need my sleep,' he said. Mr Gadget was in an upbeat mood, the confidence growing.

Tuesday was a warm, sunny day in the North East for the FA-controlled media open day inside St James's Park. On three levels, the players and manager were interviewed by TV, radio and finally the written press. Training switched from Durham to St James's.

When asked about the fitness fears of Stam, a straight-faced Gullit said: 'I think Mr Ferguson is being a little bit clever. I expect Stam to be fit.' Shearer was asked his opinions on the influx of foreigners. 'I think it's good if we can get very, very high quality foreigners in here, but if you flood it then I think it can be to the detriment of the English game in the future. There are a lot of foreigners that aren't playing, which I think is very significant indeed. I think it could be a problem if we continue to get foreigners in who aren't going to play week in, week out. if it continues to happen then it definitely will become a problem.'

Over at Old Trafford Roy Keane emerged from a night in the police cells. Their press day was bound to be more lively! The United boozers' club was not too popular with the manager, although the players felt that a fleet of police cars screeching to a halt outside Harry's Bar to cart off the captain was out of proportion to the incident involving a couple of women and a champagne glass. 'Now,' said Ferguson, allowing himself a smile for the first time, 'does anyone want to talk to me about Wembley?' Keane retained the armband for the final.

But back at St James's, Shearer was clinical in his delivery, a past master of the media interview. He talked about the shame of facing a crestfallen city twelve months earlier after the defeat by Arsenal, admitting: 'We felt guilty when we went on a parade through the city the day after losing. Around 300,000 fans turned out and most clubs wouldn't have had that many if they'd won the Cup. It was embarrassing and now I want to be around when Newcastle win a trophy. I want to see this place lift off. We have a great rapport with our fans and it suits them to see that you are giving 100 per cent, sweating blood.

'A lot of people are not expecting us to win on Saturday. But our fans are. The reasons I came here were because it was my hometown club, because of Kevin Keegan and because I firmly believed that the club were going to win things. That third part has not happened yet, but we're not far away now. It's so close and so far. And that's the Newcastle story. It's the way it's been and now I hope it's about to change. Win or lose, our fans will lift the roof off. They deserve for us to win and there's an air about this place right now.'

Charvet had missed the last seven games with a knee ligament injury, but he declared himself fit to figure in central defence alongside Dabizas. The French defender had been at Wembley last season as a Chelsea player in the Coca-Cola Cup but did not play. 'Wembley is a beautiful place,' he said. 'My family will all be there and they will see Newcastle win. It is important for the fans that we do that. The atmosphere was electric when we beat Tottenham in the semi-final. You could feel Old Trafford move. The supporters here are different. They are just not like this at Chelsea.'

Ketsbaia, in contrast, had thrown down an eve of Cup final 'Play me or I'm off' ultimatum to Dalglish the year before. Now he was at it again. 'If I'm an important player here, then I want to stay here. But if I am not, I want to leave.'

More than two hours passed and Gullit conducted his final interview. He gave an insight into his philosophies and his methods when he recapped on how he managed to turn a season of transition into one offering some tangible reward. He conceded that some players inherited from Dalglish had been 'sceptical' of him. He didn't mention any names, but the list would have included Shearer, Lee, Speed and probably the UK-based players rather then the foreign contingent, which he was rapidly adding to. 'But then they see me for real. I am more a coach than a manager. I do not let that out of my hands. I do all the preparation, all the technical work, I do it all myself. When they know that, all of a sudden their attitudes changed.'

The players discovered a totally dedicated, committed and passionate football man. Not a fashion model, not a playboy, not doing pizza ads, but desperately wanting to repeat his success at Chelsea. Gullit also dispelled the notion that he had favourites and that his rotation system was some sort of whim based on personal preferences.

Tough decisions had to be made. 'I talk all the time to all the players. We have meetings, again all the time. I am always asking "what do you think about that?" Even when it concerns tactical work, I want people to take responsibility. I suppose that is very Dutch.

'But the day they walk out on to the pitch, I can scream all I want at Wembley but nobody will hear you. I want players to take responsibility themselves to change things if necessary, to ask questions for themselves about certain things. If you can't do it when I talk, then it has to be done the hard way – sit on the bench, have a shower and think about it! I want them to do exactly as I ask, not because of me but because I want to get the best out of you.'

He was talking specifically about Gary Speed. 'Now Gary is one of my best players.' The importance was to get the message across. Shearer was not treated any differently and came under the same Gullit edict – if you play to instructions and play well, you stay in the side.

Gullit said: 'Yes, Alan has also progressed a lot, done very well as captain, also worked very hard, even though he didn't always get the right response from the press, and that was probably because they thought he wasn't scoring enough goals at the time. But that was because he needed to play with a target man, and that was not really fair on him.

'I am not afraid to make decisions. If somebody is not good enough, if he is a bad player because his attitude is not right, than I have to make decisions, and I do that. That has been done and the team plays well, everybody's nose is pointing in the same direction.'

Speed and Hamann were among the key players who had conformed and improved. Gullit said: 'Yes, there are certain players you have arguments with because you know they can play better and to persuade them to do it is the most difficult part, particularly when a player has been doing something for years and years. Gary is a good professional, he is always early for training, out there preparing, and has become better than he was – and that is his own achievement, not mine. It is something they had in them in the first place. I just had to motivate. He always thought, I must get into the box. But when? It is all about timing, the right position is everything. First you have to do a certain job for the team, everyone in every position has to do that for the team. The extra comes when you have a good shape.'

Gullit's conclusion was typically forthright. 'If you are successful everybody likes you; if you are not successful . . . I'm not here to be liked or not liked. You have to do certain things to be successful. Those players in the team, you never hear moan. Those who don't play moan. The press go to the ones who moan. I know the name of the game, I know how it goes.'

He was also busy concluding £10 million deals for Marcelino and

Goma. Goma was on Tyneside for talks. Harper signed a new three-year deal as the axed Shay Given pencilled in post-Wembley talks with Gullit.

And so Gullit led his team into the final feeling victory was possible. He insisted: 'Yes, we have a very good chance of winning it. The vibes are going through the club, and already you see it with the players that miraculously all twenty-two are fit. The concentration is incredible, and we have already showed that we are not scared of Manchester United when we played them this season.'

Gullit is synonymous with achievement, but he refuses to assess his career until it is over. At times he would like to play – and he would once again put on the boots that made him World Footballer of the Year for Jurgen Klinsmann's farewell game in Stuttgart on Monday night. 'Some moments I wish I could still play, but I know I couldn't last ten minutes! I know I take care of my body, I don't drink or smoke, and sometimes participation in training matches goes easy – but not with strength or power anymore, and it is something you miss.' All his medals are packed away in boxes, apart from a few of the more precious ones in a small display unit in the Amsterdam apartment he shares with Estelle and baby Joelle. The Chelsea FA Cup final medal is one of those, alongside European Cup and European Championship medals.

Winning the Cup wouldn't be the end of Newcastle's quest – but maybe the beginning, kick-starting the team toward much bigger goals?

On the night before the final rumours swept the North East that Duncan Ferguson would not travel with the official party, had been booked into hospital for an operation on Monday, was out of the final and would fly down on the morning of the game with one of the young players. In fact, he did travel with the squad.

But Ferguson's struggle for fitness did not avail Newcastle or Gullit as once again their final was a massive anti-climax. An apology to his chairman, a handshake with Ken Bates and a wave goodbye to the cheering fans. It was a day of mixed emotions for Ruud.

The pride of leading out the team, the bitterness of defeat. He was convinced he could win. But the team were a big disappointment. When I saw him after the game, he smiled and said: 'Wrong prediction.' I had tipped Newcastle for the Cup before he arrived and told him in January he would win the Cup. Well . . . Ruud's crucifix and powers of motivation had guided Newcastle to the final, rather than a decent team. That was the reality. Now came the tough part, to build that decent team.

Gullit had already signed two more players and was searching for more. With his defence in such disarray at Wembley, the first two summer acquisitions were to be centre-halves. To have won, his team needed to be committed throughout in the tackle – not just the first ten minutes – be solid at the back and ride their luck.

A fully fit Ferguson who came off the bench for the start of the second half, and Steve Howey tightening up the defence might have made a difference. But there had been no possibility of his starting. 'I knew he would not last two halves, it was not even an issue.' But Gullit painted a frightening picture for those clubs like Newcastle with ambitions to try to close the chasm between them and Manchester United and the rest. He observed: 'Manchester United could spend £30 million or £40 million to get the players they want. We can't do that. They can buy exactly what they need, even those players who cost a lot of money. That has got to be easier than going for different players, perhaps not the ones you really would want, but who can still do a better job than the ones you have.' Not a problem peculiar to Gullit. If anything, St James's Park is expanding as rapidly as Old Trafford, and Newcastle too possess a dedicated, massive fan base, and have invested heavily in the team. Yet no one can match Manchester United's spending power.

United fans took it for granted that one of the first to leave in the summer would be Dabizas, badly at fault for Scholes' killer goal. Said Dabizas: 'I will talk about my future with the manager and the board. I want the manager to tell me to my face that he has already brought in two new central defenders. I don't want to stay here and be fourth choice.'

There was a welcome fit for heroes on Tyneside on Sunday but once again no trophy to show off. It was enough to make Shearer weep.

Tens of thousands of loyal Toon Army fans jammed roads, pavements and bridges to catch a glimpse of the team as they travelled through the city on an open-top bus.

Had they won, hundreds of thousands were expected to jam the route from the Gosforth Park Hotel to Newcastle Civic Centre. As it was, estimates put the crowd at well under that figure. Still, the four-mile route was a sea of black and white as flags and banners hung from windows and balconies. The bus crawled along at a couple of miles an hour with its mounted escort. Despite losing, the fans still found their voices to give the players their backing. Some supporters managed to make their way to the start of the procession before following the bus along the route into the centre of the city, where a civic reception took place at 7pm.

Popular spots along the route were the Three Mile Inn at Gosforth and the nearby High Street. Many families arrived on the Great North Road as early as mid-day to make sure they had a good spot. Northumbria Police maintained a large presence to make sure there was no repeat of the trouble which had broken out in the city on Saturday afternoon after the final whistle. Police had made fifty-seven arrests after 500 fans went on a drink-fuelled rampage in the city's famous Bigg Market.

On a blustery Sunday, around 6,000 fans gathered at the civic centre where the parade was due to end. Black and white scarves, hats, flags and wigs were given their final airing of the season. Ian Gilmore, secretary of the Independent Supporters' Club, said: 'I am not surprised at the turnout. A lot of them will be those who could not get tickets, it's their way of saying thank you. We did our best but were beaten by a better side, for the second year running. I just hope we can reach those heights as well.'

John Regan from the Independent Newcastle United Supporters' Association was more pleased with the team's performance this year, but chose not to join in with the homecoming because the thought of watching another losers' parade was just too much to bear. 'Although I've supported Newcastle all my life and I'm proud of my team's achievements I just couldn't bring myself to attend another losers' parade. I think Alan Shearer summed it up for me after the final whistle when he said losers' medals mean nothing – and he's right. We've now got to take stock and look forward to next season, but I genuinely believe that Ruud Gullit is the man to take Newcastle United to glory. We need someone with a bit of sparkle in midfield to create chances for Alan Shearer. The service he got on Saturday was almost nonexistent. You can't score goals out of nothing and if Shearer doesn't get the ball then he can't be expected to score. But I firmly believe he's still the best striker in Europe and we need to create more chances for him.'

As the bus left the Gosforth Hotel for the civic reception the players' mood was sombre, showing obvious disappointment at having let down their fans. But Regan concluded: 'When Gullit went through the tunnel at the end of the game, the Newcastle fans to a man were chanting "Ruud Gullit's black and white army". He's got the backing of the supporters. We believe he's the best man for the job and can get us to where we want to be.'

13

The final showdown

Ruud Gullit was not happy with Alan Shearer's Cup final performance. In fact he was privately aggrieved. Bitterly disappointed. Shocked.

Those close to Gullit were told what he had thought of the England captain's Wembley display. Gullit trusted those in his inner sanctum implicitly to keep his private thoughts and observations strictly confidential, never to be made public. However they did impart to me how the coach felt towards the man he appointed captain.

When the going got tough against Manchester United at Wembley, particularly after the first goal, Gullit looked to Shearer to be the leader, the fighting spirit that everyone believed in. Instead Gullit felt that Shearer's head had gone down even before some of the rest of the team. The quality of leadership that Gullit sought in Shearer was not there. In fact there was a moment during the FA Cup final when Gullit turned to his coaching staff beside him on the Wembley bench. 'Look at Shearer,' implored the Newcastle coach. Gullit and his staff watched. From Gullit's perspective he didn't like what he was seeing. There was Shearer, hands on hips, static, just watching, and doing little or nothing for the half-minute they all concentrated on the England captain.

Had Gullit had the squad of players he desired from the start, had it been the kind of lavish squad he enjoyed at Chelsea where he was criticised for his rotation system, and had there been a Tore Andre Flo or a Luca Vialli on the bench, then Shearer would have been substituted in the Cup final. Gullit felt that Shearer was a disgrace. He believed that a player of his stature and earning his level of salary, ought to be an example to the younger players and the rest of the team.

Gullit had recognised Shearer's waning inspirational qualities as a result of the deficiencies in his game shortly after arriving at the club. Gullit would have left Shearer out at some stage during the season had there been an alternative. Unfortunately Ferguson was at first ill and then injured, Andersson was patently not up to standard and at times an utter disappointment, Ketsbaia erratic or injured and Paul Dalglish had been given his chance. Gullit looked at all the options, but there was never a satisfactory time to leave Shearer out. It had to be the right time. The Newcastle manager had thought about it on numerous occasions, but the opportunity had not arisen. It had to be right because Gullit knew what the consequences would be only too well. The backlash would be immense. The effects on the club traumatic. The debate endless.

He pondered the repercussions . . . foreign coach versus the national team captain. The whole issue of the purchasing policy in buying foreign players and displacing English ones, of the foreign-English divide within the dressing room would come to a head. It would not be a simple selection. Drop Shearer, and everyone would auto-matically accept there was a split within the camp, even though they might think Shearer no longer deserved an automatic place in the side. These aspects all had to be taken into consideration and it annoyed Gullit. He knew it was right to select a player in relation to his performance, but in Shearer's case the issue was far more profound.

Gullit felt there was a fixation on Shearer. He had become a special case, even though Gullit had set out to ensure that he would not be a special case. On the training ground, Gullit's policy was not to pick out the young players like Griffin, Aaron Hughes or David Beharall for critical analysis. That was far too easy. Gullit would point his finger at the more senior players. One such training ground discussion had hit the headlines as a confrontation between Gullit and Shearer. Newcastle's manager had said he was worried that there were too many players being selfish at the club. Apparently Shearer was the first to react, and did so instantly. Maybe he felt, as captain, it was his responsibility to respond to such a serious charge on behalf of other players as well as himself. However Gullit was intrigued that Shearer spoke up so quickly.

As for the perception that Gullit did not have support within a dressing room completely united behind Shearer, that too was another myth. There was growing resentment against Shearer initially among a small sector of the players. Gullit would receive calls from team-members brave enough to express their dissatisfaction with Shearer. They were honest enough to put forward the opinion that Shearer was no longer pulling his weight, that he had lost his form, and that there might not be as great an objection as one might suspect if the coach were to omit the England captain from the team.

The Cup final only served to strengthen and renew Gullit's doubts about Shearer. And it might also have reinforced some of the players' views that Shearer was no longer indispensable. But Gullit and the club knew that there would not be an acceptable offer for Shearer until the striker began to hit a rich vein of form. Paradoxically, this was the time to sell him. The coach knew that Shearer was not the Shearer of three or four years previously, and even if he was, Gullit had never been convinced of the striker's style of play. However, if Shearer resumed his goalscoring form, it would be far more complex to convince the fans it was the right course of action to sell him. But it was only going to be the right time to sell, when Shearer's form merited a big enough fee to make the parting at least acceptable in financial terms.

14

Shearer signs new five-year contract

Ruud Gullit embarked on a whirlwind of summer changes, determined to relaunch Newcastle United as a major force in the Premiership and in Europe. The one time World Footballer of the Year even made his debut in a Newcastle shirt in a pre-season friendly at Reading, coming on as a second half substitute. In his favoured sweeper's role he helped a virtual reserve side haul themselves back from two down for a draw watched by 4,500 Geordie fans in the crowd of 17,000. Gullit planned only the occasional outing, as he purchased a new defence and three centre backs in Elena Sierra Marcelino from Real Mallorca, Alain Goma from Paris Saint-Germain and Franck Dumas from Monaco. His key signing at Chelsea had been Frank Leboeuf as sweeper, the system closest to his Dutch ideology. Marcelino was outstanding against Chelsea in the European Cup Winners' Cup semi-finals when his team surprisingly went on to the final where they lost to Lazio. The 6ft 2in, 13-stone Gijon-born defender didn't make his league debut until twenty-two and was first picked for Spain last November at the age of twenty-seven. He moved from Sporting Gijon to Real Mallorca in 1996 for £200,000 and had been the rock in the club's rise in the Primera Liga.

But for Desailly, Blanc and Leboeuf, the talented Goma would have won more than his two caps. His £4.75m move to Newcastle on a five-year contract reunited him with Domi. He played largely as a right back with Auxerre before switching to centre back after his move to PSG in 1998. The twenty-six-year-old rejected Spurs because of his admiration for Gullit. 'Ruud's attitude is right. He talked about discipline, motivation and the importance of hard work, which is what I wanted to hear. He inspired players in the past because of who he was, but I believe his attitude and commitments inspire players now.'

True to his word, Gullit worked his players hard in his first pre-season training, and was not too despondent about losing all three games in Scotland, culminating with Kenny's Revenge at Celtic where John Barnes was in the opposite dug-out.

The team had been completely overhauled. Out went Dietmar Hamann. There was first an abortive £7 million bid by Arsenal, and then one for £7.2 million from Aston Villa. The German's outspoken views about wanting to go to Highbury earned him a two-week fine, before he was eventually sold off to Liverpool for £8 million.

In came Young England star Kieron Dyer for £7 million, Newcastle beating off West Ham, Middlesbrough and Leeds to win his signature. Gullit moved for Dutchman George Boateng, his offer of £3 million being turned down; subsequently he signed for Aston Villa for £4.4 million. Gullit was also linked with moves for Louis Enrique of Barcelona. But he landed the Ipswich kid. Gullit said: 'Kieron's a promising boy who can only become better and better.'

George Georgiadis headed for PAOK for £1 million, insisting: 'I've got no choice. I'm wasting my time at Newcastle because I'm not even getting a place on the substitutes' bench. I wouldn't mind if I played and performed badly, but I was never given a chance by the manager.' Philippe Albert signed for Charleroi for £600,000, while Stuart Pearce joined West Ham on a 'free'. Robert Lee's squad number went to Dyer.

Shearer signed a new five-year contract to tie him to St James's Park for the rest of his career. It was suggested there was a clause that he would eventually become the new manager but he says: 'I want to move into management one day but that can wait. I would prefer it to be at the end of my playing career. Some of the reports quite surprised me – you would have thought my move into management was imminent. Nothing could be further from the truth. Ruud Gullit could be manager here for years.'

Youth trainee Anthony Parry, seventeen, was sacked by the club after failing a drug test and becoming addicted to heroin. Gullit said: 'The club dealt with it very well. They did everything in their power for the boy but there is a limit. We can't blame anything on the club. It's all in his hands, we did our best to help him.' According to the FA, Parry admitted his heroin addiction after traces of morphine were found in his blood during the random test. He was immediately given treatment and counselling by both the FA and Newcastle staff; there were hopes he would be able to rescue his career but the club opted to release him.

Duncan Ferguson had an operation in Bradford on the Monday after the FA Cup final. Mesh in the groin had not held, the problem diagnosed two months before the final. Now he hoped this would be the final operation.

Gullit said: 'My message to the fans of Newcastle United is not to be sad. I want them to be optimistic about the future of their club because I certainly am.'

The pre-season Gullit craved to prepare his team the way he wanted had not gone well, notably the resounding defeat at Celtic, but he never saw the calamitous start coming. In fact, if anything he was full of optimism. Worried by the glut of injuries, but confident that he had a large enough squad and some promising youngsters to cover for every eventuality. His main concern was how the forward line would function with Shearer leading the attack and Ferguson still injured. Gullit's opening programme notes for the first Premiership game with Aston Villa were confident. If there were any niggling doubts, they were kept strictly private. 'We have worked very, very hard in the last few weeks to get ourselves as well prepared as possible for a demanding season ahead and I'm happy with what I've seen from the players. Pre-season preparation is about physical conditioning, but there are always going to be ups and downs and whilst it's disappointing to pick up injuries you know that they are something you have to accept and there have certainly been more ups than downs on the training pitches and in the warm-up games.

'Everybody talks about Duncan Ferguson missing the start of the season, but the programme we have set him will strengthen certain parts of his body that have needed strengthening for some years and I have every confidence that when he is fully fit here he will be fitter than he has ever been.

'The results of the nine games we have played have been unimportant. What's pleased me is the encouraging signs I have seen during those games. Of course, there have been things I didn't want to see, but when they are so apparent you can work on eradicating them and overall a busy and demanding schedule has told me much about my squad. Travelling so much has brought the players together and given the newly-signed players many opportunities to settle in with their new colleagues.

'Some of our youngster players, the likes of Paul Robinson, Jamie McClen, James Coppinger and Brian Kerr, have also done well and it's been a pleasure to see how well how they are progressing. So now it's time to run the preparation into match again and we are all conscious of the fact that our fans expect us to do better this season than last.

'As I said when I took this job at the end of August last year that the one thing I regretted was not taking the squad through the pre-season training and games. I've done that this time and I'm looking forward to seeing the players of Newcastle United doing better for fans who supported us so well even when we disappointed them last season. We can do better, we all know that. Even if we'd finished in the top three last time round we would set out to finish first or second. But we didn't finish third, we finished thirteenth and that gives us a lot of room for improvement.'

Shearer seemed to be singing from the same Gullit song sheet, at the outset at least, although the pair of them were not on first, even second name terms. No mention for Shearer in Gullit's opening address to the fans, and in Shearer's 'Captain's Corner' programme notes he never mentioned Gullit by name even though he did, at least, mention 'the manager'.

Shearer, though, said he felt settled: 'I have been more than happy to commit myself to this great club for the next five years and that means, with my twenty-ninth birthday just a few days away, that I do not contemplate kicking a ball for any other club. I have signed a new contract not simply because I'm a Geordie and this is the club I have loved for as long as I can remember. I said when I came here three years ago that I believed that it could be as big as any club in the land, I believed that I could win trophies here. I still believe those things and I desperately want to get my hands on some silverware because the fans here deserve nothing less.'

Shearer felt in peak condition. There could be no excuses later!

He was in harmony with Gullit as he spelled out what was required for the new season. 'Must do better. That's what the fans of Newcastle United are expecting from the players this season and that's as it should be. We finished thirteenth last season, the same position as the year before, and that is not acceptable for a club of this size and ambition. There were times last time round when we seemed to be getting it right, but we lacked consistency and came up with sloppy results just when our fans, whose backing never wavered, were starting to believe that we had really turned the corner. It was all so deeply disappointing, especially the way we finished the season after beating Tottenham in the FA Cup semi-final at Old Trafford. Between then and the final we had six Premier League games to play and I honestly believed that we could win them all and finish our Premier League campaign in the top six or seven. But we won none of them and then came away from Wembley without the FA Cup for the second year in a row. Expectations were so high, but the achievement was simply not there and as we face our first game of this season every player here has to be aware that our supporters deserve better.'

The shaky relationship between Gullit and Shearer was well below the surface for the outset of a new season, but it was always likely to force its way back to the top.

15

Worst start in the club's history

Ruud Gullit had wanted his first summer to build the squad of his choice. He was not able to do it. Much has been made of the collapse of the takeover by the American based media company NTL and of Gullit's frustrations of having insufficient funds to purchase the players he really wanted. But it wasn't simply lack of funds. Gullit's real headache was getting rid of the dead wood at the club to raise the funds for new players. Many of the players he inherited from Kenny Dalglish simply refused to leave. Equally, the club couldn't sustain a wage bill that was continually escalating as Gullit brought in more players without being able to sell those already there that he did not want.

For Gullit this was the insoluble problem at St James's Park. It was a cancer that he could see was slowly but surely eating away at the club. There were some players that Gullit wanted, but either the transfer fees were prohibitive at a time when Newcastle didn't have the cash flow available to make the purchase, or the players were asking ridiculous amounts in salaries. Salaries of £40,000 a week would not be uncommon to compensate a player for moving to the North-East when he might prefer London.

Gullit would not blame a board that was so supportive for going ahead with those deals. If anything he supported them on such decisions. The board did everything they could to bring in the players Gullit wanted but the Dutchman accepted there had to be reasonable financial limits. One player from Juventus in particular wanted a mind-boggling salary, and although Gullit wanted the player he accepted it did not make economic sense to go through with the financial package. Gullit had nothing but praise for Shepherd and Fletcher for the way they backed him and stood by him. When they hugged Gullit before he got into his car as he sped away from St James's Park the day he announced his resignation it was evidence enough of their mutual affection.

Gullit had to make assessments on many players and some of those decisions were unpalatable for the fans. There were a number of players he wanted to sell, but he had discovered several highly paid players were unwilling to accept a downward move for lower wages. There were players whose egos told them they belonged in the Premiership, but according to the coach's view were ready for the First Division. They were being paid too much and the club was suffering because they would not leave for less money.

Stuart Pearce, the former England defender, was one of those players on exceptionally high wages, and Gullit felt it was time for him, at the age of thirty-eight, to move on. Gullit found that Pearce was always a player he could rely on, but he was regrettably now too old. But he had no complaints about Pearce's attitude, application and professionalism. Pearce set a wonderful example for Gullit to the younger players, and his attitude contrasted with that of players such as Alessandro Pistone and Philippe Albert who were reluctant even to consider a drop in their exorbitant salaries.

Albert warned the Newcastle boss he must face the consequences if his Tyneside shake-up didn't work. Albert, now back in Belgium with his first club Charleroi, insisted: 'Gullit has brought in his own players and I really hope it works for the sake of the club and the fans, who deserve better. But the highest I can see Newcastle finishing in the Premier League is eighth. And if the changes Gullit have made don't work, he'll have to pay the consequences.'

Albert, a £2.65 million Kevin Keegan signing five years before, felt there might have been too many changes at Newcastle, with some players ditched too early. 'Gullit told me I wasn't in his plans and that put me in a similar situation to Alessandro Pistone, Stuart Pearce and Robert Lee. I knew my Newcastle career was over last season when I went on loan to Fulham for three months. I was very disappointed. I won't let the last four or five months take away what happened in my first four years. Newcastle will always be very special to me. I gave the club five years of my life and that's a big part of a footballer's career. I've got so many great memories, but I had to go.'

But not even the departure of the once-popular Albert seemed to rile the locals as much as the ostracising of Robert Lee. No one quibbled when Gullit wanted to sell Pistone, but there was a huge uproar when he made Lee available. The deposed captain had been an England World Cup star just over a year before, but he no longer existed so far as Gullit was concerned! The thirty-three-year-old midfielder, regularly described by his former manager Keegan as his best ever value-for-money signing, had suffered the ultimate snub when Gullit declined to hand him a squad number for the new season, giving the number instead to £6 million signing Kieron Dyer. The same applied to Des Hamilton and Alessandro Pistone, who failed – spectacularly in the case of Pistone, a former Italy Under-21 international – to achieve at St James's Park. But Lee, the club's second-longest serving player, a seven-year veteran and a rare remnant of the Keegan era, was another case. The closest confidant of Shearer said: 'I am stunned and I am hurt, but I will not be pushed out of this club.' Lee had signed a three-year extension to his contract only twelve months before, yet he had learnt of his fate not through talks with Gullit, but in a brief telephone conversation with Graham Courtney, the club's press officer. By that stage, the news had already been leaked to the media.

Yet Lee was a perfect example for Gullit of the kind of player who would only leave on his own terms. No one can blame Lee, who had every right to hold out for the right move. But Gullit's argument is that when Lee was made available for transfer there was hardly a rush of Premiership clubs that wanted him and only Wolves were ready to make an acceptable offer.

From Gullit's perspective, the reasoning was obvious. He had a number of players that he wished to sell. For much of the last season, he had denigrated his inherited 'relegation team' and one of its members, Stuart Pearce, had already joined West Ham. Alessandro Pistone, who became one of the most expensive defenders in the world when Dalglish paid Inter Milan £4.5 million, damaged knee ligaments during a run-out against Hartlepool. Misfit Andreas Andersson, the Swedish international, one of a host of players frozen out by Gullit, went on loan with a view to a permanent £2 million move to Spanish club Santander. Andersson had cost Kenny Dalglish £3.5 million from AC Milan. Gullit was desperate to offload a group of players whose total weekly wage bill amounted to a cool £60,000.

Nevertheless optimism was running high at the start of a new season, only to collapse with the opening game defeat by Villa at St James's Park with Shearer sent off and Gullit in a rage with the ref. Next stop a 3-1 defeat at White Hart Lane on Monday, where Gullit blamed his players, and the completion of a calamitous week with defeat at Southampton, perennial relegation fighters. Gullit was on the brink after Newcastle's worst start in forty years.

The fans had chanted his name when he arrived, wore dreadlocked wigs in his honour, and never imagined the amazing events of his first year in charge. It was a big enough shock when Dalglish was sacked and Gullit appointed all in one incredible day after just two games of the previous season. Yet, just three games into the new season and the debate centred on whether Gullit would quit.

Headlines roared from every newspaper, radio and TV bulletin about Gullit's future. Gullit's Sky TV interview at the Dell sparked the possibility he would go, when he suggested he might not see out the week. Gullit thought that with three defeats the club might sack him, but instead they backed him and he never intended to walk away from the challenge.

As the debate raged, Gullit spoke to me about the truth of his position at the club, the depth of his affection for the fans, and his determination to see the challenge through. The defeat at Southampton still burning, Gullit had a quiet meal in a Chinese restaurant with a couple of friends and thought long and hard about his future. His conclusion was that he would not walk. In fact, he was more determined than ever to transform the fortunes of the Tyneside club. 'The most frustrating issue is that there is potential in this Newcastle team. I can see it and I'll do everything in my power to show that it exists and that I can change things around. Yes, we have had a bad spell, but when we get a win everything will be different. The whole mood will change. Right now there is real tension here and I can take that. It is normal in a high-profile job. I have been disappointed by what has happened. It would be strange if I didn't react in those circumstances. After all, I'm only human. If I didn't care, I would walk away from all this. But I do care and I believe I can come through it all.'

There was a limit to his patience; girlfriend Estelle and their eighteen-month-old daughter Joelle held the key to how far he was prepared to go. 'When the family needs me desperately I will have to go away to see to them. Under those circumstances I will be there for them. They come first. I have my family's support and that is more important than anything else. I also have the support of the club and that, too, is important.

'Of course what is happening is hurting Estelle, and that hurts me. But Estelle is backing me, and certainly not insisting I come home.

Estelle has, in fact, been very understanding. She says that I must give this club a chance. She knows, as I do, that there is huge potential here. But although she wants me to succeed at Newcastle I cannot stand by and let the family suffer at all. If that happens I will have to make a decision. And if my family needs me I will always put them first.'

There was much talk of a Gullit comeback on the field. 'I won't play again unless the board tell me they want me to play. Maybe then I would consider it or if the team needs me.' Despite all his problems, Gullit was resolutely upbeat. 'I'm okay. Yes, I felt very disappointed after the Southampton game, as I am sure everyone saw. I didn't want to make any comment. We're not bad, but it's up to us to prove it.'

He was also at pains to clear up the confusion over whether he had offered to resign: 'I did not offer to resign. When I was asked, "Are you going to be there for the next game?" I said I didn't know. Why? Because it is normal for the board to think about sacking a coach that loses the first three games, so I didn't know what was happening. If that is what they had wanted, there was nothing I could do. But they have said they want me to carry on and I want to stay. So resignation is not an issue.'

But after a week of intense speculation about his future, and his private life, Gullit was cheered by the fans from the start of the match with Wimbledon and in his programme notes that day, he made it clear: 'I absolutely believe that I can be successful as the manager of Newcastle United. We need a win to restore confidence and we need that win as soon as possible. Nobody wants to get it right more than me, my staff and the players. We know what's expected of us. I can live with the weight of expectation because I know that we are better, much better, than we have shown so far.'

He clarified the position on dressing room splits, unrest, and personality clashes. 'Millions of words have been used in recent days to describe the situation at Newcastle United after our three defeats in eight days. Many of those words have been inaccurate and consequently wounding in a personal sense.

'So our problems began early and they piled up at Spurs and Southampton. Our critics had a field day and I'm perfectly happy to take constructive criticism on the chin. I've played and managed in the spotlight for many, many years and I have always been prepared to be judged on my football and coaching abilities. But the personal stuff is something else and I certainly feel that having my personal life placed under the microscope is an unfair invasion of my privacy.

'But nothing that has happened has shaken my belief that we can emerge from all the traumas and become the winning team the supporters of this club very much deserve. The loyal backing of those fans has been heartwarming and it's for them that all of us here want to get back to winning ways as soon as possible. But it's a fact that we can't expect to be at our most effective until we have more of our first team squad available. When we have then you will see a different Newcastle United.'

Gullit accepted that the team played 'badly' in the opening three games. 'We were the better side against Aston Villa until the dismissal of Alan Shearer. We dominated at Tottenham and deservedly went ahead and we were excellent in the first half against Southampton. But at White Hart Lane and the Dell we caused problems for ourselves by conceding goals far too easily and of course I am definitely not happy about the way we caved in after taking the lead. They are the disappointing, negative aspects of our opening games, but there were encouraging things, too, in the early stages of both those matches and while I fully accept that playing well in patches is not good enough at any level I much prefer to take a positive attitude.'

Kevin Keegan fully appreciated the problems which Gullit faced and the weight of expectation on the Dutchman's shoulders. 'I've sympathy for Ruud,' admitted Keegan. 'I've sympathy for any manager. We've got a sort of bond because we don't like to see any of our number coming under pressure. But with Newcastle it is a massive club and people like talking about it. It's been a very open club and it was like it when I was there.' Despite three successive defeats in Gullit's first full season in charge the fans still backed him; his name echoed around St James's Park in response to the days of intense speculation about Gullit's future.

Gullit eventually won the first point of the season against Wimbledon at St James's Park, but only after throwing away first a 2-0 lead then a 3-1 lead to draw 3-3. Gullit pinpointed the problem; the team were playing delightful football at times, but then just fell apart.

In the middle of it all was one of the most amazing confrontations in Newcastle United's history. The England captain in one corner and the former World Footballer of the Year in the other. A battle of two of the highest profile football personalities in the world.

Gullit's first twelve months on Tyneside had been equivalent to a lifetime in many managers' careers: the complete overhaul and dismantling of Dalglish's era, and during such a radical transitional period Gullit still managed to get Newcastle back into Europe and to the FA Cup final. Under normal circumstances the rejuvenation of Newcastle United would have been tough enough, but there was also the constant debate about the future of the England captain.

Speculation had persisted virtually non-stop from the moment Gullit arrived that Shearer would go. It only subsided with Gullit's decision to make him captain, and the suspicion there were no serious buyers at the price Newcastle would demand! The new season brought no new dawn, but instead even darker images of a feud between manager and skipper sure to undermine confidence within the dressing room and throughout the club.

Gullit needed a turnaround in results to pull the season together. First he had blamed referee Uriah Rennie for the Shearer sending off, then blamed his players for the debacle at Tottenham after going into the lead, and then issued an apology to clarify the position that he blamed himself for whatever was going wrong rather than the players.

Shearer's contribution had been a red card against Villa, a penalty in the 4-2 defeat at Southampton – again after Newcastle took the lead and then collapsed – and a one-match ban when Gullit got his attack into gear with three goals against Wimbledon. Yet no one in the country believed that when he completed his ban he would fail to walk straight back in the team, particularly as Kevin Keegan announced his first England squad of the new season the very next day. 'Inconceivable.' That was the word from Tyneside, inconceivable that Shearer would be left out of the Tyne-Wear derby with Sunderland at St James's Park.

If there was a test of wills, Gullit would show who was boss. But it would be a huge gamble at such a critical time. If Gullit got it right then he would be the hero. Otherwise the danger was that it would backfire on him big time.

16

Shearer dropped for the first time in his career

Successive matches at St James's Park, and they just simply had to be won for Gullit to survive. Yet for someone under so much personal pressure he had been in an upbeat mood for the first – without Shearer. Gullit had waited for this chance to prove his attack could function better without Shearer than with him. Were he to be proved right against Wimbledon, then Gullit had already made plans to leave Shearer on the bench for the Sunderland derby. Frustratingly, although Gullit's attack had scored three times, the defence conceded the same amount. Gullit couldn't quite believe that at 2-0 and then 3-1, holding winning hands, his team had again collapsed. Privately he once more thought he was cursed!

For public consumption, he explained what had gone wrong: 'In my own mind I am convinced that we definitely would have won our first game of the season if Alain Goma had not been forced to leave the field with an injury. His height and strength was a key factor against Wimbledon's big guys and there's no team better at bombarding you with high balls and giving you problems with their strength in the air than the one we played on Saturday. I give them the credit they deserve for battling back when all seemed lost, but I still get a good feeling from a game which ultimately ended so disappointingly. We did some things wrong, but we also did a lot of things right and if we can create the same number of chances every game we'll win a lot more than we lose.'

Gullit gave his first hint of the impending decision to leave out

Shearer when he talked about Robinson and the movement the attack had with the youngster rather than Shearer. 'Our movement, especially in the first half, was excellent. We were very creative and I was delighted with the part young Paul Robinson played on his debut in the Premiership. He was excellent and for a twenty-year-old with so very little experience at this level he came in and did very well indeed up front against those big Wimbledon defenders. So did Jamie McClen in midfield. He, too, played his part in an overall team performance I firmly believes bodes well for both the short-term and long-term future of this football club.'

While the opinion polls in the North-East continued to back Gullit, the crunch time had arrived. Estelle, the niece of seventies Dutch soccer megastar Johan Cruyff, had never taken to the area, and her preference to stay in Amsterdam had not exactly gone down well. Yet the city still took to a man who preferred the cappuccino café society to the working men's clubs and Newcastle brown ale. They accepted his Armani suits, Gucci loafers with no socks and fashionable leather jackets. Ruud, in fact, enjoyed the Quayside lifestyle, the relaxed atmosphere of the up-market restaurants, and made many new friends in the region. Even so, after spending much of the week in the smart Mal Maison hotel on the Quayside, he would take every opportunity to return to Estelle and Joelle in Amsterdam. But it was hardly a long journey; it was as easy as a plane journey to London. But the intrusions into his private life were reaching an intolerable level and he made it plain that once it affected his family he would know it was time to leave. There was one last chance. The derby.

Gullit knew the Tyne-Wear derby was make or break. 'Believe me, we know how important this game is. We understand how much local pride is at stake. I've played in derby games in Italy, for AC Milan and Sampdoria, so I know how passionate and committed fans are on a night like this. It's a night for big hearts, of course, and we will not be found wanting in that respect. But I also want my players to play with their heads.' More clues about Shearer being left on the bench when Gullit added: 'It is not about Ruud Gullit but about the team and most of all about Newcastle United.'

Overall Gullit was still convinced there would be a turnaround in fortunes. He said: 'Our start has been very difficult, but our focus is very much on building a better team and a brighter future for fans whose support and knowledge is just terrific. We had a bonus on Saturday with Duncan Ferguson playing for the last half hour or so and he showed us what we already knew, that when he is fully match fit he will give us new dimensions. The kids who stepped in did us proud, the fans did us proud and that's why I refuse to be downhearted at drawing a match we clearly should have won. I understand the frustrations and I understand why everybody looks at this game against Newcastle's closest rivals as such a massive one.'

Behind the scenes Gullit had spoken to key members of the board. The manager had full boardroom backing to take one of the most controversial and momentous decisions on Tyneside, to leave out the England captain.

Mirror readers woke up on the day with a massive hint that Gullit was about to leave Shearer out. In my discussions with Ruud, I got the clear indication that was exactly what he would do. It was strictly a footballing decision. Gullit no longer had faith that Shearer was the right man to lead the attack. A youngster like Robinson was a better bet. Eager, youthful, mobile, Robinson would at least contribute to the game even if he didn't score.

Even though my paper carried the back page story that Shearer might be left out, while every other paper reported 'peace in our time' after press conferences with both Gullit and Shearer, there was still an element of doubt throughout the country. No one really believed, even if Gullit was thinking about it, that he would have the nerve to go through with it. When the team sheet was handed around an hour before the kick off without Shearer's name in the starting line up, there was still complete amazement. One journalist described the team sheet as Gullit's suicide note.

17

Resignation

Ruud Gullit knew from the moment he decided to drop Alan Shearer that it was inevitable the England captain would knock on his door to demand an explanation. Gullit was not to be proved wrong. He knew precisely what he would tell him. He had been thinking about that day for many months.

And the day after Shearer was dropped, came the moment. Gullit will not divulge the contents of the conversation between himself and Shearer. However, the village gossip has numerous versions of what might have gone on behind closed doors. Perhaps the most realistic scenario is that Gullit would not have held back in his explanation. He would have explained to Shearer that his decision was not a personal one, nor was it made for any other reason than for the team. Clearly Gullit had been concerned about Shearer's form for many months and it was not a decision taken on the spur of the moment. Gullit would also have made it clear that if Shearer had any grievance against him for whatever reason then he should perform to his optimum for his own pride, his own satisfaction, knowing that he would have to maintain standards for himself.

The inside track from the Shearer camp is that the England captain told Gullit that he had been doing his best, he had no personal grievance and that he felt he still merited a place in the starting line-up. But in reality Shearer was unable to lead the attack in the way that Gullit would want his centre-forward and that was never going to change.

Gullit had more important issues to think over than his relationship

213

with Shearer, or his frustration at having the England captain, a player of such enormous stature, completely incapable of fulfilling the desired role within his team. For Gullit the results had conspired against him at a time when the pressures and intrusions into his private life had been mounting. Gullit felt that he should be judged only by events on the pitch, and that the constant intrusions into his private life were no longer at an acceptable level. Gullit was certainly being judged for the results. He was being hammered. He accepted that, and it was his place to put it right. But he was equally concerned over Estelle, Joelle, and how the media were using Estelle's father Henny to add to their problems. Gullit was coming to the only logical decision.

Gullit thought he was cursed as the shocking results piled up at the start of the season, cursed particularly at St James's Park. No doubt Ruud had premonitions about the Sunderland game. When the heavens opened up and nearly drowned the fans and his team, he knew that the omens were against him. When he sent on Ferguson before Shearer, it was making a point. When he shrugged his shoulders and observed that the score was 1-1 when Shearer came on and they lost 2-1, it was again emphasising a point.

The next day was a tough one. Gullit was not backing down in his conviction that the team would function in attack better without Shearer. But public opinion had swung against him. Whereas the local paper's opinion poll a week earlier had showed 81 per cent backing Gullit to stay, the local radio station now showed a complete split over whether he was right to axe Shearer. Clearly, had Gullit stayed then Shearer would have remained on the bench at Old Trafford. After a morning of meetings, Gullit needed a moment's peace, an opportunity to reflect and then look forward.

Then came the instant he knew it was time to quit. Ruud could always unwind and think clearly on the golf course, particularly with one close friend and confidant. As he arrived at his friend's home, a photographer leapt out of the bushes to take his photograph. Ruud approached the photographer, perplexed as to why there was a need for such an intrusion. It might seem a trivial moment, but for Ruud as for many people in his position, it summed up the kind of relentless scrutiny an individual can face. In many cases such as this there is always one incident too many. This was it. He asked the photographer whether it was all right to visit a friend's house to pick him up to play a round of golf without having all this hassle.

The photographer was simply doing his job, one of those uncomfortable assignments that are part and parcel of being in the media. There is always the risk of a reaction, although the 'snapper' probably didn't expect a philosophical debate. But Gullit had already been driven to distraction by events in Holland a week earlier when Estelle had been 'door-stepped' by a pack of photographers. Estelle had come over to Newcastle to give her moral support to Ruud, but had returned after the Sunderland match. Ruud had learned in Italy to accept the non-stop media attention, the endless headlines and detailed articles. But he had also decided to escape that degree of intensity by leaving Italy for England. He had liked the freedom he experienced in London during his time with Chelsea and did not imagine it would not be similar in Newcastle. He was shocked by the biting criticism he found in the local media in particular. He had gone through 'hell' for a year for so many intrusions into his private life. For the last two weeks he had felt 'persecuted'. He told me: 'I just wanted my life back.'

It was time to go. And there would be no pay-off. The board had wanted Gullit to stay, but there was no going back. He knew it was going to be almost impossible to manage half the side with matches at Manchester United and Chelsea coming up. And his refusal to accept the goldfish bowl he thought he had escaped when he left Italy pushed him into what he felt was the most honourable way out – resignation. Gullit had eight months left on a two-year agreement, but he did not ask for, and was not given any compensation.

He contacted Shepherd and Fletcher – no one else. Not even the Smith brothers, who were so close to Ruud. Jon had a conversation that evening with Ruud and could tell from his tone and clipped responses that all was not well. When Jon asked Ruud what he planned to do, Ruud told him he would know his decision in the morning.

Yet rumours spread that Sunderland manager Peter Reid was aware of the decision. Checks were made, denials in response. Mostly people were unaware for sure of Ruud's decision. In fact, it was hardly a surprise. The national media were predicting that Ruud would go, it was only a matter of time, although informed sources suggested that Manchester United would be the last game and that he would not be returning to Chelsea once the Premiership resumed in a fortnight, after the Euro 2000 qualifiers.

Having made up his mind to go before the match at Old Trafford, and with Shepherd and Fletcher aware of the breaking point, the word was out at 7.30 am on Thursday that a press conference was scheduled for 11 am. Gullit prepared his farewell speech personally without any input from the Smith brothers. He told me: 'At ten I dictated my thoughts to my secretary, she put it into the computer and printed it out. I read it out and would take no questions. The journalists were silent when at the end I told them, "Here it is, you can't get it wrong!"'

The full text of the resignation speech is as follows:

'The reason for my resignation is partly the bad results we have had in the last couple of weeks, but the biggest reason is something I am going to explain to you now. I am as disappointed by the results as any other person who loves Newcastle United and therefore I take full responsibility for the bad results. The fans' expectations have not been fulfilled and therefore I would like to apologise to them. I also would like to thank them for the marvellous support they gave me during this difficult time. But, of course, if the results keep on going badly you have to make a choice. I know there are still a lot of people who want me to stay and there are a lot who want me to go but I think the moment has come to resign. When all the players will be fit I still think that this team is capable of doing very good things, therefore I wish Newcastle United a very prosperous future with more luck than all the previous managers have had.

'The main reason I came to England four years ago was that I wanted to have my own private life back. The years at Chelsea I enjoyed very much because I really have the feeling that I could be myself again. The feeling of walking along the street minding my own business, being able to shop, being able to go to the cinema, being able to go out, being able to be like anyone else. These things seem very ordinary for someone who doesn't know what it is like to be me. These things are worth more to me than any treasure.

'The moment I came to Newcastle the journalists asked me if I understood how big the job was and I thought I knew – now I know what they really meant by that. In this last year my private life has been invaded in a bad way. I am used to being judged on what I do as a professional footballer or football coach, but my private life has been on the streets too much. During the last year I have had reporters, photographers, constantly around my home in Newcastle, people following me where I go to eat, go out, go to the cinema, but the worst part is that they have been harassing my family in Holland and that for me was the limit. I cannot see the point why my family has to suffer for my profession. For me my family always comes first and therefore I took this decision to resign.

'Despite all the judgements on my professional life I have some wonderful memories about my stay in England. I have made some wonderful friends and have had the opportunity to work in one of the best Leagues in the world. The enthusiasm of the game has given me enormous joy as a player and as a manager. As a player I could express the joy I had inside me and as a manager I could express that to my players, this resulted in two medals that I treasure very much. The feeling of being twice at Wembley in a final has given me in this short period of management and coaching a great satisfaction, therefore I would like to thank all the players I have been working with.

'I would like to thank also a part of the media who have been working with me in a good and professional way, I know you cannot win everyone for you. I would like to thank the Newcastle players for their efforts and their professionalism and wish every individual a very fruitful career. I would like to thank my staff that have been very supportive and helpful during my stay at Newcastle. Again I would like to thank Judith my personal secretary for all her work and energy. I would like to thank Mal Maison Hotel who have been really good to me during my stay in Newcastle. And I want to thank all the restaurants where I have been to for their marvellous food and hospitality.

'I would like to thank the fans for their support and their love for me. I would like to wish Steve Clarke good luck and I think he will be a marvellous manager for Newcastle United in the future. And last but not least, I would like to thank Freddy Shepherd and Freddie Fletcher for their support and energy and the belief they gave me. They work very hard and put all their energy into the club to make this club successful. I hope they can fulfil their dreams to make this club one of the best in Europe. Newcastle Football Club has come from a small club to a club of international standing and it is partly because of them. I wish them all the luck and happiness in their jobs and private life. Thank you for your attention and I will go on a long holiday with my family.'

18

Where it all went wrong

Ruud Gullit went to the wrong club at the wrong time in the wrong place for the wrong reasons. He had guaranteed his place in the fabric of this country's footballing history as the first foreign coach to win a major trophy. He was also the first black coach to be successful in English football; the foundations of that success were laid at Stamford Bridge and Chelsea are clearly still profiting from them. Much of Luca Vialli's team still contains Gullit's outstanding signings . . . Zola, Flo, Poyet, Leboeuf, De Goey, Le Saux, Babayaro and Di Matteo. The Newcastle board were attracted to Gullit in the first place because of his success at the Bridge, the style of football, and because they wanted a charismatic figure after the fans failed to relate to Dalglish.

After spending so much on players, Gullit had the reputation of a flawless record in his purchases at the Bridge. There was not a single failure, and some of the most stunning successes were either free transfers like Poyet or bargains like £300,000 for Flo. It is argued that Gullit bought poor players for Newcastle, that his downfall was ultimately his choice of players and the calamitous start to the new season. To a large extent that is true. But the problem lies much deeper. Gullit was at the wrong club because he could no longer attract the players that would produce his sexy football at one of soccer's great outposts.

The new breed of Continental superstar is not the kind depicted by Alan Hansen. The derogatory generalisation of Hansen's *Match of the Day* comment is offensive to the majority of imported stars of immense stature who are most definitely not 'dodgy foreigners'. Is Didier

218

Deschamps a dodgy foreigner? I am sure Deschamps, Desailly, Leboeuf, Petit, Vieira, and Henry would ask Hansen to show him the medal he won with the Scottish World Cup team. Gullit wanted Deschamps when he was at the Bridge, and there were meaningful talks, but Juventus were not ready to sell. When Deschamps was available, he wanted only to come to London. Gullit wanted him again, but not even his stature within the world game could persuade players of Deschamps' calibre to move to the North-East. Let's face it, Gullit's own partner Estelle wouldn't move there!

In fact Estelle was against Ruud taking up the appointment in the first place, and the only doubt when Gullit first arrived on Tyneside for more talks on taking the job was whether Estelle's influence would prevail and he would turn it down at the last minute. When it comes to selling the area even the weather can be an enemy, particularly when, even in the summer, it can bucket down as it did during the Sunderland game. Lifestyle is important to players who are already millionaires.

That's not to say it doesn't snow in Scandinavia. Flo came to the Bridge because of the potential under Gullit. Gullit called him Pistol Pete, and had enormous faith in his abilities as a goalscorer. In contrast, when he wanted Dion Dublin for Newcastle, the player preferred to stay in the Midlands, and instead Gullit invested £8 million in Duncan Ferguson. Gullit would have bought Dublin as well as Ferguson, or even another striker, because he quickly suspected that Alan Shearer was not the type of centre-forward to fit into his philosophy of how the game should be played.

Call it sexy football, total football, whatever, but Gullit told me why he didn't have a Shearer type even within a Chelsea side that lacked an out-and-out goalscorer. He explained that he wanted goals to come from all departments, as at Chelsea even now. That is the key to their success. They don't rely on just one player as Blackburn did with Shearer and Newcastle did for several years. His argument was that the player might be injured or marked out of the game. If the team was functional throughout at scoring then it was not necessary to have one thirty-goal-a-season player, but several players all capable of scoring into double figures. Chelsea scored 100-plus goals in a season to underline Gullit's point.

Gullit came to the conclusion that it would be best to sell Shearer. Shearer knew it. And that is the real reason behind Shearer's dislike for Gullit. Gullit, on the other hand, had a problem in rebuilding the Newcastle team with Shearer still an integral part of it. Had Newcastle received an acceptable offer from a club Shearer would have been happy to join – such as Arsenal – then Gullit would have been big enough to sell him. The board had privately sanctioned the sale. However, apart from catching Shearer's representatives getting out of a taxi at Highbury, there was no bid from Arsenal, and the level of offer being suggested from abroad would have meant the club taking a loss on their £15 million investment.

Shearer stayed. But he did not forget that the new coach would have sold him. For weeks there was non-stop speculation. Would he go, or would he stay? At the time it was not Gullit's future on the line, but Shearer's. Shearer's public comments were enigmatic. He was consistently saying he wanted to stay, but while on England duty left a rider hinting strongly that he would review his position if the team under Gullit was not going to bring the medals and trophies he craved for the club. Shearer even admitted he was embarrassed by the measure of the defeat Newcastle suffered against Arsenal. Equally, Gullit knew from the first match against Liverpool the players who had to go.

At this point Glenn Hoddle was also experiencing problems with Shearer. Hoddle, like Gullit, felt that Shearer had become too static. Both coaches wanted to see more movement, wanted the old Shearer who would work the channels and deliver penetrating crosses if he wasn't getting the service. Whether it was the Shearer publicity machine, the PR overdrive, or simply an excuse made for him by the media, the continual 'lack of service' tag began to irritate both Hoddle and Gullit.

Gullit waited for Hoddle to act, Hoddle for Gullit. Someone had to have the guts to drop the England captain. When Gullit eventually did it, there was uproar; a split in opinion among Newcastle fans and a debate in the media. The key question should have been whether Shearer's form justified his place. Instead, it was whether the England captain should be left out. The body language at St James's Park for the Sunderland game with Shearer on the bench told the sorry tale of a rift. But the split had occurred many months earlier.

In the absence of an acceptable bid, and with Shearer insisting he wanted to stay – while behind the scenes there were discussions about his departure – it was decided to call the England captain's bluff and offer him a new extended contract. Shearer took the new offer, and Gullit even made him captain, replacing Robert Lee. But even the new contract brought with it fresh sniping. Shearer, it was suggested, would be the next manager, and there was a verbal agreement if not a written one in the contract. That served only to undermine Gullit's position, and Shearer took his time admitting there was no clause stating he would be a future manager.

During Gullit's summer rebuilding I spoke with him about Shearer. I asked: 'Are you going to sell him?' Gullit laughed: 'I'll let you know if I do.' It was the sort of coded comment that both Gullit and Shearer had been engaging in for months, and the animosity intensified with the club's worst start for forty years. But even if Shearer didn't want to play for Gullit, the coach implored him to play for himself and for the club. If Shearer underperformed then it would reflect as badly on him as it would on the coach.

There were times when Gullit thought there was a glimmer of the old Shearer. Gullit had played against him and knew he could be a 'pain in the arse', always pushing, shoving, agitating until he won the ball. But there were also times when even this aspect of his game was looking tired. Uriah Rennie eventually sent Shearer off for overuse of his elbows, even though the actual red card incident was pretty tame. Gullit's concern was that Shearer had become tame all round, and without the effective hustle and bustle of his game, by Shearer's own admission he is not a great individual, blessed with dribbling prowess or the visionary pass. Gullit was finding it increasingly frustrating to buy the players he really wanted. He was often left with second, third or fourth best. When it became impossible to recruit players of the Zola class, he bought players like Maric who, more than any other player, sums up Gullit's errors in the transfer market. A player with a wonderful reputation, the Croat was not really fit when he arrived, quickly lost confidence, and more recently lost heart in the club.

Although Gullit was informed that the Newcastle job was a tough one, he didn't fully appreciate just how difficult it was until he got there. Gullit was hurt by his acrimonious departure from the Bridge, and originally told me that he felt it was best not to return to English football until he had first taken up an appointment somewhere else. When Newcastle called, he changed his mind. He recalled the wonderful atmosphere there when he played for Chelsea, and believed in joining clubs that were once great but had fallen on hard times. It was something he had followed throughout his career, and it had worked at Chelsea.

Gullit was lured back quicker than he intended, and by the wrong motives. He wanted to prove to Chelsea how wrong they were to sack him. Gullit teased his successor Luca Vialli last season when he insisted it was time for Chelsea to win the League. He left when they were second in the Premiership, and last season they should finish first. They came third, qualified for the Champions' League for the first time and are among the favourites again to win the title for the first time since 1955. In fact, Gullit has yet to return to the Bridge. Last season he had no need to. Not drawn there in the cups, with no League game at the Bridge because Kenny Dalglish's last game had been at Chelsea. So the timing of Gullit's resignation is interesting. Had he stayed for the game at Old Trafford and pulled off a shock against Manchester United, perhaps, a valiant draw as he achieved last season, he would be going back to confront Ken Bates, Vialli et al with his team bottom or second from bottom of the Premiership. That was never going to be a pleasant experience.

But it was not the real reason that Gullit quit Newcastle. It was purely and simply because he had had enough of living in a goldfish bowl. When I spoke with Ruud the first morning after his resignation he felt a blessed relief from being 'persecuted', followed by the paparazzi, hounded by the media with an intensity he had not experienced since the days he was the world's number one footballer, winning European Cups and the Scudetto with AC Milan, then the most powerful team in the world.

He woke without a care in the world, back in Amsterdam with Estelle and Joelle, mischievously answering his mobile phone. He had made it plain two weeks earlier that he would know the precise time to walk away – when it affected him so badly that it in turn rebounded on his family. That time had arrived. The name of Alan Shearer did not appear in his long and emotional farewell speech.

It may well be that Gullit will be back in English football, he did not rule out that distinct possibility. He has no intention of making any derogatory comments about Shearer or anyone else at Newcastle. In fact, in many ways he enjoyed his year at the club, making many new friends. He has appreciated their efforts on his behalf. But if Gullit is to return to the English game, it won't be for some time. He really does plan a long holiday, just as he did when he left the Bridge. He won't even want to consider any offers until the New Year. And he won't make the same mistake of taking a post in the provinces. Estelle was happy living in London, in posh Cadogan Square, between Peter Jones and Harrods at the back of Sloane Street. The apartment was luxurious, within range of all the top designer stores and best restaurants. Gullit is a cosmopolitan coach suited only to London.

Maybe Gullit might be considered again by Spurs once George Graham has enjoyed his flirtation back in North London. Maybe he'll end up in West London once more with Fulham, then Estelle will relish a move back to the trendsetters' area of Chelsea. Mohammed Al Fayed would even give her a gold card at Harrods. The alternative is that he is offered a post as a national team boss. If he does come back to England he will have to choose his destination with much more care and thought.

The timing of Gullit's return to English football with Newcastle was itself an error. Immediately he was shown the door by Bates, there were two clubs thinking seriously about recruiting Gullit. Spurs chairman Alan Sugar had been offered Gullit as a player but his then manager Gerry Francis didn't want to sign a sweeper. Glenn Hoddle did, but after six games, Gullit was switched to midfield. Now Sugar had the chance to take him on as manager, with Christian Gross's days numbered. But if Sugar has a fault, he is too loyal to his managers. He had kept Francis longer than he should have done, and he did the same with Gross. Next option for Gullit was Aston Villa. The manager's chair there was vacant. But Bates and Doug Ellis are old friends, so one can draw logical conclusions about why Gullit was never approached.

Bates, of course, will take no pleasure from Gullit's demise. There won't be a single 'I told you so' coming from the Bridge. If Gullit made many enemies in English football, he also made many friends, inside and outside the game. 'People were very, very nice to me in Newcastle, I made friends but life became more and more difficult with photographers chasing me. I accepted it in Italy but it was the reason I came to England, to escape all that. In London I could walk the streets without being disturbed. It was not the same in Newcastle.'

As Gullit departed English football for the second time in controversial circumstances, although without anywhere near the same degree of animosity as the time he left the Bridge, the old hackneyed observations were wheeled out. Aloof, arrogant, unapproachable. Yet it seemed they were peddled by the same sort of people who condemned him at Chelsea. They had a common denominator. They never knew him. Of course they knew of him, they had heard all the rumours, talked to those who had most reason to dislike him – the players left out of the team, those who fell victim to his rotation policy that has now become so fashionable at the Bridge, those who had an axe to grind.

There were also those who did know him. They had a vastly different story to tell. It was almost as if there were two people. Personally, having written his autobiography, I suppose I would fall into the category of those who know him better than most. He spent many Friday evenings on the sofa at my Chelsea flat. 'I can only stay for an hour,' he would insist, as he wanted to rush back to Estelle in nearby Cadogan Square. Once he started talking he would stay for more than three hours.

It was ironic that I reported Gullit's arrival at Newcastle from Monte Carlo when I was covering the Super Cup between Chelsea and Real Madrid, and I was in the same place a year later when he had made up his mind to resign. My mother had a stroke two weeks earlier and before I left for the Super Cup between Manchester United and Lazio, the doctors thought she might pull through. Ruud told me to tell her that he said 'it wasn't her time to go'. The next time I was able to speak with Ruud was the first day back in Amsterdam after his resignation. I told him she hadn't made it. 'I'll be going to the church shortly and I will light a candle for her.' There were far more important things in life, said Ruud, than football.

19

Life after Gullit for Newcastle and Shearer

Ruud Gullit's fate was the subject of the Manchester United fans' wicked sense of humour. During the 5-1 thrashing at Old Trafford, it began with 'Cheer up Alan Shearer . . .', then the biggest insult of all, 'Shearer for England', and finally 'Let's all laugh at Shearer'. Of course the Toon Army backed their hero, rapidly becoming a fallen hero. The striker the Manchester United fans used to fear, and whom they originally wanted in their own team, managed a solitary shot and one assist throughout the game. Shearer and Ferguson led the attack, but the only goal came courtesy of Henning Berg, amazingly the Premierships' eleventh own goal of the season.

But there were plenty of symbolic own goals still to come from Newcastle. One point from the first six games, while the champions were three points clear at the top with sixteen points. Newcastle had now conceded eighteen goals, the worst defensive record in the Premiership.

Bobby Robson was two hundred miles away watching Ipswich, still insisting he had yet to receive a call. Robson had made it clear he wanted the job and was favourite to be offered it. The former England manager said: 'I would love that job more than anything else in the world. It would truly be a dream come true for me. I know that if I was a chairman of a club I'd probably think more than twice about appointing a sixty-six-year-old as a manager, but I'd appoint me like a shot. Physically I'm as fit as a fiddle, every bit as mobile and lively as I was at fifty. Mentally I'm switched on and alert, my enthusiasm for the game is as intense as it has ever been and will endure until the day I

225

die. Now read my CV – World Cups, European trophies, championships, supercups . . . it's quite a list. I left PSV Eindhoven at the end
of last season to come home to England having clinched them a
Champions' League place they didn't expect. Not to retire, I'm not
ready for that yet. The bottom line is I have enjoyed tremendous
successes as a manager and, on top of that, I know I'm better than I've
ever been.'

But Robson had recovered from life-threatening cancer of the eye.
Although it was in 1995 and he was back on the training ground in half
the time of the six months he was told he would be off work, there was
clearly concern about his appointment.

Back at Old Trafford the game had turned from farce to Greek
tragedy with Nikos Dabizas sent off for disputing the second goal.
Caretaker Steve Clarke brought back Robert Lee for his first start of
the season and at 1-1 at half time there was no sign of the
embarrassment to follow after the interval. By the end Toon favourite
Andy Cole had helped himself to four goals and said: 'I'm gutted for
Newcastle. It's a great club and I do not want to see them in the
position they are in. There is pressure on all the players to turn things
round. But it is going to take a long time to do it.'

The biggest irony was that Cole was left out by Kevin Keegan from
his twenty-seven-man squad for the back-to-back vital Euro 2000 ties
with Luxembourg and Poland, while the England coach had made the
point of stressing that Shearer was still the 'cornerstone' of his England
team. When Shearer arrived at Bisham Abbey for international duty
Keegan announced that his captain would not be performing the
traditional day-before-the-game press conference.

The Geordie fans leaving Old Trafford, and interviewed on TV,
wanted Robson to succeed Gullit. Robson knew of the 'obsession' in
the North-East from childhood. He said: 'I'm in the market for a full-
time job. A year ago I left the best job in world football with Barcelona
simply because I wanted to be actively involved again at the sharp end.
I was travelling the world first class wherever I wanted to go, searching
out potential buys for the club. One of my greatest strengths is
judgement of players and the dossier I built up doing that job is still in
there. I find it totally incomprehensible when managers pay millions of
pounds for a player they have seen only through a carefully crafted
video recording – and they do.'

There had been an offer to take over from Keegan when he walked
out in 1996, but Robson described it as the right club at the wrong
time because of his contractual obligations as coach to Barcelona. Sir

John Hall had personally gone to Barcelona with a five-year contract. 'Barcelona told me I could not go. What they didn't tell me was they had already secured Louis Van Gaal to a long-term contract as coach. They actually denied it when I asked about the rumours. I'd have gone to Newcastle like a shot if I'd known it was true.'

Alan Shearer may have won his power struggle with Gullit, but it's a hollow victory. He was just about perfect; the ultimate role model. But in Newcastle's early-season crisis, Shearer had become a lumbering parody of the striker who topped the scoring charts at Euro 96. Squeaky-clean Mary Poppins, the man Kevin Keegan has entrusted with the England captaincy for the national side's most pivotal week, was taking a real battering for the first time in a wonderfully successful career.

Malcolm Macdonald, who wore the number nine shirt for Newcastle and England like Shearer, says it's a travesty. In a damning and forthright assessment of Shearer's declining powers, Supermac says his successor is no longer fit to lead his country from the front. 'Even Newcastle fans are beginning to have grave doubts about Shearer as a player and a captain.

'Being captain of England means much more than wearing an armband and leading your team up the tunnel at Wembley,' said Macdonald. 'More than ever, kids are looking to our sporting heroes for leadership as role models and the England captain has a responsibility to society as much as his ten team-mates. But I would not like to fight in a war as a private if Alan Shearer was captain of my platoon. And I'm afraid I would not want my kids to look up to Shearer and copy him any longer. I don't think he deserves to be England skipper any longer and he's not even worth his place in the team. For me, the day he was sent off for persistent misconduct against Aston Villa should have been enough for Kevin Keegan to revoke the England captaincy from Shearer.

'Think about those two words: persistent misconduct. In other words, Shearer was dismissed for non-stop niggling. It may have been the first red card of his career, but it was confirmation of the way his approach has changed. Ever since he came back from that terrible ankle injury, which was an achievement in itself, Shearer has had to rearrange his game. But his redefined approach is more physical and confrontational – and his reaction to being sent off was to turn round and say, "Hey – I'm Alan Shearer, you can't do that to me."

'He is in danger of demeaning a proud position and of being remembered for all the wrong reasons. You can put Luxembourg, San

Marino, the Faroe Isles or any other team of international part-timers up against England at Wembley and the result will be the same: Shearer won't fill his boots because I'm not sure he can do it any more at this level.'

Macdonald still lives on Tyneside, where he has watched hero-worship for Shearer subside. More alarming for Supermac than the England skipper's declining potency around the box, however, has been Shearer's militancy off the pitch.

He was especially dismayed by Shearer's feud with Gullit, adding: 'He follows a line of exalted professionals at Newcastle, but his behaviour in the days leading to Ruud Gullit's downfall brought discredit to those who wore the shirt before him. The day after Newcastle lost 4-2 at Southampton, Shearer repeatedly refused to back Gullit and hid behind club orders not to discuss his manager's position. When Gullit had accused his senior players of letting him down after the previous game at Tottenham, who do you think his comments were aimed at?'

Former FA chief executive Graham Kelly alleged that Shearer threatened to boycott the 1998 World Cup over pay and a disciplinary charge levelled for kicking Leicester's Neil Lennon in the face. Macdonald went on: 'When you apparently get the England captain issuing threats about not playing in the World Cup finals over money . . . good heavens, what is the game coming to? I can remember Don Revie coming into the dressing room, looking like Pooh Bear with a honeypot, and boasting that he had just negotiated win bonus and draw bonus payments with the international committee on top of our £200 appearance fees. To his credit our skipper at the time, Alan Ball, looked him in the eye and replied, "We don't need money to play for England – you just put those three lions on our chests." What a contrast with Shearer's gunboat diplomacy – pay up or I don't play. If that's the way it happened, it's a disgrace.

'And as for the way Shearer claimed he was victimised by the FA for that tackle on Lennon? For him to squeal that he was called to account over that incident just because he was the England captain is laughable. Instead of being hard done by, he got away with it. They let him off, didn't they? The case was supposedly "unproven" when the TV evidence was crystal-clear. Had he been any other player in the Premiership, he would have been banned. Of course the people in positions of power and influence were guilty of letting him get away with it.

'Politically, it was just too expedient to say "case dismissed" and leave Shearer clear to play in the World Cup. But from the moment the FA allegedly swept the whole thing under the carpet, they gave Shearer a licence to go barging his way around the Premiership.'

By the end of the week, Robson was on Tyneside taking over from Gullit. When he was unveiled at a St James's Park press conference he promised 'no panic' and 'no changes' as he wanted to steady the Newcastle ship, inheriting a side in turmoil.

Robson insisted the situation was 'retrievable' and emphasised that he was relishing the challenge ahead. The County Durham-born miner's son, who has only signed a contract until the end of the current season, said: 'I thought Barcelona was big but this has pipped it. It's great to be back and I'm proud, honoured and thrilled. It was rather ironic this morning but I followed a car from where I was staying into the club and the registration was SOS 1. I don't know how ironic that was but I get the message.

'It was the right club to come to two years ago but I was at Barcelona then and I had to fulfil my contract. I thought the chances of my coming here had gone then. I thought Kenny Dalglish would be long term. Then I went to PSV Eindhoven. After Kenny left I thought I might have been in the reckoning. But I thought Ruud Gullit was a long-term appointment. I thought it [the Newcastle job] had gone. But that is football.

'I realise I have a massive job ahead of me. It is a great challenge. I am up for it. I am not afraid of it. I don't underestimate it. I am going to enjoy working here. The priority is to bring about a change in fortunes, stabilise the club and ensure that next year Premiership status is still at Newcastle and that we have made progress. There is no panic. It is retrievable and I'm confident I can do it.'

It is his first job in English League football since leaving Ipswich to manage the national side in 1982. Robson recognised that his predecessors have spent heavily and stressed that he would not be making sweeping changes at the club in the short term. 'I need to look at the players quickly and establish in my mind what we have. The club have spent a massive sum of money on the present staff. My job is to – as quickly as I can – ascertain what the present quality is and find out if it is sufficient. It may be that we do not have to spend and change the staff. I want first to look at the staff. Everyone has a chance. Everyone starts fresh. That applies to technical staff too – they deserve an opportunity. When I decide what has to be done I will offer my views to the board. At the present moment I have no desire to change. The number two is Steve Clarke. I am very impressed with him. I asked for information. He gave it to me willingly and honestly. At this moment there are no changes, until I have had a look at the situation.'

Robson rejected the idea that the pressure of the job he has taken on could be overwhelming. 'I am not worried. We have the best group of fans in the whole wide world and they're not too demanding. They understand things. I saw the Sunderland match. I saw the crowd. It is not a pressure point when you see those fans. I've worked at Barcelona. When things are not going well 100,000 fans wave handkerchiefs at you. Then, you know it's time to go.

'I won't get that here, that's for sure. I know the public will give the players a chance. If the fans see the players are giving their best they will be patient. For such a fantastic group of people we have to bring about a set of results that the board and fans deserve.

'The club needs a win badly and I have to re-instil confidence, enthusiasm and self-belief in the players to give them the chance to stop the poor results they've had and achieve the results we all feel sure the players are capable of. We've got to plug a few holes and steady the ship. The priority is to turn the club around in terms of Premiership results.'

Asked how long he had coveted the Newcastle job, Robson replied: 'I was first interested in being manager when I saw Jackie Milburn in 1950. I thought it would be good to do that job. If you'd said a few years ago that Kevin Keegan and I would swap jobs you wouldn't have believed it. But it happened.'

Robson said he would be in touch with the England coach but did not intend ringing him while he is preparing for the Euro 2000 qualifiers against Luxembourg at Wembley and against Poland in Warsaw.

'It would not be right for me to distract Kevin Keegan from the task he has this week. They are two enormous games for the country. I'm going on Saturday [to Wembley for the Luxembourg game]. I'll be very close to him. I'll take the opportunity to wish him good luck and, at some later stage, I'm sure I'll have some dialogue with Kevin Keegan.'

Newcastle chairman Freddy Shepherd, welcoming Robson's return to his North-East roots, said: 'He is someone we have long admired. We have asked him to take over responsibility for all team affairs with immediate effect. We have asked him to undertake a look at the playing side of the club. We look forward to his contribution. Welcome home, Bobby.'

Robson addressed the 10 am press conference at St James's Park as hundreds of fans gathered outside to welcome a local hero home. He then travelled to the Chester-le-Street training quarters at 11.30 am to meet his players for the first time.

20

From Mary Poppins to the Big Bad Wolf . . . Bobby Robson tries to teach Alan Shearer new tricks

The departure lounge at Warsaw Airport and with the plane delayed on Thursday morning, something compelled me to call Ruud on his mobile. It might have been crackly reception to Amsterdam, but Gullit had watched the England match the previous night. Alan Shearer's performance did not surprise him.

After the glory of his first ever hat-trick for his country against the hapless Luxembourg defence at Wembley, it was back to reality in Poland. A dreary, goalless, lifeless, listless draw and a poor Shearer display against the Poles brought the striker more pointed criticism. No longer was it Shearer This, Shearer That, and Shearer Can't Do Any Wrong from Kevin Keegan after his seemingly endless applause for the England captain's hat-trick.

The *Mirror*'s headline was 'Fatal Attraction', accompanied with a back page editorial that Keegan had to ditch Shearer for the benefit of the nation.

The *Express* were embarrassed as their first edition gave Shearer ten out of ten in the marks for his display in Warsaw, although it was amended to seven out of ten later on.

Keegan's undiluted backing for Shearer throughout the back-to-back Euro 2000 ties seemed to wane immediately after the draw in Warsaw. Of his strike force of Shearer and Fowler, and it was the Liverpool star who had all the chances, Keegan said: 'They huffed, they puffed, but they didn't blow the house down.' From Mary Poppins to the Big Bad Wolf! And England's forlorn hopes of Euro 2000 qualification hung on the hope of Sweden beating the Poles in Stockholm to leave England in the play-offs.

Former Arsenal and England striker Alan Smith, now a TV and radio pundit, and one of the more rational of his critics, still came down firmly against Shearer. He believes that the only reason Shearer has not been dropped by the England coach is that Keegan does not possess a viable alternative. Smith argued: 'Alan Shearer is not the force of old. His overall game is not able to terrorise defenders. He has not got that pace or presence any more. He has a great reputation at international level and pointed out himself that his statistics show a great goal ratio of more than one goal in every two games. But stronger opponents have shown that they can handle him. There is not a candidate screaming out to replace him in the England team that's part of Kevin Keegan's problem. Chris Sutton can be used as a target man and I think that Emile Heskey has a physical presence. But the reason Shearer keeps his place is because there is no one pushing him that hard.'

Curiously, Keegan took off Fowler rather than humiliate the England captain when he brought on Owen, and three days later another English manager lacked the bottle to haul off Shearer. Dear old Bobby Robson, the Newcastle pensioner up against the Chelsea Pensioners, took off Ferguson instead. Yet Ferguson came closer to becoming the first to score at Stamford Bridge in the Premiership this season with a header that brought the best out of Ed de Goey. Robson did, however, confess that Shearer has become a static centre-forward, is not in the best of shape, and that defenders know how to play against him as the goals have dried up in the Premiership. In fact, Robson summoned the England striker to his hotel room on the Friday night for personal tuition on how to improve his stagnating game.

Picture the scene. The sixty-six-year-old picks up the telephone and calls the England captain on the night before his first game in charge of Newcastle United. 'Come to my room,' urges Robson. With the lavish backdrop of Chelsea Harbour, inside Robson's room at the Conrad Hotel, the two Geordies had a real heart-to-heart. Robson was probably leaping around the room as he demonstrated to Shearer how he wanted him to improve his game. Come off the centre-half, half turn, lay the ball off, don't play with your back to goal, don't back into the centre-half, and when we get you into better shape we'll have you running down the channels again crossing the ball from the flanks.

Robson explained: 'He needs help. He has got into this little static position. I had a long chat with him in my room about his game and I have also worked with him in training. I told him that he was backing into people, that if the ball comes to him slowing up that the centre-half won't wait, he will come and nick it. I impressed upon him that he mustn't lose the ball, and that he must turn and see the fellow's face, don't let him defend when he is always able to see your number because if he does then you are in the wrong position.' Whether it is self-delusion on Robson's part, whether he can teach a twenty-nine-year-old new tricks, whether it is a desperate bid to resolve a probably insoluble problem, one can be sure his motives are genuine enough. But unless Newcastle United's £15 million goalscorer can somehow find some more of those goals, then Robson will have to find the courage to drop the England captain.

Robson believes it is possible for Shearer to become a force within the Premiership again and therefore persuade all the doubters that he is still good enough to lead his country. Robson said: 'He wasn't down at all when he returned with England. I have talked to him and told him we need to do some work to build him up again. He needs to be making diagonal runs, from left to right and right to left but he can only do that if he improves his shape. He has had some criticism but he has also had a marvellous ten years. He has been a national hero but now for some reason people are turning against him. He can come through that by winning again with his club football and I'll help him.'

But Robson is gambling the club's Premiership status on finding a formula to get the best out of Shearer. Robson said: 'With Alan Shearer and Duncan Ferguson in the side the flank play is crucial. When Rob Lee curled one in Duncan got a header that only a 6ft 4in giraffe of a goalkeeper could have saved, otherwise we would have won the game.'

There is such an endearing quality about the old boy. No doubting his passion. All that boyish enthusiasm is genuine enough. The former England and Ipswich manager turned back the clock at Stamford Bridge. His sincerity is infectious. And of course the best of Booby Robson was back too. For the benefit of Gary Lineker and his *Match of the Day* interview the new Newcastle Messiah got his Popescus mixed up with is Petrescus. Of course, Robson once signed Popescu from Tottenham for Barcelona, and now he had to prepare his team for the first time against Petrescu. And dear old Pop called Kieron Dyer 'Ken', but only once and he can be forgiven for all the excitement on his return to English football after a ten-year absence. Anyway, none of the Toon Army will care if their Pop of a manager gets all the names wrong provided that he somehow halts the current slide.

Robson admitted: 'I loved it, I was emotionally excited, but with a clear head. It was a buzz to be back, marvellous. I had a gut reaction we would get a point. I made up my mind on Wednesday we would play for a point, a 0-0 or a 1-1. I didn't want to come here and play with an attractive side like they did at Manchester or Tottenham and get beaten heavily. I was not up for that.' Instead, Newcastle lost playing dreary football instead of sexy football.

It's customary in these circumstances for the players to praise the new manager, and Dyer didn't let anyone down. He said: 'Chelsea are a quality team going for the championship but didn't create very much until the last five minutes when we were pushing for the equaliser. All credit to the manager, he changed the system, he instilled great confidence by talking to all the players individually. He is a legend. I take great heart in the way we played, we were hard to break down.'

But it's easier to destroy than to create. The tricky bit is to get the team to play. And for Robson to come to terms with the Shearer Fixation. There were mocking taunts of 'Where were you on Wednesday?' aimed at Shearer and 'Ruudie, Ruudie'. Gullit was a cornerstone of building this exciting Chelsea team that is currently challenging Manchester United with only one defeat so far and without a home goal conceded. Even Shearer's work rate was in question under Gullit, and although he looked more interested under new management, the end product was the same.

Usually when Shearer has been written off, he is at his most dangerous. But against Marcel Desailly, he was never in contention. The French World Cup winner hardly needed to have one of his better games. And with Luca Vialli opting to rest Didier Deschamps and rotate his squad, Robson's conviction that the gulf between these sides is not as wide as the league tables suggest is naive, and comes from a man who has been out of touch with the development of the English game. While Robson was desperate for just one point, Vialli juggled his enormous squad knowing the real contest was reserved for AC Milan in the club's Champions' League proper debut at Stamford Bridge. Robson came to the Bridge with a specific game plan to stifle Franco Zola. Warren Barton would be man marking him, in a sweeper system that Robson last played when England manager in Italia 90 with Mark Wright. That system is reserved for tough away assignments such as Chelsea where the opposition are deemed far superior. Vialli said: 'We were expecting that with a new manager as that is always a great motivation, and it gets a response from the players. There is still room for improvement but the way they approached the game they are in the right frame of mind.' Robson added: 'I knew it would give me an examination of how far away we are from Chelsea and from Manchester United. If we were beaten 4-0 it would be a long way away. The gulf in the league would be vast. But on the field it wasn't.'

Welcome to the Premiership, Bobby. Now's the time to get real. Chelsea were far from their best, while Newcastle's spoiling tactics worked for most of the game. But as soon as they went for it themselves, and Robson reverted to his 4-4-2 style, Zola and Flo had enough chances in the final stages to have got a couple each.

21

Shearer back on the goal trail

Bobby Robson, however, did not have to wait long for the taste of success. First a win in Bulgaria, and then a record breaking 8-0 win against Sheffield Wednesday, with five goals coming from Shearer. Not a bad week for the new boss and the under-siege Shearer. Fighting to prove he is not a spent force at all levels, his first five-goal haul of his career – to equal Andy Cole's Premiership record – transformed Robson's emotional St James's Park coronation into an unbelievable one. Shearer tormented woeful Wednesday with an eleven-minute hat-trick in the first half, and rounded off the rout with the final two goals of the club's biggest Premiership win and Newcastle's biggest margin of victory since the forties. Shearer's swagger was restored.

Robson could not have had any idea of the fantasy football that lay ahead as he took his bow on the pitch ten minutes before kick off. The man who openly admitted to being envious of the men who have preceded him in the St James's Park 'hot-seat' had the Toon Army chanting 'Walking in a Robson wonderland'.

Once Aaron Hughes headed his first ever goal for the club on eleven minutes the brittle resistance of Wilson's side shattered. The rejuvenated Shearer was provided with the service he thrives on, and all the predatory instincts were back when he flicked Solano's low cross past Kevin Pressman for his first goal from open play of the season. He added his second from the penalty spot when Thome was harshly adjudged to have handled Barton's attempted cross. He completed his first Newcastle hat-trick for over two years, three minutes before half time, pouncing in the six-yard box to force home

237

another Dyer cross from the left. Shearer played a major part in the fifth goal too, twice trying to add to his haul, before Dyer forced home his second attempt from close range for a deserved goal of his own. Speed headed in Solano's corner, Pressman gifted Shearer his fourth with a poor punch which he stabbed back into an empty net, and Haslam's foul on Paul Robinson presented him with his fifth from the penalty spot.

Shearer said: 'I've said all along that if I'm given the chances I will put them away. I'm not finished. I'm delighted to have equalled Andy Cole's Premiership record and that result has taken a lot of pressure off us. That win was for those fans out there. They have stuck with us and now we have turned the corner. But we can't afford to be carried away. I hope it's a launch-pad but we need another thirty results like that.'

Shearer praised the immediate impact made by Robson, and admitted he had never before scored four goals in a game – never mind five. 'There has been a big improvement since the manager came in and everyone is playing with a smile on their faces.'

The result was the biggest of Robson's club career, but ironically he had a bigger win – 9–0 against Luxembourg – when he was boss of England. 'I hope the public don't expect results like that every game because it's a tall order. Once the first goal went in, the gates opened and I said to the players "Don't save yourselves. Give the public everything. They have been waiting months for this."'

'Alan has responded instantly to what I have asked him to do. He just needed a bit of guidance and he has done it. An 8–0 score-line helps our goal ratio and to do it in the Premiership is quite incredible. But there is still a long way to go and we must not underestimate the fragile position we are in.'

In fact this was Newcastle's first League win since April 3.

Chairman Freddy Shepherd said: 'You get what you see with Bobby Robson. He is so genuine. It's unbelievable what Bobby has done since he came here and certainly no one could have written yesterday's script. Shepherd was also delighted for Shearer: 'Alan has done his talking on the field – and don't forget that's eight goals he has scored in the space of just fifteen days. Alan Shearer had a point to prove and he has proved it. You can read between the lines on that.

'To be fair to Ruud, the players he left behind have started to perform. But the fans have had to endure a miserable six weeks and that win over Wednesday was for them. It was like winning the lottery when we beat Sofia in the UEFA cup last week and now I feel I've won it twice. Relegation, what's relegation? It's not in my vocabulary.'

Shearer's five-goal salvo was the perfect response to critics who had already penned the twenty-nine-year-old striker's soccer obituary. 'I didn't think I could score five goals, or is that just at international level?' he joked in a pointed reference to the barbs of former Newcastle favourite Malcolm Macdonald.

Shearer praised the contribution of Dyer: 'He's made a hell of a difference.' Shearer also paid tribute to the football intellect of the new Magpies manager. 'He's down-to-earth and he's honest and genuine, and I don't think you can ask any more than that. He came in and he's got his little one-liners which have everyone laughing at times. But he's serious at times as well when he wants hard work and you don't cross him because you'll feel the force of it, which is important. He has the respect because he's been a success wherever he's been. Everyone gets on with him and he has everyone smiling. We don't work physically that hard in training. A lot of it is technical and he likes to conserve our energy for a Saturday. We're getting the rewards at the moment. It has to continue, but I'm sure it can.'

Mick Wadsworth's recruitment as head coach is part of that programme, as was his challenge to young Hughes to take his chance with Nikos Dabizas suspended for the Wednesday game. 'I was proud of Hughes,' said Robson. 'I called him in on Friday and said "What do you want me to do, give you a chance or send you out on loan and bring in (Colin) Hendry, as an example? That's the choice I've got. Are you going to do it for me? Are you going to panic?" We were down to the bare bones. We had one centre-half. But he gave me the answer in two minutes, so I said "Right, you won't let me down so I'll play you", and I was pleased with him. We have to make a lot of our players better players. If the club has spent its money and doesn't have much left, the only answer is to make the present players better players. There's only one way to do that and that's on the pitch. We need some top coaches who will work with the players individually and in small groups. There'll be a lot of afternoon work here. I had no money when I was at Ipswich. I had to work with the players on the pitch. We have to do that here.'

Lee believes that everything is now in place for Shearer to enjoy one of his most successful seasons of his career. 'Al is still the great, old-fashioned England centre forward. He's the best we have got in this country. I have always backed Alan to score goals if he gets the service. If the right players are around him he'll do the rest. Now that he's getting that service he'll prove that he's still the number one. I honestly believe there is nobody better, and if there is I haven't seen him.

'Bobby Robson has come in, training is enjoyable again and it's showing in Alan's football. He wants to go out there and express himself for this manager. The body language has got to be different after you've scored five goals to when you are on a losing side every week, and he has had the extra responsibility of being captain. How could anybody expect him to be walking around with a smile on his face then? He has great respect for Bobby Robson, and players like Kieron Dyer have been encouraged to put in the sort of crosses that Alan hasn't enjoyed for a long time.'

Shearer added: 'I didn't like it when Ruud Gullit left me out but I like to think I reacted to his decision in the right way. If it's true that we didn't see eye to eye it's also true that I always played my heart out when I pulled on the black and white shirt.'

Compare the tone of that with his comments on Robson. 'Bobby Robson understands the Geordies. He shares their deep-seated passion for the game and knows how much it means to so many. Everyone who knows him has told me about his honesty and passion. I have seen those qualities for myself in the past few days and I know that better times lie ahead. He understands people. We are enjoying life again and we have a smile on our faces.

'You are never too old to learn in this game and it's definitely paying off. He has told me what he wants from me and I have faith in what he says. There is a mutual respect between us. He is keen for me to play on the half-turn, which suits me fine. He wants me to run at defenders rather than have my back to goal and that's great. Mind you, he told me at half-time against Sheffield Wednesday that if I scored six he would buy me a Mars bar. I suppose I'll have to buy my own now!'

Substitute Paul Robinson cheekily asked Shearer whether he could take the late penalty that gave the England skipper his fifth goal . . . and was politely told where to go. Robinson joked: 'I told him "that's a shambles, you've already got four. How greedy do you want to be?" Seriously, Alan has just shown again that he's the top man and it's amazing some people can say he's past it. I'm sure Kevin Keegan would have been delighted when he saw the result.'

So Shearer isn't quite finished yet. As always he's most menacing when he's being written off. Even by Shearer's standards its been an amazing start to this new season. But of course, it's how it all ends that counts . . .